King Power
in
Chess

Also by Edmar Mednis:

Practical Endgame Lessons

How Karpov Wins

How to Beat the Russians

King
Power
in
Chess

Edmar Mednis
International Grandmaster

David McKay Company, Inc.

New York

To Baiba, my Queen

Library of Congress Cataloging in Publication Data

Mednis, Edmar, 1937–
King power in chess.

1. King (Chess)   I. Title.
GV1451.5.K5M42   794.1'47   80–12142
ISBN: 0–679–13450–6

1 2 3 4 5 6 7 8 9 10

MANUFACTURED IN THE UNITED STATES OF AMERICA

Preface

Feel like tucking your King in some corner in the beginning of the game and letting it remain there forevermore? A natural enough feeling, since losing the King means losing the game. Yet to play without the King means playing without one potentially useful piece. Mikhail Tal, a former world champion, has intriguingly suggested that in many positions the value of an active King is about "3 points," i.e. equivalent to a minor piece.

The experienced player is generally familiar with the concept that most of the time it is profitable to activate the King in the endgame. But how about the opening and middlegame? Much less is known and understood about the role of the King during these phases. Yet already in the last century Wilhelm Steinitz demonstrated that in the context of King's Gambit type openings the King can often be both active and safe. More recently, the current world champion Anatoly Karpov has added much insight into the successful utilization of the King during middlegame play.

This book, then, is about the role of the King throughout the three phases of a complete game: opening, middlegame and endgame. It is about what to do to be successful—and almost equally important, what not to do. Since this is the first book on the subject, I have tried to impart as much instruction as seemed practical. Nevertheless, to be truly useful, a book must also be enjoyable and entertaining. Otherwise the student simply will not tackle it! Therefore, even though I have tried to be scientifically rigorous, the major emphasis throughout is on readability.

So that the reader and author are on the same wavelength regarding the characterization of moves, the following list contains the presently accepted meanings:

! = a strong move
!! = a very strong move; a fantastic move
? = a bad move; a weak move
?? = a horrible move; a blunder
!? = an enterprising move; a move worthy of consideration
?! = a dubious move for theoretical or practical reasons

Since the book's subject is an original one, of necessity the exposition and analysis of the concepts is my own. The specific examples have been chosen from the following standard sources: personal knowledge, personal contacts, leading chess books and periodicals. When appropriate, direct credit is given in the text. As for all of my previous books, my partner here too has been my wonderful blonde wife Baiba. My deepest gratitude goes to her for typing the entire manuscript and for continuous moral support.

Because chess is both complicated and inexhaustible, some errors of analysis are almost inevitable. The author accepts responsibility for all of these. Your assistance in bringing them to my attention will be appreciated.

New York, 1982   Edmar Mednis

Contents

Preface

PART I: THE OPENING

Part I
THE OPENING

Everything must have its beginning and in chess this is called "the opening." The basic purpose of opening play is to get ready for the fight. Therefore in general the following three goals and principles should be observed: (1) Castling, (2) Development of pieces towards the center, (3) Control of the center, either by actual possession or short or long range action of pawns and pieces. There is no sharp dividing line between the end of the opening phase and the start of the middlegame. Technical books on the opening quite often give variations more than twenty moves long. In such cases, however, it is quite clear that the middlegame has been reached. Once the primary development activities have been completed, the game can be considered to have passed into the middlegame stage. As a broad range, this should occur within the first 10–20 moves. Usually no later than Move 15 the players have to start paying particular attention to middlegame factors.

It is in the opening that the King has the least absolute power. This does not mean that it is not important. On the contrary, great care must be taken in regard to King status and movements. It is just that correct King play consists of many more defensive considerations than opportunities for active play.

1

CHAPTER 1
Castling

SECTION 1. When to Castle

By far the most unique and important King movement is castling. Though a relatively recent (15th century) addition to the rules of chess, its introduction quickly revolutionized some major facets of opening play. This is due to the two significant benefits that castling provides: (1) King safety (the castled King is generally safer than the King left in the center) and (2) The castled Rook is activated for central play. From this it follows that early castling is a generally desirable part of good opening play. Examples from modern chess theory abound. For instance, in the normal variations of the Ruy Lopez, White castles on Move 5 (1 P–K4 P–K4 2 N–KB3 N–QB3 3 B–N5 P–QR3 4 B–R4 N–B3 5 0–0). And if Black chooses the Berlin Defense to the Ruy Lopez by playing 3 . . . N–B3, then most accurate for White is the immediate 4 0–0!. A look at the Scheveningen Variation of the Sicilian Defense shows both sides castling early in one main line: 1 P–K4 P–QB4 2 N–KB3 P–K3 3 P–Q4 PxP 4 NxP N–KB3 5 N–QB3 P–Q3 6 B–K2 B–K2 7 0–0 0–0. Similarly, watch the castling in the Normal Variation of the Pirc Defense: 1 P–K4 P–Q3 2 P–Q4 N–KB3 3 N–QB3 P–KN3 4 N–B3 B–N2 5 B–K2 0–0 6 0–0. Both sides have mobilized their Kingside forces as quickly as possible, with castling having been an integral part. For an example of maximum speed of castling for Black in a QP opening, consider this popular line in the Nimzo-Indian Defense: 1 P–Q4 N–KB3 2 P–QB4 P–K3 3 N–QB3 B–N5 4 P–K3 0–0. Maximum flexibility in early opening play is one of the characteristics of modern master strategy and there is no better illustration of this than the beginning moves of the various Reti/King's Indian Reversed complexes: 1 N–KB3 N–KB3 2 P–KN3 P–KN3 3 B–N2 B–N2 4 0–0 0–0—with both sides castled before Move 5!

Yes, early castling as a general goal is incontrovertible. Yet there is a corollary to this principle which goes as follows: *"Castle only when you have nothing better to do."* In other words—when in the position there is something specific that requires immediate attention—do that first, instead of "automatic" castling.

DIAGRAM 1

BLACK

WHITE

Mednis–Boskovic
Manhattan Int 1976
after Black's 9th move

A good example is Diagram 1, E. Mednis–M. Boskovic, Manhattan International 1976, after Black's 9th move. In an English Opening Black had committed an inaccuracy (the previous moves were: 1 P–QB4 P–K4 2 P–KN3 N–KB3 3 B–N2 N–B3 4 N–QB3 B–N5?! 5 N–Q5! B–B4 6 P–QR3! P–QR4 7 P–K3 0–0 8 N–K2 NxN 9 PxN N–K2) and the diagram shows White with a noticeable advantage in the center. White's next step should be to safeguard it and if possible enlarge on it. Therefore the active, forcing **10 P–Q4!** suggests itself. Black has nothing better than **10 . . . PxP** and after **11 NxP!** White's central superiority is secure since after e.g. 11 . . . P–QB3,

White can play 12 N–N3 B–Q3 13 P–K4 or perhaps even the immediate 12 P–K4!? (12 . . . Q–N3 13 B–K3 QxP 14 0–0 seems a promising pawn sacrifice). I of course saw 10 P–Q4, but the thought struck me, "What's the hurry—I'll play it next move!" and with *no actual thinking* I automatically played 10 0–0?!. It was only after my opponent had played the active 10 . . . P–QB3! that I started to rue my thoughtless castling. Now 11 P–Q4 KPxP 12 NxP?! allows 12 . . . NxP, and 12 KPxP leads to nothing after 12 . . . B–N3. Therefore I continued with 11 Q–B2 P–Q3 12 P–Q4 KPxP 13 KPxP, but accurate play by Black allowed him to neutralize White's slight advantage and achieve a draw (13 . . . B–N3 14 PxP NxP 15 B–K3 B–N5! 16 N–B3! NxP 17 Q–K4 B–KB4 18 QxP R–N1 19 Q–Q5 B–K3 20 Q–K4 N–N6! 21 QR–Q1 BxB 22 QxKB N–B4 23 R–Q2 N–N6 24 R/2–Q1 N–B4 25 R–Q2 N–N6 26 R/2–Q1 N–B4 27 R–Q2 draw).

DIAGRAM 2

BLACK

WHITE

Foguelman–Reshevsky
Buenos Aires 1960
after White's 12th

At first glance the situation in Diagram 2, Foguelman–Reshevsky, Buenos Aires 1960, after White's 12th move, appears less capable of giving a clearly defined sense of direction for Black. Yet with the benefit of the actual moves up to then (1 P–K4 P–QB4 2 N–KB3 P–Q3 3 P–Q4 PxP 4 NxP N–KB3 5

P–KB3?! P–K4   6 B–N5ch QN–Q2   7 N–B5 P–Q4!   8 PxP
P–QR3 9 B–R4 P–QN4   10 B–N3 N–N3   11 N–K3 B–QB4   12
N–B3) the analysis is considerably simplified. White has chosen
against the Sicilian Defense the non-developmental 5 P–KB3?!
(instead of the normal 5 N–QB3) and Black has reacted with the
theoretically recommended pawn sacrifice, thereby freeing his
position at the temporary cost of a pawn. At the moment White
already has four defenders protecting the QP and thus it appears
logical that Black has nothing better than first to complete his
development in a riskless way by playing 12 . . . 0–0 and then
go about regaining the QP. However, a concrete analysis shows
that after 12 . . . 0–0?! 13 0–0! Black lacks a good followup,
e.g. 13 . . . B–N2 14 N–K4! or 13 . . . P–N5 14 N–K4 NxN 15
PxN P–B4 16 PxP BxP 17 K–R1 and in each case the regaining
of the pawn by Black leads to positional advantage for *White*.
Therefore Reshevsky goes directly into action:

12 . . . B–N2!

Now after 13 0–0 QNxP 14 QNxN NxN 15 R–K1 0–0 Black has
regained the pawn while retaining a slight initiative. Even so this
was the best that White had.

13 N–B5?!

Of course, here 13 N–K4? fails to 13 . . . NxN 14 PxN Q–R5ch
15 P–N3 QxKP. With the dangerous looking text White tries to take
advantage of the fact that Black's QB has just moved off this
diagonal.

13 . . . P–N3!

Again there is no time for 13 . . . 0–0? because of 14 N–K4! as
after 14 . . . NxN 15 PxN Black's Queen can't check on KR5.

14 N–N7ch K–B1   15 B–R6 K–N1

The position Black had to evaluate when deciding on his 12th
move. His King and KR are awkwardly placed, but can White do
anything about this? If he cannot, then White's KN could easily go
lost. Black's concrete analysis showed that he is safe and this feeling
was reinforced by the fact that his minor pieces are actively placed.

16 Q–Q2 P–N5   17 N–K2

17 N–K4? fails to 17 . . . NxN 18 PxN Q–R5 ch.

17 . . . P–R4   18 P–Q6!? KN–Q4!

And not 18 . . . P–R5? 19 N–K6! QxP 20 Q–N5! KN–Q4 21 NxB QxN 22 QxKP (Reshevsky). Neither are 18 . . . QxP? 19 Q–N5 nor 18 . . . BxQP?! 19 0–0–0! satisfactory for Black.

19 N–N3 BxP

Black has regained the pawn advantageously and threatens to win the trapped Knight, starting with 20 . . . B–KB1. White therefore sacrifices the Knight for some attacking chances, but Black skillfully combines defense with counterattack to win in good style:

20 N(7)–B5!? PxN   21 NxP Q–B3!   22 P–N4 B–KB1!   23 B–N5 Q–N3   24 P–KR4 P–R3   25 B–K3 NxB   26 NxN P–R5   27 B–B4 NxB   28 NxN BxP   29 R–KB1 Q–K5 ch   30 Q–K3 QxQ ch   31 NxQ P–K5   32 N–Q5 K–N2   33 K–B2 R–Q1   34 N–B4 B–B4 ch   35 K–N3 B–Q3   36 QR–B1 KR–K1   37 P–B3 R–K3   38 P–N5 RPxP   39 RPxP R–N3 White resigns

Of course, it should go without saying that one should castle only when the benefits of castling—primarily greater King safety—exist. The next section will cover the general question of where the King should be. Yet it is very much worth emphasizing the point that castling should be done only when actual thinking has led to the conclusion "Yes, castle—it's safe and worthwhile to do so!" Otherwise, the same fate will await you as happened to Black in A. Alekhine–I. König, Vienna 1922, after White's 10th move. After a passively played opening (1 P–Q4 N–KB3 2 P–QB4 P–QN3 3 N–QB3 B–N2 4 Q–B2 P–Q4?! 5 PxP NxP 6 N–B3! P–K3 7 P–K4 NxN 8 PxN B–K2 9 B–N5ch! P–B3 10 B–Q3), Black finds himself in a position without counterplay opportunities. He should now try to complete his minor piece development with 10 . . . N–Q2, having in mind a potential . . . P–QB4, and in the meanwhile await White's decision of where he will put his King. Instead, Black "automatically" rushed his castling:

10 . . . 0–0?   11 P–K5! P–KR3   12 P–KR4!

After White's last two moves it is clear that he has five pieces (Q, KR, N and both Bishops) and the KRP trained against Black's insecurely defended castled King. It is easy to see that on any kind of an immediate basis, Black's King would have been considerably more secure in the center. On the other hand, note Alekhine's handling of the question of castling. He doesn't castle because he sees that there is something better to do: an immediate attack against Black's insufficiently protected King.

12 . . . P–QB4   13 R–R3!

Black's last prevented the threatened 13 N–N5 because of 13 . . . PxP!, as then the combination 14 B–R7ch K–R1   15 B–N8? is refuted by 15 . . . P–Q6!. Therefore White brings the KR into the game with decisive effect. Alekhine points out that if now 13 . . . P–B4   14 PxPe.p. BxP   15 N–N5! and White wins easily.

13 . . . K–R1   14 BxP! P–B4

Mate follows in short order after 14 . . . PxB 15 Q–Q2.

15 PxPe.p. BxP   16 B–KN5 PxP   17 N–K5!

Going all out for Black's weakened Kingside.

**17 . . . N–B3   18 Q–K2! P–N3   19 BxP K–N2   20 B–R6ch!
K–N1   21 NxN BxN   22 QxPch K–R1   23 BxR QxB   24 QxQB
Black resigns**

Section 2. Where to Put the King?

There are three things that can be done with the King: castling Kingside, castling Queenside or leaving the King in or near the center. In general, the castled King is safer than the King left in the center; also, in general, Kingside castling leads to greater King safety than Queenside castling. On the Queenside there is somewhat greater territory to protect in front of the King; in particular, the QRP is unprotected, and if the King moves over to protect it this not only costs a tempo but to a lesser extent also distances the King from the protection of the QR. Additionally, the Q-file is usually at least semi-open, and this again makes access to the castled King on QB1 easier. However, from the above it does not follow that preference must always be given to Kingside castling whenever it's safe to do so. There may well be other considerations involved. For instance, consider the "old" or safer method for White against the Sicilian Dragon: 1 P–K4 P–QB4 2 N–KB3 P–Q3 3 P–Q4 PxP 4 NxP N–KB3 5 N–QB3 P–KN3 6 B–K2 N–B3 7 B–K3 B–N2 8 0–0 0–0. There is nothing at all wrong with White's build-up, yet the fact that both sides have castled on the same side means that White has few chances for a massive attack against Black's King and must satisfy himself with strategic, centrally directed maneuvering. If he wants to be able to mount direct attacks against Black's King, White should select the sharp Yugoslav Attack: 1 P–K4 P–QB4 2 N–KB3 P–Q3 3 P–Q4 PxP 4 NxP N–KB3 5 N–QB3 P–KN3 6 B–K3 B–N2 7 P–B3 N–B3 8 Q–Q2 0–0 9 B–QB4 B–Q2 10 0–0–0. White now will be able to generate a strong attack by throwing his Kingside pawns forward, but at the same time Black will obtain strong counterplay against White's King along the QB file. Objectively, both approaches are equally promising for White; the character of play is significantly different, however. There is no objective basis for making a choice. Instead, the basis for the decision must involve personal and/or psychological factors.

Most of the time, however, there are valid strategic bench marks for deciding where to put the King. Let us first consider A. Alekhine–M. Euwe, Match Game No. 7, 1935, after White's 10th move of a French Defense (1 P–K4 P–K3 2 P–Q4 P–Q4 3 N–QB3 B–N5 4 KN–K2 PxP 5 P–QR3 B–K2 6 NxP N–QB3 7 P–KN4?! P–QN3?! 8 B–N2 B–N2 9 P–QB3 N–B3 10 N/2–N3). White has sent his KNP forward to try to get something going on the Kingside. As Alekhine has pointed out, Black should now continue with 10 . . . Q–Q2, followed by 11 . . . 0–0–0. Black's King would be quite safe there, because White has nothing pointing in that direction, while Black has lots of defenders around his King. Such a plan would give Black virtual equality, as there would be no way for White to capitalize on his slight space advantage. However, Black "preferred":

10 . . . 0–0?

In the trade we call such action "castling into it," as rather obviously White is already aiming at Black's Kingside.

11 P–N5 NxN   12 NxN K–R1   13 Q–R5! Q–K1?!

Safer is 13 . . . N–R4!, after which White's best is 14 B–B4 followed by Q-side castling.

14 N–B6! BxN

Or 14 . . . PxN 15 PxP N–R4 (15 . . . BxBP? 16 B–K4) 16 PxB QxP 17 BxB NxB 18 B–N5 P–KB3 19 B–R6 R–KN1 20 0–0–0 N–Q3 21 KR–K1 with advantage to White (Alekhine).

15 PxB PxP 16 Q–R4 Q–Q1 17 B–B4! P–K4 18 B–N3 P–B4 19 PxP R–KN1 and now, instead of 20 B–B3? Q–Q6! which gave Black sufficient counterchances for equality (White won in 41 anyway), practically decisive, according to Alekhine, would have been 20 **Q–R3!**: 20 . . . Q–Q6 21 B–R4! or 20 . . . R–N5 21 0–0! followed by 22 P–B3.

DIAGRAM 3

BLACK

WHITE

Corzo–Capablanca
Havana 1913
after White's 14th

What should Black do with his King in Diagram 3, J. Corzo–J. R. Capablanca, Havana 1913, after White's 14th? The course of the unusual King's Indian type of opening (1 P–Q4 N–KB3 2 P–QB4 P–Q3 3 N–QB3 QN–Q2 4 P–K4 P–K4 5 P–B4?! PxQP 6 QxP N–B4 7 B–K3 Q–K2! 8 N–Q5 NxN 9 KPxN B–B4 10 N–B3?! P–KN3! 11 K–B2 R–KN1 12 R–K1 B–N2 13 Q–Q1 N–K5ch 14 K–N1) has allowed Black to activate his minor pieces while chasing White's King into an awkward spot. With White's Rook on K1 pointing at Black's Queen/King battery, it is clear that Black's King must get out of the way. Kingside castling is impossible and Queenside castling is inadvisable. Capablanca says laconically "not 14 . . . 0-0-0 which would expose Black to very strong attacks." Golombek provides the following specific variation after 14 . . . 0-0-0?: 15 BxP! P-N3 16 Q-R4 K-N2 17 P-B5!! and White wins. From a strategic basis such a result is not surprising, since after Queenside castling Black's King is bereft of defenders, whereas White can quickly generate attackers. Therefore correct for Black is Capablanca's:

14 . . . K-B1!

Note that here, with defenders all around him, the King feels quite comfortable.

15 B-Q4 P-KN4! 16 BxBch

16 NxP? is refuted by 16 . . . BxBch 17 QxB NxN 18 RxQ N-R6mate.

16 . . . RxB 17 N-Q4 B-Q2 18 P-KB5 Q-K4 19 Q-Q3 R-K1 20 N-K6ch PxN 21 BPxP RxP!

A very strong sacrifice of the Exchange, made quite sound by virtue of White's playing without his KR. In what follows too, Capablanca plays perfect chess to win.

22 PxR B-B3 23 Q-B3ch Q-B5! 24 Q-K3 K-K2! 25 P-QN4 P-N3 26 P-N5 B-N2 27 P-N3 N-Q7 28 Q-QB3?! N-B6ch 29 K-B2 Q-B1 30 P-B5 N-K4ch 31 K-N1 N-B6ch 32 K-B2 NPxP 33 Q-R5 N-K4ch 34 K-N1 Q-B6 35 QxPch K-B3 36 QxQP QxRch 37 K-B2 QxPch White resigns

Consider now the situation in Z. Lanka–M. Minasyan, USSR 1978, after White's 21st move. In the course of a very sharp variation in the Sicilian, which was very popular in the late 1970s, Black sacrificed the Exchange for more than full compensation: 1 P-K4 P-QB4 2 N-KB3 N-QB3 3 P-Q4 PxP 4 NxP N-B3 5 N-QB3 P-K4 6 N/4-N5 P-Q3 7 B-N5 P-QR3 8 N-R3 P-N4 9 BxN PxB 10 N-Q5 P-B4 11 P-KN3?! PxP 12 B-N2 B-K3 13 BxP B-N2 14 Q-R5 R-QB1 15 0-0 N-K2 16 QR-Q1 R-B4 17

N–K3 P–Q4 18 P–QN4 R–B6! 19 N–N1 RxN! 20 PxR Q–N3 21 Q–N5. Black has a very strong center and the Bishop pair, and excellent play against various weak pawns. With his last move White protected his KP and attacked Black's KB. Black's Bishop must be protected—and is there anything simpler and more purposeful than castling? I don't think so, and after 21 . . . 0–0! 22 B–N2 P–B3 Black would win the KP with check and have the better chances. Instead Black unaccountably played:

21 . . . K–B1??

How can this be better than castling? The King is less safe and the KR is boxed in—the very benefits that castling can provide! Castling should always be the first choice; only when it is unsuitable should a King move be preferred. Note also that this is inherently an *attacking position for Black*, and yet as played he can't utilize his Rook at all.

22 B–N2 P–R3 23 Q–R5 QxP ch 24 K–R1 P–K5 25 B–R3!

Compared to the situation possible after Black's castling, this is completely unsatisfactory for him: his King is unsafe and he's playing without his Rook. No wonder that already White has a winning attack!

25 . . . Q–N3 26 R–B4 P–B4 27 R/1–KB1 B–K4 28 RxPch! BxR 29 BxB B–B3 30 N–B3! Q–K6 31 B–K6 Black resigns

He'll be mated in short order. What a drastic turn of events!

But if we look at Diagram 4, A. Bisguier–S. Gligoric, Bled 1961 also after White's 21st move, we see that Black's situation is significantly different. As a result of time-wasting in a Scheveningen Sicilian (1 P–K4 P–QB4 2 N–KB3 P–Q3 3 P–Q4 PxP 4 NxP N–KB3 5 N–QB3 P–QR3 6 B–K2 P–K3 7 0–0 Q–B2 8 P–B4 QN–Q2 9 B–B3 B–K2 10 K–R1 N–B1? 11 P–KN4! P–R3 12 P–B5 P–K4 13 KN–K2 B–Q2 14 P–QR4 B–B3 15 B–K3 N/1–Q2 16 N–N3 R–QB1 17 Q–K2 Q–N1 18 P–R5 Q–B2 19 P–N4 Q–N1 20 R–B2 N–R2 21 N–R5) Black finds himself in a very passive position. The clear need is for *defense*, and the immediate point that needs defending is the KNP. Here the obvious 21 . . . 0–0 does not work out well, as after e.g. 22 Q–Q2 B–KN4

DIAGRAM 4

BLACK

WHITE

Bisguier–Gligoric
Bled 1961
after White's 21st

23 R–Q1 Black has difficulties with both his backward QP and in preventing White's dangerous pawn storm on the Kingside via P–KR4 and P–KN5. Therefore better is:

21 . . . K–B1!

Not only is the King closer to the QP here, but the Rook on KR1 is better placed defensively because in case of White's potential P–KR4 and P–KN5 the Rook is opposite the White King. This not only makes it harder for White to get in P–KN5 but, even if he does achieve it, Black can hope to get some counterchances along the KR file.

22 R–Q1 B–KN4 23 BxB NxB 24 B–N2?

Speed in attack was of the essence here: 24 P–R4!, with White better whether Black exchanges or retreats. The Bishop retreat is even counterproductive because the KNP is left insufficiently protected.

24 . . . N–R2! 25 P–R4?!

25 Q–Q2 N/R–B3! with approximate equality was White's best.

25 . . . N/Q–B3 26 N–N3 B–Q2 27 N–Q5 NxN 28 PxN?

Leaves White completely without counterplay and allows Black to start walking in via all the weaknesses in White's position. Correct was 28 RxN, with White having chances along the Q-file.

28 . . . B–N4   29 Q–B3 N–B3   30 B–B1 BxB   31 NxB R–B5   32 N–K3 RxQNP   33 P–B4 Q–R2!   34 K–N1 R–N6   35 R–K1 Q–Q5 36 R–KN2 K–K2   37 Q–B2 K–Q2!

A King move to negate White's threat: e.g. if 37 . . . R–QB1? 38 P–N5 PxP   39 PxP N–K5   40 P–B6ch PxP   41 N–B5ch.

38 R–N3 R–QB1   39 Q–QR2 RxN! White resigns

The need for King safety via castling greatly diminishes as exchanges take place. In endgame-type positions, there is usually no need at all to castle, and very often the King in the center is both safe and desirable. In A. Karpov–V. Korchnoi, World Championship Match 1978, Game No. 16, after Black's 13th move, the game has transposed directly from the opening into the endgame (1 P–K4 P–K3   2 P–Q4 P–Q4   3 N–Q2 P–QB4   4 KPxP KPxP   5 B–N5ch B–Q2   6 Q–K2ch Q–K2   7 BxBch NxB   8 PxP NxP   9 N–N3 QxQch   10 NxQ NxN   11 RPxN B–B4   12 B–Q2 N–K2   13 N–B4 0–0). Karpov now played 14 0–0 KR–Q1   15 N–Q3 B–N3 16 P–B3 P–B3   17 KR–Q1, but after 17 . . . K–B2 there was nothing better for White than getting his King closer to the center with 18 K–B1—yielding a very minute advantage for White. True, Black still has the isolated QP, but White has lost valuable time with his King "moves." Tal therefore recommends as stronger the immediate:

14 N–Q3! B–N3   15 B–R5

Black has nothing better than to exchange and after

15 . . . BxB   16 RxB KR–Q1   17 K–Q2! White is clearly better.

His King is actively placed in the center, his Rooks have play along the QR file (Black's 17 . . . P–QR3 allows White's QNP to move forward to N5 as an attacker) and Black's QP remains a chronic weakness.

Section 3.
Keeping the Castled King Position Safe

It is all well and good to have gotten the King to relative safety by castling, but the effect will be short lived if the player then forgets about his King. The King needs help from two quarters for reasonable safety: (1) There must be sufficient pieces nearby to repel any attack, and (2) The pawn formation in front of him must be sound. It is difficult to generalize regarding the amount of defensive help required, as it obviously depends on the particular position. Capablanca has suggested, as a general principle, defending "with as few pieces as you can," since this means having available as many pieces as possible for offensive work someplace else. I would add that, whenever in doubt, choose to err on the side of safety; obviously, the end of your King is the end of the game.

The subject of soundness of pawn chains in front of the King is easier to tackle. For maximum safety the pawns should not be moved, which means that for the Kingside–castled King the KB, KN and KR pawns should be on the second rank; similarly for Queenside castling, the QR, QN and QB pawns should remain unmoved. Such pawn configurations impart strength in two ways: (1) A maximum number of squares in the immediate vicinity of the King are well guarded, and (2) The opponent will experience maximum difficulties in forcing open lines by means of throwing his own pawns forward. From this it follows that if you expect a direct attack on your King, you should be most reluctant to move any of your Kingside pawns and thus create an object of attack. For example, if you expect Black to play . . . P–KN4, don't play P–KR3, as this will give Black the chance to attack your KRP with the simple . . . P–KN5.

The following two examples will demonstrate the proper defensive handling of pawn chains under intensive attack both on the Kingside and Queenside. Diagram 5, S. Reshevsky–B. Malich, Siegen Olympiad 1970, arose after Black's 10th move in a Sicilian Scheveningen (1 P–K4 P–QB4 2 N–KB3 P–K3 3 P–Q4 PxP 4 NxP N–KB3 5 N–QB3 P–Q3 6 B–QB4 B–K2 7 B–N3 0–0 8 B–K3 N–R3! 9 P–B3 N–B4 10 Q–Q2 P–QR3). Black has employed optimum piece development against White's somewhat premature KB maneuver and has good equality here. White

DIAGRAM 5

BLACK

WHITE

Reshevsky–Malich
Siegen Olympiad 1970
after Black's 10th

therefore decides that his best practical approach is a violent pawn storm against Black's Kingside. Black's defensive strategy is a model for coping with such storms:

11 P–N4 Q–B2!

Black gets ready for Queenside counterplay. Definitely wrong would be 11 . . . P–R3?, since after 12 P–KR4 followed by 13 P–KN5 White would get open lines on the Kingside for nothing.

12 P–N5 KN–Q2   13 P–KR4 P–N4   14 P–N6!? N–K4!!

14 . . . BPxP?! would leave the KP hanging and after 14 . . . RPxP 15 P–R5! White would get open KN and KR files against Black's King for his sacrificed pawn. By allowing White's KNP to live Black allows White to open only the KN file, while he readies at the same time central and Queenside counterplay.

15 PxRPch K–R1!

By not capturing it, Black is able to use the forward KRP as a shield to minimize White's attacking power along the KR file.

16 P–R3 R–QN1   17 K–B2

White doesn't want to castle Queenside because of Black's

imminent attack there. Nevertheless, his King would have been somewhat safer there than in the center.

17 . . . B–N2   18 QR–KN1 P–B4!

Both attacking White's King and allowing a multipiece defense of the KNP—Black's remaining vulnerable Kingside point.

19 K–K1 PxP   20 Q–N2 B–KB3   21 PxP QR–K1! Draw!

Partly out of respect for his famous opponent, Black here accepted White's draw offer. With all of his pieces well placed for both defense and offense, Black's prospects are the superior ones.

And now for optimum handling of defense/offense for White, after castling on the Queenside. We'll start our action with an example that developed out of another sub-variation of the Sicilian Scheveningen in E. Mednis–J. Timman, Sombor 1974, after White's 11th move (1 P–K4 P–QB4   2 N–KB3 P–K3   3 P–Q4 PxP 4 NxP N–KB3   5 N–QB3 P–Q3   6 P–KN4 N–B3   7 P–N5 N–Q2   8 B–K3 N–B4?!   9 Q–Q2 P–QR3   10 0–0–0 B–Q2   11 P–B4). Compared to the previous game, Black's . . . N–QB4 maneuver is not successful here, because White, by not having lost time with his KB, is able quickly to set up a harmonious attacking position:

11 . . . P–N4   12 B–N2!

Developing while protecting the KP. Again 12 P–QR3? would only serve to create a vulnerable point for Black's eventual . . . P–QN5 advance.

12 . . . P–N5   13 N/3–K2 R–QN1   14 K–N1! Q–B2   15 P–KR4

White has completed his development, safeguarded his King as much as is reasonable and now continues his attack on Black's Kingside.

15 . . . P–QR4   16 P–R5 P–R5   17 P–N6 P–N6?!

Black's King position will now be too vulnerable. It was imperative to keep the lines against the King as closed as possible by playing 17 . . . BPxP 18 PxP P–R3.

18 PxPch KxP   19 BPxP PxP   20 P–R3! P–R3

Preventing 21 P–R6. It is clear that Black has nothing in particular available on the Queenside, because (1) White, by playing his King away from QB1, has negated any immediate chances for Black along the QB file and (2) White has—in effect—kept the QR and QN files closed. Thus White has more than sufficient time to carry out his own attacking plans.

21 KR–KB1! NxN 22 NxN K–K1 23 Q–KB2! B–B1 24 P–K5! R–N3

Or 24 . . . B–R3 25 B–B6ch N–Q2 26 Q–N3! BxR 27 Q–N6ch K–K2 28 QxKPch K–Q1 29 RxB and Black is defenseless.

25 P–B5! B–N2 26 PxKP PxP 27 Q–N3! BxB?!

After 27 . . . P–N4!? White's fastest win is 28 PxPe.p.! BxB 29 QxB PxN 30 BxQP R–KN1 31 P–N7!.

28 Q–N6ch K–Q1 29 N–N5ch R–Q3

29 . . . B–Q3 loses a Rook: 30 NxQ B–K5ch 31 QxB NxQ 32 BxR.

30 QxB Black resigns

SECTION 4. Castling "by Hand"

Because of the desirable King and Rook placements that result after castling, it is often advantageous to achieve such placements by artificial means if the natural castling move is impossible. "Castling" this way is called castling "by hand." A relatively simple example is shown in Diagram 6, E. Mednis–J.J. van Oosterom, Antwerp 1955, after Black's 12th move. The somewhat extravagant variation of the Two Knights' Defense chosen by Black has prevented White from castling, but this has cost Black time (1 P–K4 P–K4 2 N–KB3 N–QB3 3 B–B4 N–B3 4 N–N5 P–Q4 5 PxP N–QR4 6 B–N5ch P–B3 7 PxP PxP 8 B–K2 P–KR3 9 N–KB3 P–K5 10 N–K5 Q–Q5 11 P–KB4 B–QB4 12 R–B1 Q–Q1). White must play resolutely to try to take advantage of this:

13 P–Q4! B–N3

This natural retreat leads to insufficient counterchances for the sacrificed pawn. Also unsatisfactory are 13 . . . BxP 14 P–B3 and

DIAGRAM 6

BLACK

WHITE

Mednis–Van Oosterom
Antwerp 1955
after Black's 12th

13 . . . QxP 14 QxQ BxQ 15 P–B3, in both cases with big endgame advantages for White. Black's best practical chance is 13 . . . PxPe.p.!? 14 QxP Q–B2 to keep the position as open as possible.

14 P–B3!

By safeguarding the center White gets ready for the coming King flight.

14 . . . N–Q4   15 K–B2! 0–0   16 K–N1!

White has gotten his King to safety by artificial castling and is in secure possession of the gambit pawn. Black's attempts at counterplay after opening the position are easily turned away.

16 . . . P–QB4   17 PxP BxPch   18 K–R1 B–K6?   19 P–QN4! N–N2?!

Loses immediately, but even after the better 19 . . . BxB   20 QxB N–N2   21 R–Q1 the pin along the Q-file is devastating.

20 N–B6 Q–B2

Resigned to his fate. Black saw that 20 . . . Q–Q3 allows 21 QxN QxQ 22 N–K7ch. White now takes the piece and wins easily.

21 QxN BxB 22 RxB N–Q3 23 R–Q1 N–B4 24 QxP P–N3 25
P–N5 B–N2 26 P–B4 KR–K1 27 Q–B3 R–K6 28 Q–B2 QR–K1
29 B–N4 R/6–K5 30 BxN RxKBP 31 Q–N3 BxN 32 PxB Q–K4
33 N–B3 QxB 34 N–Q5 RxP 35 N–K3 **Black resigns**

Remembering the possibility of castling "by hand" can often
help to get one out of a tough spot. Consider W. Heidenfeld–H.J.
Hecht, Nice Olympiad 1974, after Black's 12th move. After
opening errors (1 P–K4 N–KB3 2 N–QB3 P–Q4 3 P–K5 N–K5 4
P–Q4?! NxN 5 PxN P–K3 6 B–Q3? P–QB4 7 P–KB4 N–B3 8
N–B3 Q–R4 9 B–Q2 Q–R5 10 B–K3 P–B5 11 B–K2 B–R6 12
B–QB1 Q–R4), White finds himself with an apparently in-
defensible forward QBP (13 B–Q2 allows 13 . . . B–N7, while 13
Q–Q2 BxB forces White to choose between losing his QR or QB
pawns). Yet White fashions a way both to protect his weak
Queenside pawns and get his King castled:

13 K–Q2! B–K2 14 Q–K1! B–Q2 15 K–K3! P–B3 16 R–B1 PxP
17 BPxP 0–0 18 K–B2! B–K1 19 K–N1 and White is out of all
immediate trouble.

I would have liked to say that this story had a happy ending, but
it didn't. The fundamental weaknesses in White's Queenside
remain, and by playing outstanding chess Black won in 54 moves.

A sophisticated version of Queenside "castling" is shown starting
from Diagram 7, G. Ligterink–E. Geller, Wijk aan Zee 1977, after
White's 13th move of an ultra–sharp Sicilian Najdorf (1 P–K4
P–QB4 2 N–KB3 P–Q3 3 P–Q4 PxP 4 NxP N–KB3 5 N–QB3
P–QR3 6 B–KN5 P–K3 7 P–B4 Q–N3 8 Q–Q2 QxP 9 N–N3
Q–R6 10 BxN PxB 11 B–K2 N–B3 12 0–0 B–Q2 13 K–R1). In
order to win the "poisoned" QNP Black has lost valuable
development time. However, because White's QNP is missing,
there are basic weaknesses in his Queenside position. Black aims for
counterplay against White's Queenside before White has sufficient
time to get at Black's loosened Kingside:

13 . . . R–B1! 14 P–B5 N–K4!

Activity is of utmost necessity here. After 14 . . . P–KR4? 15
PxP PxP 16 RxP White has advantageously recoved his pawn.

15 PxP PxP! 16 B–R5ch K–Q1! 17 N–K2

DIAGRAM 7

BLACK

WHITE

Ligterink–Geller
Wijk aan Zee 1977
after White's 13th

After 17 RxP Q–N5! 18 Q–N5 K–B2! Black's King is safe and he threatens both 19 . . . QxN and 19 . . . B–K2. After 19 Q–N3 K–N1! the double attack on the Knight forces White to move it, and this leaves White's KP unprotected.

17 . . . K–B2! 18 N–B4 K–N1! 19 Q–B2 B–R3

Black has castled the "Kingside" way on the Queenside, making his King safe and the Rook ready for action along the QB file. According to Geller White should now continue with 20 N–Q4! BxN 21 QxB KR–B1 22 Q–R6, with Black having only a slight edge after 22 . . . Q–B4. Instead, White tries a combination—with a hole!

20 NxP? BxN 21 QxP B–QB5

Overlooked by White. Since 22 QxB BxR is hopeless for White, he plays on a few moves with a piece down and then resigns.

22 KR–K1 N–N3 23 P–K5 PxP 24 QR–N1 KR–B1 25 Q–N6 R–QB3 White resigns

SECTION 5. Castling as a Surprise Weapon

Anyone who has read this far is fully aware of castling. Isn't every master familiar with castling? Yes, of course . . . but in competitive chess strange things sometimes happen. One of these is not noticing the possibility of castling when considering prospective play. This is generally a problem which hits the attacker much more than the defender. The defending side is usually looking at various ways to get out of or stay out of trouble. However, the attacker is so preoccupied with his own threats that he may neglect to look at castling as a possible move by the opponent. A legendary example is Hoffman–Petroff, Warsaw 1844, after White's 12th move. In a Giuoco Piano, after 1 P–K4 P–K4   2 N–KB3 N–QB3   3 B–B4 B–B4   4 P–B3 N–B3   5 P–Q4 PxP   6 P–K5 N–K5?!   7 B–Q5 NxKBP   8 KxN PxPch   9 K–N3 PxP   10 BxNP N–K2, instead of continuing with the developmental 11 N–B3, White thought the time ripe for the combinational 11 N–N5? NxB 12 NxBP. The idea was 12 . . . KxN?   13 QxNch followed by 14 QxB. Yet Black can ignore White's threat:

12 . . . 0–0!!   13 NxQ

White wants to be shown. There is nothing better, as 13 QxN RxN   14 QxB leads to mate starting with 14 . . . Q–N4ch. Note the importance throughout this example of getting the KR into the game.

13 . . . B–B7ch   14 K–R3 P–Q3ch   15 P–K6 N–B5ch   16 K–N4 NxKP!

A quiet move, yet White has no way of getting his King to safety (e.g., 17 Q–Q5 R–B5ch 18 K–R3 R–KR5mate).

17 NxN BxNch   18 K–N5 R–B4ch   19 K–N4 P–R4ch   20 K–R3 R–B6mate

In the above example, castling was as much of an attacking move as a defensive one. The next three examples show it as a defensive move—to the surprise of the attacker. In S. Lyman–E. Mednis, New England Open 1964, White tried to refute a complicated variation of the Sicilian Richter by ultra-sharp play. In the process, however, he first neglected to note Black's considerable chances for counterplay and then a defensive resource by Black.

DIAGRAM 8

BLACK

WHITE

Lyman–Mednis
New England Open 1964
after Black's 17th

For our purposes the decisive action starts with Diagram 8, after Black's 17th move (1 P–K4 P–QB4 2 N–KB3 N–QB3 3 P–Q4 PxP 4 NxP N–B3 5 N–QB3 P–Q3 6 B–KN5 P–K3 7 Q–Q2 P–QR3 8 0–0–0 B–Q2 9 P–B4 B–K2 10 N–B3 P–N4 11 P–K5 P–N5 12 PxN PxN 13 QxBP PxP 14 P–B5?! P–Q4! 15 PxP PxP 16 B–K2?! N–N5! 17 K–N1 R–QB1). White seems to be in trouble, since his Queen is attacked, and, if it moves from the QR1–KR8 diagonal, White's QB hangs, while 18 Q–Q4 is refuted by 18 . . . NxBP. Yet White had anticipated this position and had counted on the following surprising move:

18 N–K5!?

With the pretty idea 18 . . . RxQ? 19 B–R5ch K–B1 20 B–R6ch K–N1 21 B–B7mate. Also losing for Black are 18 . . . PxN? and 18 . . . PxB?. However . . .

18 . . . 0–0!!

Black's King now is safe and the monkey is on White's back: he has three pieces *en prise*. Black wins one of them by force and with it the game:

19 Q–KN3 PxB 20 P–KR4 Q–B2 21 P–B3 B–KB3! 22 PxP QxN White resigns

Another example of castling foiling the reckless attacker occurred in B. Spassky–A. Suetin, 1963 USSR Team Matches. The first part of the Queen's Gambit Accepted opening developed routinely: 1 P–Q4 P–Q4 2 P–QB4 PxP 3 N–KB3 N–KB3 4 P–K3 P–K3 5 BxP P–B4 6 0–0 P–QR3 7 Q–K2 P–QN4 8 B–N3 B–N2 9 R–Q1 Q–B2 10 N–B3 QN–Q2 11 P–K4 PxP. But now in place of the normal 12 NxQP with a slight advantage to White, Spassky ventured the sharp but unsound 12 P–K5?. He had in mind the position resulting after 12 . . . PxN 13 PxN NxP 14 N–K5 B–B4 15 B–KB4 Q–N3, and now was ready to bamboozle Black with:

16 NxP

With the plan 16 . . . KxN? 17 R–Q6!!, and after 17 . . . BxR, 18 QxKPch followed by devastation. But Black, being a pawn up, can simply ignore the Knight!

16 . . . 0–0!! 17 N–N5?!

Taken aback by Black's unexpected shot, White reacts too meekly. The only way to get some play was with 17 N–Q6.

17 . . . PxP 18 QR–N1 QR–K1 19 RxP Q–B3 20 N–B3 N–K5! and Black soon won.

Not only is Black a pawn up, but it is now he who has the attack!

Note that the name of the defender who sprang the surprising castling move was Aleksei Suetin. Couldn't one feel secure in thinking that the Soviet GM would always look out for such possibilities? Yet ten years later look at what happens to him when in the role of the attacker. Diagram 9 shows A. Suetin–B. Ivkov, Portoroz/Ljubljana 1973, after Black's 17th move. By decidedly superior opening play (1 P–K4 P–K4 2 N–KB3 N–QB3 3 B–N5 P–QR3 4 B–R4 P–Q3 5 0–0 B–Q2 6 P–Q4 N–B3 7 P–B4!? B–K2?! 8 P–Q5! N–R2 9 BxBch QxB 10 N–B3 P–B4?! 11 PxPe.p. QxP?! 12 B–N5! QxBP?! 13 BxN BxB 14 QxP N–B1 15 Q–R3 N–K2?! 16 QR–B1 R–QB1 17 NxP! Q–K3) White has won a good pawn and can easily consolidate his advantage with 18 N–Q3! BxN 19 RxB RxR 20 QxR 0–0 21 Q–N4. But why such a prosaic line, he thought, when there is a sparkling winning combination?

DIAGRAM 9

BLACK

WHITE
Suetin–Ivkov
Ljubljana/Portoroz 1973
after Black's 17th

18 Q–R4ch?? P–QN4   19 NxNP

White of course had expected Black's 18th and had prepared this response. The plan is clear: 19 . . . PxN? 20 QxPch K–B1 21 N–Q7ch K–N1 22 RxRch! NxR 23 R–B1 and White wins. As Suetin tells it, he was horror-stricken when he noticed, as he was playing this move, that it's legal for Black to castle.

19 . . . 0–0!

Now both of White's Knights are *en prise* and one must be lost.

20 RxR NxR   21 N–B4 PxN   22 QxP QxP

White has two connected passed pawns for the piece, but the pawns cannot be quickly mobilized, whereas Black's forces rapidly come into play. Black won without difficulties as follows:

23 P–QN3 Q–K7   24 P–QR4 R–Q1!   25 P–R3 B–Q5   26 Q–KB5 P–N3   27 Q–B4 Q–K3   28 Q–B3 N–Q3!   29 N–R5 N–K5   30 Q–K2 BxPch!   31 RxB R–Q7   32 N–B4 RxQ White resigns

A more complicated version of neglecting to consider the opponent's right to castle occurs in our last example, V. Korchnoi–J. Timman, 1977 Dutch Championship, after White's 21st move. As

a consequence of a sharply played opening (1 P–QB4 P–K4   2
N–QB3 N–KB3   3 N–B3 N–B3   4 P–K3 B–N5   5 Q–B2 P–Q3   6
P–Q3 B–N5   7 B–K2 BxNch   8 QxB Q–Q2   9 P–KR3 B–R4   10
P–KN4 B–N3   11 P–K4 P–QR4   12 B–K3 P–N3?!   13 N–R4?!
Q–K2   14 P–N5 N–R4   15 BxN BxB   16 N–B5 Q–B1   17 P–B4
0–0–0   18 N–N3 P–R3!   19 PxRP RxP   20 PxP R–R2   21 P–Q4!)
Black has sacrificed a pawn to open lines against White's position.
After the simple retreat   21 . . . B–N3! Black's prospects would be
fully equal, e.g. 22 0–0–0 PxP   23 P–Q5 N–N5 or   22 P–R3 PxP   23
P–Q5 N–Q5!   24 BxN PxB   25 QxQP Q–Q3!. But isn't there
something sharper?

21 . . . B–B6?   22 0–0!

The King is safe enough here, and the tempo gained by the
attack on the Bishop is of crucial importance. Not wanting to
remain down a clear pawn after 22 . . . B–R4   23 PxP, Black
decided to "complicate" with. . .

22 . . . BxP?!   23 NxB PxP   24 P–Q5 RxRP

. . . but White consolidated without too much difficulty and won
convincingly:

**25 K–N2! R–R5   26 N–N3! N–Q5   27 BxN PxB   28 Q–Q2 R–Q3
29 R–B4 Q–R1   30 RxR QxR   31 R–R1 Q–N5   32 Q–K2! Q–N3
33 Q–K4 P–N4   34 QxQ RxQ   35 PxP R–Q3   36 N–B5 R–N3ch
37 K–B3 Black resigns**

SECTION 6. Closing the Door on Castling: Does It Create a Serious Disadvantage?

As was discussed earlier, castling is a very desirable operation in
general. Yet a frequently occurring question is: How hard should
we strive to ensure that we keep the option of castling? Should we
take time out to prevent a check which would force a King move
and thereby prevent future castling? Are winning chances
significantly increased (without incurring a proportional increase
in risk of a loss) by forfeiting the right to castle in order to keep
more material on the board? This section will attempt to answer
the above questions; the general subject of having the King in the
middle of the board will be taken up in Chapters 2 and 3.

A. FORFEITING RIGHT OF CASTLING BY VOLUNTARILY ALLOWING A CHECK

Some openings almost seem to require that the opponent be tempted to give an early check, the answer to which must be a King move. By far the best example of this is the King's Gambit Accepted (1 P-K4 P-K4 2 P-KB4 PxP). What does the temptor hope to gain by his dare? Basically he counts on driving back the checking piece with a gain of time and thereby gain an advantage in development. In the King's Gambit this is joined by the expectation of achieving a considerable central superiority. It is hoped that these two factors will outweigh the inherently loose King position. An excellent illustration of these principles is provided by the game A. Planinc-B. Ivkov, 1978 Yugoslavian Championship:

1 P-K4 P-K4 2 P-KB4 PxP 3 N-KB3 B-K2 4 N-B3!? B-R5ch?!

Black can't resist making White's King move. Yet the check works out to be a loss of time, since the passively placed Black pieces cannot follow up with an attack against the centrally placed White King. Better chances for equality are given by the developmental 4 . . . N-KB3 5 P-Q4 P-Q4.

5 K-K2 P-Q3 6 P-Q4 B-N5 7 BxP N-QB3 8 Q-Q3 KN-K2 9 K-Q2!

By unpinning the Knight White now threatens Black's KB.

9 . . . BxN 10 PxB Q-Q2 11 R-Q1! 0-0-0 12 K-B1!

Notice how White has gotten his King to safety by castling "by hand."

12 . . . K-N1 13 Q-K3 P-QR3, with a nice advantage for White.

White has a sound central superiority, the two Bishops in a fairly open position, and his King is quite safe. On the other hand, Black's position is still passive, while the "checking" KB is doing nothing on the edge of the board, and Black will need to spend a move to get it usefully placed. White has several logical ways to proceed; one is to conclude minor piece development by

DIAGRAM 10

BLACK

WHITE

Planinc–Ivkov
1978 Yugoslavian Cham-
pionship
after Black's 13th

playing 14 B–B4. Instead he rushes into an attack, sacrifices unnecessarily and blunders in time pressure. The game continued:

14 P–Q5?! N–K4   15 R–Q4 B–B3   16 R–N4 P–B4!   17 PxP e.p. N/4xQBP   18 R–N3 N–Q5   19 R–R3 B–K4   20 B–N3 P–KN4! 21 K–N1 R–QB1   22 B–B2 P–R3   23 BxP?! PxB   24 Q–Q3 N–N4 25 NxN PxN   26 R–R5 R–B2   27 Q–R3 Q–B3   28 P–QB4 P–QN5! 29 QxPch R–N2   30 R–N5 R–QB1   31 Q–R5 R/1–B2! 32 R–QB1? RxR   33 QxRch QxQ   34 PxQ RxRch   35 KxR BxP White resigns

An important position in the Meran Defense of the Queen's Gambit Declined results after 1 P–Q4 P–Q4   2 P–QB4 P–QB3   3 N–KB3 N–KB3   4 N–B3 P–K3   5 P–K3 QN–Q2   6 B–Q3 PxP   7 BxBP P–QN4   8 B–Q3 B–N2   9 P–K4 P–N5   10 N–QR4 P–B4   11 P–K5 N–Q4   12 NxP NxN   13 PxN BxP.

White's most fruitful continuation now is 14 0–0!. Black can't respond with 14 . . . 0–0? because White can play either 15 Q–B2 or 15 BxPch. Black's best is 14 . . . P–KR3, and then with 15 N–Q2! White starts a successful regrouping and keeps a slight advantage, as in L. Polugaevsky–E. Mecking, Manila 1975. But doesn't White have a way to put more pressure on his opponent? Let's now follow W. Uhlmann–B. Larsen, Match Game No. 6, Las Palmas 1971:

14 B–N5ch?!

Prevents Black from castling—but as the previous note showed, Black wasn't threatening it anyway. The cost of the move is that the Bishop is misplaced, and to reposition it will require another move. Because of the active placement of Black's minor pieces and Black's strong central presence, White will have no meaningful way to follow on this check.

14 . . . K–K2 15 0–0

Even less promising is 15 B–N5ch?! P–B3 16 B–KR4 Q–R4!, and it is already Black who is attacking.

15 . . . Q–N3 16 B–Q3 P–KR3 17 Q–K2 KR–Q1! 18 B–Q2 K–B1! 19 QR–B1 QR–B1, with a slight advantage to Black.

Black has, in effect, almost castled by hand and his King is normally safe on KB1. Black has completed his development with all of his pieces standing well and actively. Black's slight superiority derives from having the more active piece placement— a direct consequence of the time lost with 14 B–N5ch?!. In the following course White played inexactly and Black won in good style:

20 R–B2 P–QR4 21 KR–B1 K–N1 22 P–KR3 N–K2 23 N–K1?! B–Q5 24 RxR RxR 25 RxRch NxR 26 P–QN3? N–K2 27 N–B3 B–B4 28 B–K1 N–B4 29 K–B1 Q–B3! 30 B–N5 Q–B2 31 B–Q3 N–Q5 32 NxN BxN 33 P–B4?! Q–B8 34 Q–Q2 Q–R8 35 Q–QB2 B–QB6 36 Q–N1 B–R3! White resigns

In each of the above examples, the failure to castle was not dangerous because the uncastled side had general strengths and no particular problems. If these conditions do not exist, then the dangers can easily outweigh any advantages. But even in such cases, the opponent must play resolutely to take advantage of the non-castled King. The game A. Alekhine–A. Muffang, Margate 1923 illustrates these points well. A Queen's Gambit Declined,

Orthodox Variation, led to the following well-known position after Black's 9th move (after 1 P–Q4 P–Q4 2 P–QB4 P–K3 3 N–KB3 N–KB3 4 N–B3 B–K2 5 B–N5 QN–Q2 6 P–K3 0–0 7 R–B1 P–B3 8 Q–B2 PxP 9 BxP N–Q4)—see Diagram 11. Because White's QB is under attack he should now play 10 BxB, and after 10 . . . QxB continue with 11 0–0 or 11 N–K4!?. Current theory suggests that the latter offers more chances for a slight opening advantage. Alekhine instead aims for more active play with an immediate:

DIAGRAM 11

BLACK

WHITE

Alekhine–Muffang
Margate 1923
after Black's 9th

10 N–K4?! Q–R4ch! 11 K–K2

The only consistent follow-up. 11 (either) N–Q2? fails to 11 . . . N–N5; 11 Q–Q2 is met by 11 . . . B–N5, and 11 K–B1 forces White to play without the KR.

11 . . . P–B3!

This, as pointed out by Alekhine, is Black's logical plan, in order to take advantage of the do-nothing position of White's QB. In the game Muffang played the routine 11 . . . R–K1? 12 KR–Q1! N/2–N3 13 B–N3 Q–N4ch, and after 14 Q–Q3 White obtained a significant endgame advantage which Alekhine had no difficulty in transforming into a thirty-move win.

12 B–R4 N/2–N3, with at least full equality for Black. White must allow the exchange of his KB, since 13 B–QN3?! N–N5! is very strong for Black, with 14 . . . Q–N4ch or 14 . . . Q–R3ch as the follow-up. Note that in this variation White hasn't had a chance yet to develop his KR.

An objectively playable, though very double-edged example of voluntary renunciation of castling occurred in R. Vaganian–G. Forintos, Moscow 1975. The start was another sub-line of the Queen's Gambit Declined, Orthodox Variation:

1 P–Q4 N–KB3 2 P–QB4 P–K3 3 N–KB3 P–Q4 4 N–B3 B–K2 5 B–B4 0–0 6 P–K3 QN–Q2 7 Q–B2 P–B3 8 PxP NxP 9 NxN KPxN

Both sides have good positions, with no particular weaknesses. A check-preventative move such as 10 P–QR3 would cost valuable time, so White proceeds directly with his development:

10 B–Q3!? B–N5ch! 11 K–K2!?

Again White eschews an anti-developmental move (11 N–Q2).

11 . . . N–B3 12 N–K5 R–K1 13 P–N4!? P–KN3?!

Black will not get too far in this game by defensive measures; the position instead calls for a counterattack. Forintos suggests the following two possibilities (1) 13 . . . BxPch! 14 NxB NxN 15 BxPch K–R1! and (2) 13 . . . P–B4! 14 PxP N–K5 15 P–B3 Q–R5 16 PxN RxN!—in each case with great complications and approximately even chances. Throughout this game we see the advantages and disadvantages of White's early King move: speed of development contrasting with a shaky King position.

14 QR–KN1 B–Q3 15 P–KR4! P–B4! 16 P–R5 BPxP?!

Best moves in such positions are exceedingly hard to find over the board. Subsequent analysis showed that with 16 . . . P–B5! 17 BxNP! BxN! 18 PxB P–Q5! Black could still have retained equality.

17 RPxP

Of course 17 KPxP? allows 17 . . . BxPch.

17 . . . BxN 18 P–N5!

"Maximum energy into the attack," is White's credo. Only with 18 . . . N–K5! would Black have obtained some practical chances of coping with the attack.

18 . . . B–N5 ch?! 19 RxB! R–QB1

The pretty win after 19 . . . NxR 20 PxBPch KxP is 21 B–N5!!— Black no doubt overlooked this last move in his earlier calculations.

20 PxRPch K–R1 21 BxB! RxB 22 PxN! RxQch 23 BxR P–Q6ch 24 BxP R–K1 25 R/1–KN1 Black resigns

There is nothing to be done about the coming 26 R–N8ch. White gave a perfect demonstration of the advantages of his 11th move; Black did not grasp his inherent opportunities for counterplay.

B. MOVING THE KING TO PREVENT EXCHANGES

The more of one's pieces remaining on the board, the greater one's practical winning chances. The corollary to this is that the losing chances also increase proportionally. Successful practical play consists of always maximizing one's own chances while minimizing the opponent's. With this principle as our guiding light, let us look at some examples of moving the King.

A formerly popular line of the Tarrasch Variation of the French Defense goes as follows: 1 P–K4 P–K3 2 P–Q4 P–Q4 3 N–Q2 N–KB3 4 P–K5 KN–Q2 5 B–Q3 P–QB4 6 P–QB3 N–QB3 7 N–K2 Q–N3 8 N–B3 PxP 9 PxP B–N5ch—see Diagram 12. The smoothest way to react to the check is the developing 10 B–Q2. However, this gives Black the opportunity to achieve exchanges with 10 . . . BxBch 11 QxB Q–N5. True, the resulting endgame after 12 R–QB1 QxQch 13 KxQ is somewhat in White's favor, but to hope to win it one must be a consummate endgame specialist. There is, however, also an excellent middlegame plan, utilizing a King move:

10 K–B1!

Preventing any and all exchanges. Because of White's central superiority and Black's incomplete development White's King can expect to be safe. As a matter of fact, it is Black who must be careful, as the immediate 10 . . . 0–0? allows a devastating attack

DIAGRAM 12

BLACK

WHITE

*French Defense
after Black's 9th*

starting with 11 BxPch! KxB 12 N–N5ch. Actually Black's best move now is the careful retreat 10 . . . B–K2. Of greatest practical importance to our theme, however, is an attempt to exploit White's King location. For this we will follow the game Rotaru–Diaconescu, Rumania 1961:

10 . . . P–B3?! 11 N–B4! PxP

There is no way to stop now.

12 NxKP/6 N–B3

The tempting 12 . . . P–K5 is refuted by 13 B–KB4!, with the dual threats 14 B–B7 and 14 N–B7ch.

13 NxPch K–B1

13 . . . K–B2 is foiled by 14 N–R5! NxN 15 N–N5ch, followed by 16 QxN.

14 B–KR6! K–N1

There is no defense, as 14 . . . N–N5 is also met by 15 Q–B1!.

15 Q–B1! P–K5 16 Q–N5 K–B2 17 N–R5 NxN 18 QxNch K–K2 19 B–N5ch K–B1 20 N–K5! NxN 21 B–R6ch K–K2 22 QxNch, with a winning attack for White.

We see that White's King was safe enough on KB1, whereas the attempt by an underdeveloped Black to open the position boomeranged.

In K. Regan–G. Kuzmin, Budapest 1978, the American posed a practical problem for Black after the moves 1 P–K4 P–QB4 2 N–KB3 N–QB3 3 P–B3 P–K3 4 P–Q4 P–Q4 5 KPxP KPxP 6 B–K3 PxP 7 BxP NxB 8 NxN B–Q3 9 B–N5ch. Interposition by 9 . . . B–Q2 comes easy, but after 10 BxBch QxB 11 0–0 White has pretty much completed his development, while Black has no visible compensation for the isolated QP. Black, of course, has good chances for a draw, yet winning hopes are at an absolute minimum. Therefore Black chooses a more dynamic possibility:

9 . . . K–B1!

Black reckons that with White's development incomplete, the King will be safe enough. This allows Black to keep the Bishop pair as compensation for the isolated QP. Additionally, Black sees that White will have to expend an extra tempo to redeploy his KB. All in all, Black gains in winning prospects while risking no measurable increase in losing chances.

10 0–0 N–B3 11 N–Q2 Q–B2 12 N/2–B3 P–QR3 13 B–K2

Black now played the unmotivated, Kingside–weakening 13 . . . P–KN4?!, and had to struggle to achieve a draw on Move 40. With the sensible:

13 . . . P–KN3! Black has comfortable equality.

Black will complete "castling" with 14 . . . K–N2, play his Bishop to Q2, develop the Rooks along open or half open files, and be fully ready for the middlegame.

Nevertheless, it must be continually remembered that renunciation of castling can only be fruitful if there are general or specific strengths in the position. Otherwise, such "playing for the win" will most often turn out instead to have been "playing for the loss." Consider Diagram 13, S. Tarrasch–A. Alekhine, St. Petersburg 1914, after Black's 10th move. This position was reached after some inexact play—only discovered much later—by both sides (1 P–K4 P–K3 2 P–Q4 P–Q4 3 N–QB3 N–KB3 4

DIAGRAM 13

BLACK

WHITE

Tarrasch–Alekhine
St. Petersburg 1914
after Black's 10th

B–KN5 B–N5   5 PxP?! QxP?!   6 BxN BxNch   7 PxB PxB   8 N–B3?
P–N3!   9 P–N3 B–N2   10 B–N2 Q–K5ch). White's development is
incomplete, and the doubled QB pawns are a chronic weakness—
which Black can hope to pressure after a possible . . . N–Q2,
R–QB1 and P–QB4. White has no particular strengths to balance
these negatives. On the other hand, Black's QB has an excellent
diagonal, while even the doubled KBPs are not much of a handicap
at present, as it can't be seen how White can try to exploit their
"doubleness." With such an analysis in mind, it becomes clear that
White should play the modest 11 Q–K2. The endgame after 11 . . .
QxQch 12 KxQ N–Q2 is a shade better for Black because of
potential play along the QB file, yet a good defensive effort by
White would guarantee a draw. Apparently Tarrasch wants more:

11 K–Q2?

With the threat 12 N–R4, but once that threat is parried,
White's King is shown to be dangerously exposed in the center.
Also inferior is 11 K–B1?!, as tried subsequently in Reti–
Bogolyubov, Berlin 1920.

**11 . . . Q–N3!   12 N–R4 Q–R3ch   13 P–KB4 N–B3!   14 Q–K2
0–0–0**

The King is at least as safe here as on the Kingside, while the QR is immediately brought into the game.

15 K–B1 K–N1   16 K–N2 N–R4!   17 BxB NxB   18 QR–Q1 R–Q4

The absence of White's Bishop gives Black's pieces access to this key square.

19 P–B4 R–QR4   20 N–N2?

Defensive chances remained with 20 R–Q3! R–Q1 21 KR–Q1! Q–B1 22 R–N3, as pointed out by Alekhine. Now White is lost. Black wins convincingly, though not in the fastest possible way:

20 . . . R–Q1!   21 N–K3 Q–B1   22 P–QB5 PxP   23 P–Q5 P–B5!
24 NxP Q–N5ch   25 K–R1 Q–B6ch   26 N–N2 R–Q3!   27 Q–B4
R/3–R3!   28 PxP PxP   29 K–N1 RxP   30 QxR/R2 RxQ   31 KxR
QxBP   32 R–QB1 Q–Q7   33 K–N1 N–Q3   34 R–B2 Q–N5   35
R–Q1 N–N4   36 R–Q8ch K–N2   37 R/2–Q2 P–K4   38 PxP PxP 39
K–B1 N–Q5   40 R–Q3 Q–K8ch   41 R–Q1 Q–K5   42 R–Q3
Q–R8ch   43 R–Q1 QxP   44 K–N1 QxP   45 R–Q3 Q–K8ch   46
K–R2 P–KR4   47 R–K8 Q–K5   48 R–QB3 N–N4   49 R–B5
Q–QN5! White resigns

White's decision is much more difficult to make in S. Reshevsky–L. Polugaevsky, Palma de Majorca Interzonal 1970, after Black's 17th move. (Previous play was 1 P–Q4 N–KB3 2 P–QB4 P–B4 3 N–KB3 PxP 4 NxP P–K3 5 N–QB3 B–N5 6 N/4–N5 0–0 7 P–QR3 BxNch 8 NxB P–Q4 9 B–N5! P–KR3 10 B–R4 P–KN4 11 B–N3 P–Q5 12 N–N5 N–B3 13 P–K3 PxP 14 PxP P–K4 15 B–Q3 B–N5 16 Q–B2 P–K5 17 B–K2 Q–R4ch.) Now 18 N–B3? allows 18 . . . N–N5!, and 18 Q–B3 QxQch 19 NxQ BxB 20 KxB N–QR4 leads to an approximately even endgame. Therefore White plays:

18 K–B2!!

Looks dangerous, yet as Reshevsky tells it he felt that his King would be *fairly* safe because Black's forces are not well coordinated. In addition he was encouraged by the loose position of Black's Kingside and therefore expected to be able to launch a vigorous and rapid attack. Over-all, White's winning chances were tremendously increased over those after 18 Q–B3, while losing chances were correctly thought to be kept within reasonable bounds.

18 . . . BxB 19 KxB!

To allow the Queen to maintain its attack on the KP.

19 . . . QR–B1?! 20 N–Q6 R–R1

20 . . . R–B2? is refuted by 21 P–N4.

21 QR–Q1 N–R4 22 B–K1 Q–N3 23 P–KN4!

The start of the decisive attack.

23 . . . N–B3 24 B–B3! NxP 25 QxP P–B4

25 . . . P–KR4 is zapped by 26 R–Q5.

26 Q–K6ch K–R2 27 NxBP N/3–K4 28 R–Q7ch! NxR 29 QxNch K–N3 30 P–KR4!! P–KR4 31 N–K7ch K–R3 32 PxPch KxP 33 Q–Q5ch Black resigns

Note how White's pieces were coordinated both to protect his King and to attack Black's.

CHAPTER 2
King in the Center—
Open Positions

Open files, diagonals open toward the enemy camp, generally free ("open") space: these are what make a position an "open" position. Most open positions result from KP openings, since these naturally tend toward openness. Nevertheless, QP openings in the hands of someone eager for immediate battle can also provide open positions through an appropriate choice of variations. One of the great attacking players of all time was Frank Marshall, U.S. Champion, 1909–1936. The fact that his first move invariably was 1 P–Q4 was of little consequence for the type of play to follow.

SECTION 1. The King Is Unsafe

The King is always uncomfortable in the center when the position is open. Most of the time he is decidedly unsafe. In the center the King can be attacked from the front, right side and left side, a total of three directions. In an open position the attack can come almost simultaneously from these directions. If the defending side is even a bit behind in development, the attack can quickly become overpowering.

Whenever the defending side becomes complacent about his King's safety, disaster can strike instantaneously. Witness the following three quickies from master practice:

(1) Caro-Kann Defense: 1 P–K4 P–QB3   2 P–Q4 P–Q4   3
     N–QB3 PxP   4 NxP N–Q2   5 Q–K2!? KN–B3??   6 N–Q6
     Mate.
(2) Alekhine's Defense: 1 P–K4 N–KB3   2 P–K5 N–Q4   3
     P–Q4 P–Q3   4 N–KB3 P–KN3   5 B–QB4 N–N3   6 B–N3
     P–QR4?!   7 P–K6! P–R5? (Required is 7 . . . BxP   8 BxB
     PxB   9 N–N5, and Black will get only one black eye.
     Instead he thinks he can afford to win White's Bishop.) 8
     PxPch K–Q2   9 N–K5ch!! PxN   10 PxPch K–B3   11 QxQ,
     and White has won the Queen.
(3) Center Counter (B. Rumyantsev–V. Lomonosov, USSR
     1978): 1 P–K4 P–Q4   2 PxP N–KB3   3 B–N5ch B–Q2   4
     B–B4 P–QN4   5 B–N3 B–N5   6 P–KB3 B–B1   7 Q–K2
     B–R3?!   8 N–B3 P–N5?!   9 B–R4ch KN–Q2   10 N–N5
     B–N2?   11 P–Q6! Black resigns. The threats are 12
     NxBPch and 12 PxBP; 11 . . . BPxP is refuted by 12
     NxQPmate, while 11 . . . N–R3 gets a similar response: 12
     PxBP NxP   13 N–Q6mate!

Now we shall consider three more substantive examples from
grandmaster play. The major point to note is how inherently
unsafe the King is in such open positions. Conversely, we can
learn how to take advantage of a King unsafe in the center. The
first two illustrations are from games by Robert J. Fischer,
World Champion from 1972–75. There has never been anyone
better than Fischer in exploiting the advantages of a strategically
clear open position.

White: R. Fischer
Black: E. Geller

Played at The Bled (Yugoslavia) International Tournament,
1961

RUY LOPEZ

1 P–K4 P–K4   2 N–KB3 N–QB3   3 B–N5 P–QR3   4 B–R4
P–Q3   5 0–0 B–N5   6 P–KR3! B–R4?!

According to current theory Black has better equalizing
prospects with the crazy looking 6 . . . P–KR4!?.

7 P–B3 Q–B3?

Fischer convincingly refutes this early Queen sortie. Indicated was 7 . . . N–B3 8 P–Q4 N–Q2.

8 P–KN4!

Fischer comments thus: "I realized the danger inherent in weakening my Kingside, but felt that I could capitalize on Black's lack of development [i.e. on the K-side—EM] before he could get to my King."

8 . . . B–N3 9 P–Q4!

And here Fischer simply comments that it's worth a pawn to open up the game.

9 . . . BxP 10 QN–Q2 B–N3

10 . . . B–Q6 is foiled by 11 BxNch PxB 12 R–K1, and after 10 . . . BxN 11 NxB P–K5 12 R–K1 P–Q4 Fischer gives the following definitive line: 13 B–KN5 Q–Q3 14 P–B4! PxP 15 P–Q5! P–N4 16 PxN PxB 17 RxPch N–K2 18 BxN BxB 19 Q–K2, with a won position for White.

11 BxNch! PxB 12 PxP PxP 13 NxP! B–Q3 14 NxB!

DIAGRAM 14

BLACK

WHITE

Fischer–Geller
Bled 1961
after White's 14th

Throughout the game Fischer applies maximum energy in going after the Black King, which is unsafe in the center. If now 14 . . . RPxN   15 N–K4 Q–R5   16 NxBch PxN   17 QxP, and 17 . . . QxP? is not playable because of 18 R–K1ch.

14 . . . QxN   15 R–K1ch K–B1

If 15 . . . N–K2   16 N–B4 0–0–0   17 Q–R4 (Fischer).

16 N–B4 P–KR4   17 NxB PxN?!   18 B–B4 P–Q4?!   19 Q–N3! PxP   20 Q–N7! PxPch   21 B–N3 R–Q1   22 Q–N4ch Black resigns

Black now loses his Knight and QR.

In the above game White had to watch out for the safety of his own King, but hardly had to invest any material in obtaining the attack. In the following game, White's King is supersafe, but exploitation of the initiative requires sacrificing.

White: R. Fischer
Black: M. Najdorf

Played at the Varna Olympiad, 1962

SICILIAN DEFENSE

1 P–K4 P–QB4   2 N–KB3 P–Q3   3 P–Q4 PxP   4 NxP N–KB3 5 N–QB3 P–QR3   6 P–KR3 P–QN4?!   7 N–Q5!? B–N2?

Black has to take the bull by the horns and risk 7 . . . NxP!   8 Q–B3 N–B4.

8 NxNch NPxN   9 P–QB4!

Fischer remarks here that White must play sharply, otherwise his advantage evaporates. Black should now try to keep the position as closed as possible by playing 9 . . . P–N5.

9 . . . PxP?!   10 BxP BxP   11 0–0 P–Q4   12 R–K1! P–K4?

Black is in serious trouble already because of White's vast advantage in development. According to Fischer, Black's best defense was 12 . . . PxB   13 RxB Q–Q4   14 Q–B3 P–K3.

13 Q–R4ch N–Q2

13 . . . Q–Q2 is met by 14 B–QN5.

14 RxB! PxR   15 N–B5 B–B4   16 N–N7ch! K–K2   17 N–B5ch K–K1   18 B–K3!

White sacrificed the Exchange to open lines against Black's King. Note how he made sure that Black was robbed of castling as a defensive tool. With Black's King stuck in the center, White completes the development of his Queenside so that he will have maximum firepower directed against the King.

18 . . . BxB   19 PxB Q–N3   20 R–Q1! R–R2   21 R–Q6! Q–Q1 22 Q–N3 Q–B2   23 BxPch K–Q1   24 B–K6 Black resigns

Najdorf trusts Fischer to finish the job. Fischer himself gives the following potential variation: 24 . . . R–N2   25 Q–R4 Q–B1   26 Q–R5ch K–K1   27 QxRP K–Q1   28 BxN RxB   29 RxRch QxR   30 QxPch K–B2   31 QxPch K–N3   32 QxR.

As mentioned earlier, open positions can result from so-called closed openings. In Y. Balashov–A. Miles, Bugojno 1978, Black made an inadvisable attempt to hold on to the gambit pawn in a Queen's Gambit Accepted (1 P–Q4 P–Q4   2 N–KB3 N–KB3   3 P–B4 PxP   4 N–B3 P–QR3?!   5 P–K4 P–QN4   6 P–K5 N–Q4   7 P–QR4 NxN   8 PxN Q–Q4   9 P–N3 B–K3?!   10 B–KN2 Q–N2   11 0–0 B–Q4). This first important position is shown in Diagram 15. Black is trying to keep the position closed and looks forward to the development of the Kingside with 12 . . . P–K3. But White has different ideas:

12 P–K6!!

Throwing another pawn into the oil to make it really hot. To expect to capitalize on his large edge in development, White must have an open position. After 12 . . . PxP   13 R–K1 Black's Kingside is in a straightjacket; therefore Black chooses to be "two sound pawns" up.

12 . . . BxP   13 N–N5! B–Q4   14 BxB QxB   15 PxP PxP?!

Too optimistic. A shade better was 15 . . . P–R3, with White then having the pleasant choice between 16 N–R3 and 16 Q–B3.

16 RxR QxR   17 Q–N4!

DIAGRAM 15

BLACK

WHITE

Balashov–Miles
Bugojno 1978
after Black's 11th

The second important position. White has all of his four pieces ready to go after the Black King. Black's undeveloped forces can not offer sufficient help to the in-the-center monarch. Balashov concludes forcefully:

17 . . . N–B3 18 Q–B3! P–B3 19 N–K6 Q–N2 20 Q–Q5! P–N4 21 B–B4!! B–R3

21 . . . PxB loses the Queen: 22 Q–R5ch K–Q2 23 N–B5ch.

22 R–K1 Q–N3 23 NxPch K–B1 24 R–K6 PxB 25 RxN Q–N1 26 N–K6ch K–K1 27 R–B7 K–B2 28 NxPch K–B1 29 Q–QB5 Black resigns

Section 2. The King Is Safe

When we speak of the King being safe while in the center of an open position, the reference is to *theoretical* safety. In other words, if we defend the King perfectly, it will be safe. Nevertheless, such King placements are inherently "unsafe," and thus continuous care is required for the King to remain truly safe.

For the King to be safe, there must be either great strength in one's own position or something defective in the opponent's. If both of these conditions exist, then the King can feel quite safe. The key example of strength is a strong central pawn formation, accompanied by smooth, sound development. If the opponent is behind in development or has his pieces scattered aimlessly around the board, this obviously lessens his chances for an attack against the central King. And if he even has to worry about the defense of his own King, then his prospects for a successful attack are almost nil.

An excellent example of great inherent strength in a position is shown by the course of the game D. Bronstein–T. Petrosian, 1960 USSR Championship. After some antipositional play by White in an unusual Caro-Kann Defense (1 P–K4 P–QB3 2 N–K2?! P–Q4 3 P–K5 P–QB4! 4 P–Q4 N–QB3 5 P–QB3 P–K3 6 N–Q2 KN–K2 7 N–B3 PxP 8 N/2xP? N–N3 9 NxN PxN 10 B–Q3 Q–B2 11 Q–K2), the position of Diagram 16 was reached. The exchange of Knights has significantly strengthened Black's center, and all that is left of White's center is the advanced KP. Black immediately starts to undermine it:

11 . . . P–B3!   12 PxP PxP   13 N–Q4 K–B2!

DIAGRAM 16

BLACK

WHITE

Bronstein-Petrosian
1960 USSR Championship
after White's 11th

The exchanges on Move 12 have led to a sound four-pawn central phalanx for Black, while pretty much annihilating White's central influence. Since White has no particular chances for an attack and, to put it bluntly, hasn't even completed his piece development or castled, Black's King can feel comfortable enough just off the center. Note that because of the King location, 13 . . . P–K4? is not playable because of 14 NxP! (14 . . . QxN?? 15 B–QN5).

14 P–KB4 P–QB4!

Getting his center going and forcing White's well posted Knight to move. White's position is inferior, with the best chances offered by 15 N–N5 followed by 16 P–B4. Instead White thinks that he should try to get at Black's King. Since White's development is incomplete, King uncastled and strengths nonexistent, no objective basis exists for expecting success. Petrosian's response ignores White's threats and goes after White's weaknesses:

15 Q–R5? PxN! 16 BxNch PxB 17 QxR PxP 18 Q–R7ch B–KN2

After seemingly winning the Exchange, White's position is actually in shambles: it is *his* King that is unsafe; his Queen is out of play, and Black already has a pawn for the Exchange and an absolutely safe King. After 19 0–0 B–QR3 White can't move his Rook since 20 . . . R–KR1 would trap the Queen. What happens is not much better.

19 B–K3 PxP 20 R–Q1 B–QR3 21 P–B5 KPxP 22 Q–R3 Q–B7 23 Q–B3 B–B5 White resigns

What is considered the main line in the MacCutcheon Variation of the French Defense goes as follows: 1 P–K4 P–K3 2 P–Q4 P–Q4 3 N–QB3 N–KB3 4 B–KN5 B–N5 5 P–K5 P–KR3 6 B–Q2 BxN 7 PxB N–K5 8 Q–N4 P–KN3 9 B–Q3 NxB 10 KxN. The White King is in the center, but will be safe enough for the following reasons: (1) The French Defense is more of a defensive than offensive opening, and thus Black can't be expected to generate any fast attacks. Black has even been left with no developed pieces. (2) White's Bishop is more active than Black's. (3) White has greater control of the center. (4) White's King serves a valuable defensive purpose by protecting the QB3 pawn. (5) White has excellent attacking chances against Black's King. This very important factor means that Black will not be able to devote all of his energy to attacking White. Over-all, it should be considered that White has a normal type of advantage.

For a thematic demonstration of the possibilities of such positions let us follow the course of R. Fischer–N. Rossolimo, USA Championship 1965–6:

10 . . . P–QB4   11 N–B3 N–B3   12 Q–B4 Q–B2

More active is 12 . . . Q–R4!. After the text White should have continued with 13 Q–B6! R–KN1   14 P–KR4, as pointed out by Fischer.

13 P–KR4 P–B4!   14 P–N4 PxQP   15 PxQP N–K2?!

Development with 15 . . . B–Q2 is preferable.

16 PxP KPxP   17 B–N5ch! K–B1?

After 17 . . . B–Q2   18 BxBch QxB White opens lines with 19 P–K6!. According to Fischer Black's King would be relatively safe after 17 . . . K–Q1!. It is demonstrably unsafe on the Kingside.

18 B–Q3! B–K3   19 N–N1!

Heading for a great location on KB4.

19 . . . K–B2   20 N–R3 QR–QB1   21 KR–KN1 P–N3?!   22 P–R5! Q–B6ch   23 K–K2 N–B3

Going for counterplay. The defensive 23 . . . QR–KN1   24 PxPch RxP is too slow after 25 Q–R4, and 23 . . . P–KN4 leads to a decisive White attack after 24 NxPch!.

24 PxPch K–N2   25 QR–Q1! NxPch   26 K–B1 KR–K1   27 R–N3! N–B3   28 Q–KR4 NxP

28 . . . QxKP gets the same reply.

29 N–B4 N–N5   30 NxBch! RxN   31 BxP Q–B5ch   32 K–N1! Black resigns

Too many things are hanging, and the combinational 32 . . . NxP is parried by 33 QxQ RxQ   34 KxN R–B5ch   35 R–B3. A game played in the dynamic Fischer manner.

Defending the King is considerably easier to do when this can be combined with an attack against the enemy King, thereby keeping the opponent off balance. The defender quickly became the attacker in Macles–E. Sveshnikov, Le Havre 1977. A sharp variation in the Sicilian Defense led to the position shown in Diagram 17 after White's 15th move (1 P–K4 P–QB4 2 N–KB3 N–QB3 3 P–Q4 PxP 4 NxP P–K3 5 N–QB3 N–B3 6 N/4–N5 P–Q3 7 B–KB4 P–K4 8 B–N5 P–QR3 9 BxN PxB 10 N–R3 P–B4 11 PxP BxP 12 N–B4 B–K3 13 Q–R5?! P–N4 14 N–K3 Q–R4 15 0–0–0). The Sveshnikov Variation is characterized by a certain inherent looseness in the Black King position—hopefully to be compensated for by the two Bishops, the central pawn presence and the attacking chances that result from the above two factors. In this example, White, with his aggressive 13th and 15th moves, has made clear that he plans to aim directly for Black's King. Black's response:

15 . . . R–B1!

DIAGRAM 17

BLACK

WHITE

Macles–Sveshnikov
Le Havre 1977
after White's 15th

It is no secret that White's King can't be all that secure on the Queenside with Black's Q, QB, QN and QNP pointing toward him. By also bringing his QR into action, Black now has five attackers in position.

16 N–B5 K–Q2!

Protecting the important QP. The King is safe enough behind his central pawns because White's Kingside development is incomplete and he will have to react to Black's attack on the Queenside. White should now prevent Black's next move by playing 17 N–Q5!, which also would get another piece into the attack. Instead, White's 17th move is a serious loss of time.

17 Q–B3? N–N5   18 P–QR3 RxN!

Ripping open the King position, as 19 PxN? loses a piece and 19 QxR?? loses the Queen.

19 PxR QxPch   20 K–Q2 N–Q4   21 R–R1 Q–B4   22 RxP N–B2 23 R–R5 P–K5!

While Black's King, surrounded by pieces and pawns, is quite safe, White's King and Knight are precariously placed. As a starter the Knight is lost.

24 QxP QxKBPch   25 K–B1 BxN   26 BxPch NxB   27 Q–QR4 B–R3ch   28 K–N1 R–QN1 White resigns

After 29 RxN BxPch! White's Queen and King will be lost.

CHAPTER 3
King in the Center— Closed Positions

A strict formal definition of a closed position would describe it as one where there are no open lines (particularly files) at all. Often such a situation exists, yet this definition is too limiting. As long as there are no apparent chances for quick attacks, the pawn chains are fixed rather than in tension, and the presence of much of the original material gives the position a cluttered appearance, then we should consider the position to be of the "closed" type. It follows that most closed positions result from the use of closed openings, i.e., those starting with 1 P–Q4, 1 P–QB4, 1 N–KB3 and 1 P–KN3. Yet what is of maximum significance is not the first move but the chosen follow-up. For instance, closed-type positions usually follow from the Sicilian Defense, when after 1 P–K4 P–QB4 2 N–KB3 P–K3, instead of 3 P–Q4, White chooses the closed 3 P–Q3. This build-up, incidentally, has been a recurring favorite of Robert Fischer's.

The absence of open central lines or lines open toward the center means that in closed positions the King can feel quite safe in the center. Even though in many closed openings quick castling is employed (e.g. the Nimzo-Indian after 1 P–Q4 N–KB3 2 P–QB4 P–K3 3 N–QB3 B–N5 4 P–K3 P–QB4 5 B–Q3 0–0 6 N–B3 P–Q4 7 0–0 or in the King's Indian after 1 P–Q4 N–KB3 2 P–QB4 P–KN3 3 N–QB3 B–N2 4 N–B3 P–Q3 5 P–KN3 0–0 6 B–N2 N–B3 7 0–0), this is often done more to complete the mobilization of the Kingside pieces than for King safety. Rapid castling is also employed more often for Black than for White. White often delays castling because (1) he wants to use the tempo to initiate concrete action and (2) anticipating pawn storms on either flank, he is not really sure which is the ultimately safest side for his King.

Play starting from T. Petrosian–A. Lutikov, 1959 USSR Championship, after Black's 12th move, demonstrates these points very well. The position is unquestionably a closed one, and because of some clumsy maneuvers by Black (1 N–KB3 N–KB3 2 P–QB4 P–KN3 3 N–B3 B–N2 4 P–K4 0–0 5 P–Q4 P–Q3 6 B–K2 P–K4 7 P–Q5 N–R3 8 B–N5 P–R3 9 B–R4 P–B4 10 N–Q2 B–Q2?! 11 N–N5 B–K1 12 P–QR3 Q–Q2?!) also clearly favorable for White, who has an undisputed space advantage and more active piece placement. Petrosian now played:

13 P–KN4!

Of course White could have routinely castled and aimed for Queenside play via P–QN4. Considering Black's passive position Petrosian wants more: play on *both* flanks. For this the King is presently safest in the center.

13 . . . N–B2   14 N–QB3 P–R3   15 P–R4 Q–B1   16 P–R3! R–N1   17 Q–B2 B–Q2   18 P–N3 P–N3   19 N–Q1 P–QN4   20 P–R5!

Played to contain the Black QN. White need fear neither 20 . . . PxP 21 PxP R–N5 because of 22 N–N2 and 23 N–Q3, nor 20 . . . P–N5, since the closing of the Queenside would give White a free hand on the Kingside.

20 . . . K–R1   21 B–N3 N–N1   22 N–K3 N–K2?!   23 B–R4! Q–K1?!   24 P–N4!

After suitable preparation White is ready to start undermining Black's Queenside pawn formation. Since 24 . . . BPxP? is hopeless after 25 P–B5!, Black must allow White to do the capturing.

24 . . . N–B1   25 NPxP QPxP   26 PxP NxNP   27 BxN! RxB?!

Some chances for counterplay would have resulted after 27 . . . BxB. Note that the pawn exchanges have created definite weaknesses in Black's position. A necessary consequence of the exchanging, however, has been an opening of the position. Therefore White now brings his King to safety by castling.

28 0–0! P–B4   29 P–B3! R–B2   30 N/2–B4 R–N5?!

Allowing White to redeploy his Bishop, with a gain of tempo, makes Black's prospects nonexistent. As GM Suetin points out, some defensive chances were offered by 30 . . . P–B5.

31 B–K1 R–N2   32 B–B3 P–R4   33 NPxBP!

Winning a pawn while advantageously opening the position for the side with active piece placement.

33 . . . PxP   34 PxP P–K5   35 K–R2!

The King is safe here and the KN file cleared for the Rook. Petrosian finishes the strategically won game with energy and accuracy:

35 . . . PxP   36 RxP B–Q5   37 Q–Q3 B–KB3   38 R–KN1 K–R2   39 BxB RxB   40 Q–B3 Q–B1   41 R–N6 R–KB2   42 R–N5 Black resigns

After 42 . . . Q–R3   43 R–N6 Q–B1   44 N–K5 White wins easily. Of course White could have played the immediate 42 N–K5.

Diagram 18, V. Korchnoi–L. Szabo, Leningrad–Budapest match 1961, was reached after the moves 1 P–KN3 P–KN3   2 P–QB4 B–N2   3 P–Q4 P–QB4   4 P–Q5 P–K4   5 N–QB3 P–Q3   6 P–K4 N–Q2? (Better 6 . . . N–K2)   7 B–Q3 N–K2   8 P–KN4! N–KB3   9 P–KR3?! (Correct is 9 P–B3! and if 9 . . . P–KR3, 10 P–KR4!)   9 . . . P–QR3? (9 . . . P–KR3!)   10 P–B4! PxP   11 BxP N–Q2   12 N–B3 Q–B2   13 Q–Q2 P–R3   14 Q–R2! N–K4   15 NxN PxN   16 B–K3. White has a significant advantage here: more space, protected passed QP, potential play along the half-open KB file. White has prospects both on the Queenside (against the QBP) and on the Kingside. The closed nature of the position makes his King safe enough in the center, and thus White doesn't yet have to determine his preferred scene of action. Black's pieces are generally passively placed, and the least he should have done is to activate his Knight with 16 . . . P–KN4! followed by 17 . . . N–N3. As played, he gets no breathing room at all:

16 . . . B–Q2?!   17 Q–N1 R–QB1   18 P–KR4 N–N1?!

DIAGRAM 18

BLACK

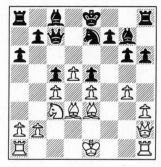

WHITE

Korchnoi–Szabo
Leningrad–Budapest 1961
after White's 16th

Hardly in the right direction! There was nothing better than 18 . . . 0–0, after which Korchnoi was planning to continue with 19 P–R5, and after the forced 19 . . . P–KN4, White would have soon castled Kingside (where because of the blocked nature of the position the King would have been safe) and then prepared the Queenside break P–QN4.

19 B–K2 Q–Q3 20 P–N5 P–KR4 21 R–R2 N–K2 22 R–B2 0–0 23 0–0–0!

The next scene of action is expected to be the KB file, so White castles Queenside to have the QR ready for doubling along that file. White can then also offer a very strong Exchange sacrifice on KB6. Black's future holds nothing but determined, careful defending; Korchnoi suggests 23 . . . K–R2 24 R/1–B1 B–K1. Yet positions as poor as Black's contain the seeds of their own destruction, and here too Black immediately allows a winning combination.

23 . . . R–B2? 24 R–B6! BxR 25 PxB QxBP

After 25 . . . N–B1 26 Q–N5 Black's King will soon be lost; the text move loses lots of material.

26 P–Q6 N–B3   27 PxR N–Q5   28 BxP Q–Q3   29 N–Q5 B–B3
30 B–R6 BxN   31 BxR QxP   32 BPxB KxB   33 B–N4 P–B5   34
Q–N3 **Black resigns**

Some unambitious opening play by White (1 N–KB3 P–QB4
2 P–KN3 P–Q4   3 B–N2 N–QB3   4 0–0 P–K4   5 P–Q3 B–K2   6
P–K4 P–Q5   7 P–QR4 P–KN4!   8 QN–Q2 B–K3   9 N–B4 P–B3
10 P–R4 P–KR3) in B. Larsen–L. Ljubojevic, Bugojno 1978 led
to a situation in which not a thing has been exchanged, the
pawn chains are rather fixed, and it is Black who has more
space. The position is of the closed type, with White's pieces
inactive. Larsen now tries to sharpen White's play:

11 N–R2

With the threat of a long Queen check. But the nature of the
position, as described earlier, allows Black to ignore the check.

11 . . . PxP!   12 Q–R5ch K–Q2!

The King will be safe in the center. By playing thus Black
enables his QB to remain on the active K3 square.

13 QxRP/4 P–B4

Equally good and less committing was 13 . . . P–KR4!   14
N–B3 N–R3, planning 15 . . . N–KN5.

14 Q–R5 N–B3   15 Q–K2 PxP   16 PxP?

Keeping the position closed makes sure that Black's King
remains secure. Ljubojevic suggests 16 BxKP NxB   17 QxN BxB
18 PxB Q–KN1, with approximately even chances.

16 . . . Q–KN1   17 P–N3 P–KR4   18 P–B4 BxN   19 QxB?!

In the endgame White will have no compensation for his
many pawn weaknesses. A better move for practical purposes
was 19 PxB.

**19 . . . QxQ   20 PxQ QR–KN1   21 PxP QNxP   22 B–B4
B–Q3!   23 QR–N1 K–B2**

Black's King is satisfactorily sheltered while White's King and
pawn weaknesses remain. Black won as follows:

24 N–B3 NxNch   25 RxN NxP   26 R/3–N3 P–N3   27 BxBch NxB   28 B–Q5 R–N4!   29 R–K1 R–R2   30 K–N2 R/2–N2   31 K–R2 N–B4   32 P–R5 N–K6   33 PxPch PxP   34 R–QR1 NxB   35 PxN K–Q3   36 RxPch KxP   37 R–R3 P–R5   38 PxP R–N7ch   39 K–R3 R–N8 White resigns

CHAPTER 4
Coping With Sacrifices

In the opening the mobilization of pieces is just starting. Therefore the opportunities for successful sacrificial attacks on the King are few and far between. By far the most common thematic attack is on the castled King starting with the KBxKRPch sacrifice. Because of its importance we shall take a closer look at the various ramifications of this sacrifice.

SECTION 1. The King Accepts the Sacrifice

As a general rule the King both should and must accept the sacrificed Bishop. Not doing so will leave the defender down a pawn, with a denuded Kingside and, under normal circumstances, subject to imminent mating attacks. The Bishop sacrifice is a recurrent possibility in many openings and the defender must always look out for it when considering the safety of his castled King. Even leading grandmasters are not immune to surprise devastation. Witness the game V. Hort–I. Radulov, Bulgaria 1974, a Richter Variation of the Sicilian Defense: 1 P–K4 P–QB4 2 N–KB3 P–Q3 3 P–Q4 PxP 4 NxP N–KB3 5 N–QB3 N–B3 6 B–KN5 P–K3 7 Q–Q2 B–K2 8 0–0–0 0–0 9 P–B4 P–Q4 10 P–K5 N–Q2 11 BxB QxB 12 N–B3 P–QR3 13 B–Q3 R–N1 14 Q–K3 P–QN4?? 15 BxPch! KxB 16 N–N5ch K–N3 17 Q–R3 Black resigns. There is nothing reasonable to be done about 18 Q–R7mate. No better for Black would have been the retreat on Move 16 to KN1, as again 17 Q–R3 would have forced mate (or the win of Black's Queen).

Once the sacrifice hits and must be accepted, the next question is where to place the King after the Knight check. As a general principle the retreat to KN1 is the safest location for the King and this move should always be considered first. As a matter of firm principle we say: *Always play the King to KN1 unless a definitive analysis shows that this loses by force.* Let us look at our first example. Diagram 19 shows the position reached in the French Defense (1 P–K4 P–K3 2 P–Q4 P–Q4 3 N–QB3 N–KB3 4 B–KN5 B–K2 5 P–K5 KN–Q2 6 BxB QxB 7 Q–Q2 0–0 8 P–B4 P–QB4 9 PxP N–QB3 10 N–B3 QxP 11 0–0–0 R–N1 12 B–Q3 P–QN4) Maslesha–V. Raicevic, Sarajevo 1978, after Black's 12th move. White's pieces are poised for a potential BxKRPch sacrifice, and Black could have taken steps to minimize its potential effect by having played, for example, 12 . . . R–Q1. Instead, Black started his own attack and challenged White. The challenge was accepted:

13 BxPch!? KxB   14 N–N5ch K–N1!

DIAGRAM 19

BLACK

WHITE

Maslesha–Raicevic
Sarajevo 1978
after Black's 12th

The only rational move. Suicidal is 14 . . . K–N3? 15 Q–Q3ch P–B4 and White has his choice of wins, including 16 PxPe.p.ch and 16 Q–R3.

15 Q–Q3 R–K1! 16 Q–R7ch K–B1 17 KR–K1?

In playing this waiting move White overvalues his attacking prospects. According to Raicevic, correct was 17 Q–R8ch K–K2 18 Q–R4, and White's attacking chances are a fair compensation for the missing piece. After the text, Black can consolidate his position and then initiate counterattacks. The resulting play is interesting, but as it is outside our theme I give it without further comment:

17 . . . N–Q5! 18 Q–R5 K–K2! 19 QxPch K–Q1 20 RxN QxR 21 NxPch RxN 22 QxR QxPch 23 K–N1 R–N3 24 QxP B–N2 25 Q–Q3 Q–B5! 26 Q–B5 Q–K3 27 Q–N5ch Q–K2 28 Q–Q2 P–R3 29 N–Q5 BxN 30 QxB K–B2 31 Q–R8 N–B4 32 Q–Q5 R–K3 33 P–QR3 N–Q2 34 Q–R8 K–N3! 35 P–KN3 RxP 36 RxR QxR 37 Q–Q8ch Q–B2 38 Q–K7 N–K4 39 Q–N5 N–B5 40 Q–N6ch K–R2 41 Q–Q3 Q–K4 42 Q–Q7ch K–N3 43 Q–Q8ch K–B3 44 Q–R8ch K–Q2 45 Q–N7ch K–K1 46 Q–B6ch K–B2 47 Q–Q7ch K–B3 48 Q–B6ch K–N4 49 P–B3 Q–K7 50 Q–Q5ch K–R3 White resigns

In this case it was easy to decide that the King had no choice but to go to KN1. The decision is more difficult in the next example, E. Colle–O'Hanlon, Nice 1930, after the moves: 1 P–Q4 P–Q4 2 N–KB3 N–KB3 3 P–K3 P–B4 4 P–B3 P–K3 5 B–Q3 B–Q3 6 QN–Q2 QN–Q2 7 0–0 0–0 8 R–K1 R–K1 9 P–K4 QPxP 10 NxP NxN 11 BxN PxP. Black's position is quite sound, and since White's over-all development has not been completed, Black can feel theoretically secure. Nevertheless, White—a dangerous, creative tactician—plays:

12 BxP ch!?

Not a winning move, but theoretically playable and promising in practice. If Black defends correctly, White draws; if Black errs, White wins.

12 . . . KxB 13 N–N5ch K–N1!

Since there is no forced win against this retreat it should be chosen on general principles of King safety. Clearly, the King feels much safer here than in the open on KN3. Not that White's win is obvious then, but there is a forced win. Black in fact played 13 . . .

K–N3?? and the game ended as follows: 14 P–KR4! R–R1   15
RxPch!! N–B3 (15 . . . PxR   16 Q–Q3ch K–B3   17 Q–B3ch K–N3
18 Q–B7ch K–R3   19 NxPch)   16 P–R5ch! K–R3   17 RxB! Q–R4
18 NxPch K–R2   19 N–N5ch K–N1   20 Q–N3ch and Black
resigned.

14 Q–R5 N–K4!

According to Euwe and Kramer, also sufficient for equality was
14 . . . Q–B3 with the following continuation being best for both
sides: 15 Q–R7ch K–B1   16 N–K4 Q–K4   17 PxP QxRPch!   18
QxQ BxQch   19 KxB, with an equal endgame.

15 RxN!

Ensuring the draw. Attempts at winning only achieve the opposite, e.g. 15 P–KB4? leads to nothing after 15 . . . N–N3. After
15 Q–R7ch? Euwe and Kramer give the following line as leading to
advantage for Black: 15 . . . K–B1   16 N–K4 N–N3   17 NxB QxN
18 P–KR4 K–K2   19 P–R5 R–R1   20 B–N5ch K–K1!   21 QxP RxP
22 Q–B6 Q–K2!.

15 . . . BxR   16 QxPch K–R1   17 Q–R5ch Draw

White has perpetual check, but no more.

Of course, if retreating to KN1 is suicide, then obviously (for
better or worse) the King must head out. Diagram 20 shows the
position in J. R. Capablanca–L. Molina, Buenos Aires 1911, after
the following moves: 1 P–Q4 P–Q4   2 P–QB4 P–K3   3 N–QB3
N–KB3   4 B–N5 QN–Q2   5 P–K3 P–B3   6 N–B3 B–K2   7 PxP
NxP?!   8 BxB NxB?!   9 B–Q3 P–QB4   10 0–0 0–0?!   11 PxP NxP.
Capablanca now played:

12 BxP!?CH

. . .and gives the following discussion thereof: "A combination
somewhat out of the ordinary, as it is generally impossible, in well
balanced positions, to obtain an attack with only a few pieces to
play. It should be noticed, however, that White can quickly bring
a Rook and Knight to the attack."

12 . . . KxB   13 N–N5ch K–N3!

DIAGRAM 20

BLACK

WHITE

Capablanca–Molina
Buenos Aires 1911
after Black's 11th

13 . . . K–R3? loses the Queen to 14 NxPch. The "desirable" 13 . . . K–N1? is refuted by 14 Q–R5 R–K1   15 QxPch K–R1, with White having a multitude of wins, including 16 P–QN4!. Thus the King must come out.

14 Q–N4 P–B4!   15 Q–N3 K–R3   16 Q–R4ch K–N3   17 Q–R7ch! K–B3!   18 P–K4! N–N3!   19 PxP?!

Up to here both have played the best moves. But here White risks throwing away his edge. According to Capablanca, decisive was 19 P–B4!, to continue after 19 . . . PxP with 20 QR–Q1 Q–N3   21 R–Q6!.

19 . . . PxP   20 QR–Q1 N–Q6   21 Q–R3 N/Q–B5?

Now White wins. As Shamkovich has shown, after 21 . . . N/N–B5!   22 Q–N3 R–R1   23 R–Q2 B–K3   24 KR–Q1 B–B5   25 N–B3 P–KN3! White's progress is problematical.

22 Q–N3 Q–B2   23 KR–K1 N–K7ch?

Better is 23 . . . B–Q2, though Black still is lost after 24 N–Q5ch! NxN   25 N–R7ch K–B2   26 QxQ NxQ   27 RxBch K–N1   28 NxR.

24 RxN QxQ   25 N–R7ch! K–B2   26 RPxQ R–R1   27 N–N5ch K–B3   28 P–B4 Black resigns

A quiet QP opening (1 P–QB4 P–QB4 2 N–KB3 N–KB3 3 N–B3 P–K3 4 P–K3 P–Q4 5 P–Q4 N–B3 6 BPxP KPxP 7 B–K2 B–Q3 8 0–0 0–0 9 P–QN3 PxP 10 KNxP NxN 11 QxN R–K1 12 B–N2 B–K4 13 Q–Q2 B–N5 14 BxB) in A. Miles–L. Ljubojevic, Bugojno 1978, led to the position in which Black's natural response is of course simply 14 . . . NxB, and after 15 P–KR3 N–B3 White would have a slight plus because of pressure against the isolated QP. This, however, seemed too little for Black, and instead he played:

14 . . . BxP ch?

Strictly on general principles the sacrifice seems unsound, because Black does not have that much attacking power left and White's development is complete.

15 KxB NxBch 16 K–R3!

The retreat 16 K–N1? clearly gives Black a dangerous attack after 16 . . . Q–R5 17 KR–K1 Q–R7ch 18 K–B1 Q–R8ch 19 K–K2 QxP etc. Counting on his completed development and the fact that Black at present has only three attackers, White definitely wants more than what could be available after 16 K–N1?. Playable may be 16 K–N3, but the text offers Black fewer tactical possibilities.

16 . . . Q–N4 17 Q–Q4!

Centralizing the Queen, so that it is both an effective defender and attacker. Too slow for Black now would be 17 . . . P–B4 because of 18 P–N3, and White's King escapes to safety via KN2 and KB3. Therefore, Black must press on immediately.

17 . . . Q–R4ch 18 K–N3 N–R3! 19 R–R1! N–B4ch 20 K–B4

Around here the game becomes a demonstration of King power. White's King turns out to be safe because his pieces are well placed, he is a piece up and Black just doesn't have enough attackers. The endgame after 20 . . . QxR? 21 RxQ NxQ 22 PxN is clearly unsatisfactory for Black.

20 . . . Q–N3 21 QxQP! R–K3 22 QxN!

One of the major strategies for successful defense when ahead in material is to give back some of it to break the attack. According to

Miles, feasible also was a purely defensive strategy with 22 K–B3! QR–K1 23 N–Q1!.

22 . . . R–KB3 23 QxR!

In the game, White weakened his Kingside with 23 P–KN4?! and Black obtained some real counterchances after 23 . . . RxQch 24 PxR Q–N7 (White still won on Move 40). The text is considerably better, since it keeps White's Kingside pawns intact.

23 . . . QxQch 24 K–N3, with a winning material advantage for White.

Having a Rook and 2 minor pieces for the Queen, White has a significant material advantage; with his King inherently safe, White has a theoretically won position.

SECTION 2. The King Declines the Sacrifice

The times when it pays to decline the sacrifice are few. If in a normal position with material equality the sacrifice is so sound that acceptance leads to an immediate end, declining it will only postpone the inevitable. Such cases will not be considered here. Declining the sacrifice is promising only in the following two general cases: (1) The defender is already ahead in material, and (2) The material and/or positional situation on the board is such that declining the sacrifice prevents the attacker from completing his plan, and thus a situation inherently favorable to the defender stays in effect. These abstract-sounding principles can be enlivened by actual examples. First let's follow the course of F. J. Marshall–A. Burn, Ostend 1907, a King's Indian Defense: 1 P–Q4 N–KB3 2 N–KB3 P–Q3 3 B–B4 QN–Q2 4 P–K3 P–KN3 5 B–Q3 B–N2 6 QN–Q2 0–0 7 P–KR4?! ("Anti-positional, but I was determined to play for attack at all costs," is what Marshall says here.) 7 . . . R–K1 8 P–R5?! (Marshall: "Consistent, but also almost unavoidable since Black was threatening very strongly 8 . . . P–K4 followed by 9 . . . P–K5.") 8 . . . NxP 9 RxN?! (And here Marshall admits "Not analytically sound, but. . .") 9 . . . PxR 10 BxRPch!!. White's sacrifices on the 8th and 9th moves were dubious and it was correct to accept them. However, the Bishop sacrifice is sound and cannot be accepted safely: 10 . . . KxB?? 11 N–N5ch K–N3 (11 . . . K–N1? leads to an elementary finish: 12 QxP N–B3 13 QxPch K–R1 14 0–0–0, followed by 15 R–R1ch) 12 N/2–B3 P–K4 13 N–R4ch K–B3 14 N–R7ch K–K2 15 N–B5ch K–K3 16 NxBch K–K2 17 N–B5ch K–K3 18 P–Q5ch! KxN 19 QxPch K–K5 20 0–0–0, with 20 . . . PxB allowing 21 R–Q4 mate and otherwise 21 P–B3 mates. This was the course of the actual game, with Black resigning on move 20. This variation appears long and complicated, yet it is not so difficult to see that Black's King will be in great danger out in the open. The key point, however, is that there is no practical need for Black to play 10 . . . KxB??. If we go back to the position after White's 10th move we see that Black is an Exchange up and can readily afford to nudge his King into safety with **10 . . . K–B1!**. White's incomplete development will not allow him to develop a decisive attack and Black, with . . . P–K4 and/or . . . N–KB3 can develop while chasing away White's pieces. The unbalanced nature of the position does give White certain practical attacking chances, but in theory Black is fully O.K.—and we know that the greedy 10 . . . KxB?? must lead to a certain loss.

A similar example of successful sidestepping is demonstrated in R. Fischer–A. Bisguier, Buenos Aires 1970, Ruy Lopez after: 1 P–K4 P–K4 2 N–KB3 N–QB3 3 B–N5 P–QR3 4 B–R4 N–B3 5 0–0 P–QN4 6 B–N3 B–N2 7 P–Q4 NxQP 8 NxN PxN 9 P–QB3 NxP 10 R–K1 B–Q3? 11 N–Q2! BxPch. Black had optimistically prepared this sacrifice by his erroneous 10th move (correct was 10 . . . B–K2), but Fischer has seen that the key element in the position is the pin along the K-file:

12 K–B1!

Black has perpetual check after 12 KxB? Q–R5ch 13 K–N1 QxPch 14 K–R2 Q–R5ch etc. Despite a momentary three-pawn disadvantage, White is not about to acquiesce since he sees that because of the Black King's central position he will win material.

12 . . . P–Q4 13 Q–R5! 0–0

A Bishop retreat allows the simple 14 NxN, and Black can't recapture because of mate on his KB2. Also unsatisfactory is 13 . . .

Q–Q3 14 NxN PxN 15 QxBPch K–Q1 16 PxP (Trifunovic), and Black's King rather than White's is in mortal danger.

14 QxB PxP 15 NxN PxN 16 PxP P–QB4 17 R–K3!

On a strictly material balance, Black's three pawns are adequate compensation for the piece. But Fischer demonstrates that in this open middlegame White's attack with Queen, 2 Rooks and 2 Bishops is not to be parried:

17 . . . P–B5 18 B–B2 Q–B3 19 R–B3! Q–K3 20 R–R3 Q–B4 21 B–K3 QR–Q1 22 R–K1! R–Q2 23 B–Q4 R–K1 24 R–R5! P–N4 25 P–N4! Black resigns

In our last example we shall see the King heading in the other direction—to KR1. The obscure Riga Variation of the Open Ruy Lopez leads to the position of Diagram 21 as follows: 1 P–K4 P–K4 2 N–KB3 N–QB3 3 B–N5 P–QR3 4 B–R4 N–B3 5 0–0 NxP 6 P–Q4 PxP 7 R–K1 P–Q4 8 NxP B–Q3! 9 NxN BxPch!. Considerable analytical and practical experience has demonstrated that White's only way to try for an advantage is with:

10 K–R1!!

DIAGRAM 21

BLACK

WHITE

Riga Variation
Open Ruy Lopez
after Black's 9th

Looks suicidal, and is only feasible because of the coming combination. Instead 10 KxB?! again allows perpetual check after 10 . . . Q-R5ch 11 K-N1 QxPch etc. 10 K-B1 does not attack the Bishop, and after 10 . . . Q-R5 Black retains approximately equal chances in the coming complications, as demonstrated by the games Maroczy–Berger, Vienna 1908 and Nyholm–Leonhardt, Copenhagen 1907.

10 . . . Q-R5 11 RxNch! PxR 12 Q-Q8ch! QxQ 13 NxQch KxN 14 KxB with a slight advantage to White.

This conclusion is not obvious. Materially, in fact, Black is perfectly O.K., having a Rook and 2 pawns for two minor pieces. Considerable experience has shown, however, that White's pieces have good play against the Black pawns on both sides of the board. The immediate course of J.R. Capablanca–Ed. Lasker, New York 1915 was: 14 . . . B-K3 15 B-K3 P-KB4 16 N-B3 K-K2 17 P-KN4! P-KN3 18 K-N3! retaining a slight edge, as the two White minor pieces have more chances for action than the respective Black Rook, while the Black Kingside pawn majority can be kept in check.

CHAPTER 5
The King on a Forced Flight

During the opening stage the board is full of pieces and thus the
King has an army of attackers to worry about. Necessarily, the
King can not feel comfortable when he is chased across the
board. Whether he will live or not depends on how far into the
enemy camp he gets chased and how well developed the enemy
forces are. If he gets chased into the waiting arms of a well
developed army, his chances of survival are slim. If he can stay
in his own territory and his forces are no worse developed than
the enemy's, then he may live. From the practical standpoint the
real question is how much material to sacrifice to send the King
on a flight. To achieve this at no cost is always pleasant; but is
it worth giving up a pawn, Knight, Bishop, Rook or Queen for
it?

Section 1. The King Is Dead

The first principle to keep in mind is that the King shouldn't
enter on a forced flight unless there is no choice—either practical or theoretical. The opening (a Ponziani) of Lipsky–Gasik,
Chehanov (USSR) 1977, developed as follows: 1 P–K4 P–K4   2
N–KB3 N–QB3   3 P–B3 P–Q4   4 B–N5 PxP   5 NxP Q–N4?!   6
Q–R4 QxNP   7 BxNch?! PxB   8 QxPch. The opening has not
been handled accurately by either side. White's best chances for
initiative rest with 4 Q–R4; Black's 5 . . . Q–N4?! is inferior to 5
. . . Q–Q4, and on Move 7 White should play 7 R–B1!. Back to
the game: Black's King must move, but where?

8 . . . K–K2?

Heading with the King out in the open is suicidal. A closer look will show that both Kings are uncomfortable. It was therefore imperative for Black to safeguard his with 8 . . . K–Q1!, and after 9 R–B1 B–KR6! 10 QxRch K–K2 he would have good chances to get at White's. This would leave the result of the game uncertain. After the text, White, *being on move*, scores first.

9 QxPch! K–B3 10 QxPch! KxN 11 P–Q4ch K–Q3

11 . . . PxPe.p. allows 12 B–B4ch K–K5 13 N–Q2mate.

12 B–B4ch K–B3 13 P–Q5ch K–N4 14 Q–K8ch

Black resigned here and the forced mate runs as follows:

14 . . . K–B5 15 Q–B6ch K–Q6 16 Q–N5ch K–B7 17 Q–K2mate

This result is logical. There is no way that Black's King can take on the whole White army. To bring about this final position, White needed to sacrifice only a single Knight.

In the next example the cost of luring the monarch out is much higher. The position shown in Diagram 22 arose in a skittles game Ed. Lasker–Sir George Thomas, London 1912, after Black's 10th move (1 P–Q4 P–KB4 2 N–KB3 P–K3 3 N–B3 N–KB3 4 B–N5 B–K2 5 BxN BxB 6 P–K4 PxP?! 7 NxP P–QN3?! 8 N–K5 0–0 9 B–Q3 B–N2?! 10 Q–R5 Q–K2?). Black's play has been very lackadaisical: he has paid no attention to the center, neglected Queenside development, allowed White a strong attacking formation and now pays insufficient attention to his King. The punishment is swift and dramatic:

11 QxPch!! KxQ 12 NxBdbl ch K–R3

Obviously forced, since 12 . . . K–R1? allows 13 N–N6mate. For his Queen White has gotten only a N and P—peanuts. Yet the prospect of getting the King onto White's side of the board was tantalizing. White will have 3 minor pieces, three pawns and potentially both Rooks to attack the King. A forced mate probably wasn't "seeable" when White sacrificed his Queen, but he felt 99 + % certain that it must be there somewhere!

DIAGRAM 22

BLACK

WHITE

Lasker–Thomas
London 1912
after Black's 10th

13 N/5–N4ch! K–N4   14 P–R4ch K–B5   15 P–N3ch K–B6   16 B–K2ch

Already there is more than one way to finish the job. Perhaps more elegant was 16 0–0, followed by 17 N–R2mate.

16 . . . K–N7   17 R–R2ch K–N8   18 K–Q2mate.

Here too there is a "cook": 18 0–0–0mate!

Whereas in the game above there was a bolt from the blue, in the next game a series of forceful sacrifices build up to a final crescendo. In a blindfold game P. Morphy–Amateur, New Orleans 1858, the first American World Champion gives a textbook illustration of drawing the enemy King into the open and then annihilating him. The beginning moves of the Two Knights' Defense were: 1 P–K4 P–K4   2 N–KB3 N–QB3   3 B–B4 N–B3   4 P–Q4 PxP   5 N–N5?! (An "amateur" move, played against an amateur. Correct is 5 0–0.) 5 . . . P–Q4   6 PxP NxP? (Just what Morphy was counting on. After the only correct move, 6 . . . Q–K2ch!, it would already be Black who is slightly better.) 7 0–0! B–K2. In a very open position White is ahead in Kingside development; to take advantage of this factor Morphy knows that he must strike immediately:

8 NxBP! KxN   9 Q–B3ch K–K3?!

To hold on to the piece Black's King must head into the open. Because of White's edge in development he will be able to get at the King by force. Better was 9 . . . B–B3   10 BxNch K–B1 with "only" a horrible position for Black.

10 N–B3!!

Maximum force along open lines is what is required to get at the King. The QN–sacrifice opens the Q-file and allows the QR to get into action quickly.

10 . . . PxN   11 R–K1ch N–K4   12 B–B4 B–B3

Black has no defense, anyway, and the text gives Morphy the chance to continue the fireworks.

13 BxN BxB   14 RxBch! KxR   15 R–K1ch K–Q5   16 BxN

Now that Black's King has been chased onto White's part of the board, the end is near. After 16 . . . PxP White starts mating with 17 R–K4ch K–B4   18 Q–QR3ch! KxB   19 Q–Q3ch K–B4 20 R–B4ch etc.

16 . . . R–K1   17 Q–Q3ch K–B4   18 P–N4ch KxP   19 Q–Q4ch Black resigns

Mate is forced: 19 . . . K–R4   20 QxBPch K–R5   21 Q–N3ch K–R4   22 Q–R3ch K–N4   23 R–N1. Another demonstration that in the opening a King caught behind enemy lines faces sure death.

The neglect of defense in Morphy's time often made violent attacks possible during the opening phase. In more modern times, considerable sophistication is required to achieve the same goals. What could be considered a positional type of sacrifice occurred in J. R. Capablanca–E. Bogoljubov, Moscow 1925. A Queen's Gambit Accepted variation led to Diagram 23 as follows: 1 P–Q4 P–Q4 2 P–QB4 P–K3 3 N–KB3 PxP?! 4 P–K4 P–QB4 5 BxP PxP 6 NxP N–KB3 7 N–QB3 B–B4?! 8 B–K3 QN–Q2?!. Black has allowed White too much central influence and—under the assumption that all is safe in a closed opening—

DIAGRAM 23

BLACK

WHITE

Capablanca–Bogoljubov
Moscow 1925
after Black's 8th

neglected the safety of his King. This gives White the opportunity for a long range sacrifice:

9 BxP!! PxB 10 NxP Q–R4

Black has to withstand equally strong pressure after 10 . . . Q–N3 11 NxB! NxN 12 0–0! Q–B3 13 R–B1.

11 0–0!

For the sacrificed piece White has two pawns, some edge in development and the prospect of keeping Black's King in the center. The relatively closed nature of the position means that no immediate shot is possible. Therefore White correctly completes his Kingside development. Inferior would be 11 NxPch?! K–B2 12 N–B5 N–K4 13 0–0 B–K3 (Golombek) and Black will follow up with . . . QR–Q1 and good piece play.

11 . . . BxB 12 PxB K–B2

The KNP needs protection and thus the King starts its journey. Hopeless is 12 . . . R–KN1 13 Q–Q6! K–B2 14 N–Q5.

13 Q–N3 K–N3 14 R–B5 Q–N3 15 N–B4ch K–R3

Black's King has been forced into a precarious position on the edge of the board. Capablanca now erred with 16 P–N4? and after 16 . . . P–N4! found himself already inferior (he, nevertheless, won in 31). Subsequently he demonstrated the following consistent winning method:

16 Q–B7! P–N3   17 P–KN4! QxPch   18 K–N2 PxR

Black loses the Queen after 18 . . . NxNP 19 R–R5ch! PxR   20 QxP/5ch K–N2   21 QxNch K–B1   22 N–K6ch K–K1   23 Q–R5ch K–K2   24 N–Q5ch.

19 P–N5ch! KxP   20 Q–N7ch KxN   21 R–B1ch K–K4   22 Q–K7ch K–Q5   23 R–Q1ch K–B5   24 Q–K6ch K–B4   25 P–N4ch! KxP   26 Q–N3ch K–R4   27 Q–N5mate.

Thus, despite the relative slowness of the early stage, in due course Black's King was forced to walk the plank with the expected result.

SECTION 2. The King May Live

Remember that trekking around the board early in the game is never the King's cup of tea. There are times, however, when the opponent, by speculative sacrifices, forces such wanderings, as well as times when the alternatives look at least as unattractive. How to decide on a practical course of action, i.e. keeping the odds in our favor? A valuable example of this comes from the course of the opening in A. Karpov–A. Zaitsev, Kuibyshev (USSR) 1970: 1 P–K4 P–QB3   2 P–Q4 P–Q4   3 N–QB3 PxP   4 NxP N–Q2   5 N–KB3 KN–B3   6 NxNch NxN   7 N–K5 B–B4?!   8 P–QB3 P–K3?!   9 P–KN4! B–N3?!   10 P–KR4 B–Q3   11 Q–K2! P–B4   12 P–R5? B–K5   13 P–B3 PxP!   14 Q–N5ch N–Q2!. White could have refuted Black's inaccurate handling of the Caro-Kann by 12 B–N2!; instead, his careless and hasty 12 P–R5? has turned the tables, and White finds himself in a difficult position. Seeing that normal continuations are gruesome (15 NxN B–B3!   15 QxNch QxQ   16 NxQ BxP   15 PxB BxN), Karpov decides that going for complications is the only sensible course. True, his King may be the first one to suffer—but there are at least fair *practical* chances for survival:

15 NxP! B–N6ch   16 K–K2 P–Q6ch

A tempting and perfectly good move, forcing the King out, because 17 K–Q2? KxN   18 PxB N–K4! puts White's pieces in a straightjacket and Black threatens the decisive 19 . . . Q–N4 ch. Also promising for Black was the simpler 16 . . . Q–B3   17 PxB QxN.

17 K–K3! Q–B3

A good alternative was 17 . . . KxN. In a certain sense Black suffers from something like an embarassment of riches. Almost everything *looks* good—yet this doesn't mean that everything must be good!

18 KxB!

By capturing with the King White keeps his Kingside pawn formation intact and the KB file closed.

18 . . . QxN   19 R–R3! P–QR3   20 Q–N5

A critical position. Black has succeeded in driving the White King into the center of the board at no material cost. Black would like to keep things this way, but as will be seen it can't be done. White's Queen and other pieces offer reasonable defensive support, and Black's Rooks aren't as yet developed. As demonstrated by several Soviet analysts, in order to succeed here Black had to start increasing the tempo of his attack by sacrificing the KB: 20 . . . P–K4!   21 RxB (Prospectless is 21 KxP QxPch   22 B–K3 N–B4ch 23 K–B2 Q–K5ch   24 K–B1 N–K3!) 21 . . . N–B4ch   22 K–K3 0–0!, and White seems devoid of a satisfactory defensive plan, as among other things, Black threatens 23 . . . Q–KB5ch   24 K–B2 N–K5ch; 23 K–Q2 is refuted by 23 . . . N–K5ch!, and 23 R–R3 QR–Q1!   24 B–Q2 N–K5!   25 KxN Q–Q4ch   26 K–K3 Q–B4ch 27 K–K4 R–Q5ch! leads to mate.

20 . . . P–R3?

Counting on 21 Q–N6? N–B4ch and Black wins after either 22 K–Q4 0–0–0ch or 22 K–K3 B–B5ch   23 K–B2 P–Q7. Yet after the centralizing Queen retreat (preventing Black's . . . N–B4ch) White will be quite safe.

21 Q-K3! P-K4?

It is understandable that Black still dreams of an attack, though with White's Queen defensively well placed on K3, White is in fact already safe. The text's cheap trap (22 RxB?? Q-QB5ch and Black wins) is easily parried. Objectively Black's correct plan was 21 . . . N-B3ch 22 KxP NxNP! 23 PxN! QxBch 24 K-B2 QxR 25 QxKPch with perpetual check for a draw: 25 . . . K-Q1 26 Q-Q5ch K-B1 27 Q-KB5ch K-B2 28 Q-B7ch K-N1 29 B-B4ch!.

22 KxP! B-B5 23 Q-N1! 0-0-0 24 K-B2 BxB 25 RxB! QxRP 26 R-R2! KR-B1 27 R-Q2! Q-R5ch 28 K-N1 Q-B3 29 B-Q3 with advantage to White.

Because of the threatened 30 B-B5 pin Black can't grab the KBP. After 29 . . . K-B2 30 B-K4, White's King and KBP were safe, and after due preparation Karpov went after Black's chronically weak KP, won it and eventually also won the game on Move 71. A triumph for the active Karpov King!

When the King's travels are essentially lateral, the chances that he will escape unscathed increase significantly. A model for correct judgment of King safety was provided by Capablanca in the historically famous and important game J. R. Capablanca–F. J. Marshall, New York 1918, where Marshall first sprang the Marshall Gambit of the Ruy Lopez. The Gambit remains a viable part of modern chess theory and it is noteworthy how close Capablanca came in his first try to finding the absolutely best moves. Our stage will be set after the moves: 1 P-K4 P-K4 2 N-KB3 N-QB3 3 B-N5 P-QR3 4 B-R4 N-B3 5 0-0 B-K2 6 R-K1 P-QN4 7 B-N3 0-0 8 P-B3 P-Q4!? 9 PxP NxP 10 NxP NxN 11 RxN N-B3 (11 . . . P-QB3!) 12 R-K1! B-Q3 13 P-KR3 N-N5 14 Q-B3! Q-R5 15 P-Q4! NxP (15 . . . P-KR4!? is objectively stronger) 16 R-K2 (16 B-Q2! leads to advantage for White)—Diagram 24. According to present day theory Black should now play 16 . . . N-N5! with approximate equality, since White has nothing better than to go for exchanges with 17 R-K8. Instead Marshall plays a much more forcing move:

16 . . . B-KN5?! 17 PxB!

DIAGRAM 24

BLACK

WHITE

Capablanca–Marshall
New York 1918
after White's 16th

When contemplating his 16th, White had to consider Black's response and decide that the coming King flight would end happily for him. There is no choice here anymore since 17 QxN? B–N6 18 Q–B1 BxR 19 QxB QR–K1 wins for Black.

17 . . . B–R7ch 18 K–B1 B–N6

After 18 . . . N–R8?! 19 B–K3 N–N6ch 20 K–K1 NxRch 21 KxN White's King is safer than in the game.

19 RxN! Q–R8ch 20 K–K2

White's King will be safe because of the following five factors: (1) The King can stay in his territory with lots of defenders around him, (2) White has a material advantage, (3) Black's shortage of minor pieces means that he lacks nimble attackers, (4) White controls the center, (5) White's pieces along open lines can threaten Black's King. Inadequate for Black now is 20 . . . QxB 21 QxB QxPch because of 22 K–Q3! QxR 23 K–B2 P–N5 24 P–N5 PxP 25 QxBP/3, with a significantly superior endgame for White (Tartakower).

20 . . . BxR 21 B–Q2! B–R5 22 Q–R3 QR–K1ch 23 K–Q3 Q–B8ch 24 K–B2

White's King now is safe as his minor pieces control the key first–rank squares. White has retained the material advantage of having two minor pieces for a Rook. His next step is to mobilize the Queenside so as to get his superior material into action. Capablanca does this superbly, while also parrying all of Marshall's attempts at a continuing attack:

24 . . . B–B7 25 Q–B3! Q–N8 26 B–Q5! P–QB4 27 PxP BxP 28 P–N4! B–Q3 29 P–R4! P–QR4 30 PxNP PxP 31 R–R6! PxP 32 NxP B–N5 33 P–N6! BxN 34 BxB P–R3 35 P–N7 R–K6 36 BxPch! RxB 37 P–N8 = Qch K–R2 38 RxPch KxR 39 Q–R8ch K–N3 40 Q–R5Mate

And now for a King flight almost impossible to evaluate from a game between two "supposed" amateurs, Hamppe–Meitner, Vienna 1872: 1 P–K4 P–K4 2 N–QB3 B–B4 3 N–R4? BxPch?! 4 KxB Q–R5ch 5 K–K3! (Otherwise the QN goes lost) 5 . . . Q–B5ch 6 K–Q3 P–Q4 7 K–B3 QxKP 8 K–N3 N–QR3 9 P–QR3!. In order to keep his material advantage, White has been forced to scamper across the board with his King. Black hasn't been able to put the King away, because his incomplete development has meant that Black has been playing only with the Queen. With his last move White prevents 9 . . . Q–QN5 and gives the King a flight square on QR2. Having 2 pawns for the piece, with a strong center and attacking chances, Black has fair compensation for the slight material disadvantage. He now decides on a truly eye-opening plan:

9 . . . QxNch?! 10 KxQ N–B4ch

With the Queen sacrifice Black will force White's King into Black's territory, but under circumstances where Black has little firepower left. This latter consideration should mean that White's King will live. The position has been much analyzed in chess literature, but the ultimate truth is not yet completely certain.

11 K–N4?!

In effect giving Black a tempo. This will mean that although White's King will live, he won't be able to escape the constant attacks which lead to a perpetual–check draw. Strong winning chances are offered by the more active 11 K–N5!. Black still must play 11 . . . P–QR4, after which 12 Q–K2 (Heidenfeld) is parried by 12 . . . N–K3!! (Seidman). The threatened 13 . . . B–Q2 mate forces 13 K–R4 N–B4ch 14 K–N5 N–K3 etc., with repetition of moves for a draw. Therefore, in order to win, White must try other defensive methods. Two promising ones are 12 P–QN4!? (Kastner) and 12 P–B4! (Presley).

11 . . . P–QR4 ch! 12 KxN N–K2 13 B–N5ch! K–Q1! 14 B–B6! P–N3ch 15 K–N5

White has been straining hard to prevent the mate threat of . . . P–N3ch and . . . B–Q2. He seems close to success, yet. . .

15 . . . NxB!!

With the threat 16 . . . N–Q5ch and 17 . . . B–Q2mate to which 16 K–R4? is no defense because of 16 . . . N–Q5!, anyway! Therefore the King must capture.

16 KxN B–N2ch!! 17 K–N5

King daringness must have some sense. Foolhardy is 17 KxB?? K–Q2! 18 Q–N4ch K–Q3, and with White's King too deep behind enemy lines there is no defense to 19 . . . KR–QN1mate.

17 . . . B–R3ch 18 K–B6!

But some daring is required! The retreat 18 K–R4?? allows 18 . . . B–B5! followed by 19 . . . P–QN4mate.

18 . . . B–N2ch 19 K–N5 Draw by perpetual check

Black has just enough attackers for a draw but not enough for a win.

CHAPTER 6
The Active King as a Power

As already mentioned earlier, the chances that aggressive King play in the opening phase will bring happiness are very slight. Nevertheless, it is quite wrong automatically to dismiss a continuation just because it requires the King to be active and aggressive. Be very suspicious of such a plan, but give it a fair evaluation. Chess is inexhaustible enough to create a few such opportunities, and dogmatism should never be the reason not to take advantage of them.

Let us look first at Diagram 25, Belova–I. Ramane, USSR 1976, which arose after White's 15th move in an Alekhine's Defense (1 P–K4 N–KB3 2 P–K5 N–Q4 3 P–QB4 N–N3 4 P–Q4 P–Q3 5 P–B4 PxP 6 BPxP P–QB4 7 P–Q5 P–K3 8 N–QB3 PxP 9 PxP P–B5 10 Q–Q4?! N–B3! 11 Q–K4 N–N5 12 P–Q6 P–N3! 13 N–N5? B–B4 14 QxNP Q–R5ch 15 K–K2). By going for a premature attack without completing his development, White has exposed her King to a dangerous counterattack. It is not too surprising that White is on the verge of being punished:

15 . . . B–K5!

The position cries for an attack. In the game Black played the gutless, defensive 15 . . . N/5–Q4? and lost quickly: 16 N–KB3 Q–K5ch 17 K–B2 B–N2 18 N–B3! Q–B7ch 19 B–K2! B–QB1 (The threat was 20 N–Q4, trapping the Queen) 20 P–Q7ch! BxP 21 N–Q4 B–QB1 22 Q–B6ch B–Q2 23 QxRch Black resigns.

16 N–KB3 Q–N5 17 N–B7ch

DIAGRAM 25

BLACK

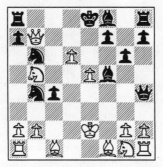

WHITE

Belova–Ramane
USSR 1976
after White's 15th

After 17 Q–B7 quite unpleasant is 17 . . . N–R3! (Gipslis).

17 . . . K–Q2   18 N–Q5ch K–K3   19 N–B7ch K–B4! and Black wins

Black's King is quite secure on KB4, and White can't prevent heavy material damage. If 20 P–KR3 Q–N6   21 N–Q4ch, Black's King continues his activity with 21 . . . KxP.

The idea of the "active King" led to a change in the theoretical judgment of the following variation of the Queen's Gambit Declined: 1 P–Q4 P–Q4   2 P–QB4 P–K3   3 N–QB3 N–KB3   4 B–N5 B–K2   5 P–K3 0–0   6 N–B3 P–QN3   7 BxN BxB   8 PxP PxP   9 B–Q3 B–N2   10 P–KR4?! P–B4!. Based on some earlier games by Marshall (where Black had played 10 . . . P–N3?) and a later one (R. Spielmann–S. Rubinstein, Vienna 1923), the whole variation was judged good for White. Finally, in R. Teschner–B. Spassky, Riga 1959, Black showed that active and cool play can refute White's premature attempt at an attack:

11 BxPch?! KxB   12 N–N5ch K–R3!   13 Q–B2 P–N3

Obviously Black's last two moves were forced, but now he plans to retreat the King to safety with 14 . . . K–N2. Therefore, White must press on:

14 P–R5!? KxN!!

"Why not?" is what Spassky must have said to himself: "Now I am two pieces up, and let White prove a forced win with his incomplete development." White, of course, threatened 15 NxPch and 14 . . . BxN? is inferior because of 15 PxPch K–N2 16 R–R7ch K–B3 (forced) 17 P–B4! and White wins one piece back while retaining good attacking chances. The reader must have noticed by now that White's sacrifices follow the same theme as discussed in Chapter 4; what is different is the uncommonly *successful* activity exhibited by Black's King. White now has nothing better than the text because both 15 PxP B–N2 and 15 P–R6 B–R1, with Black's King retreating to KB3, are prospectless.

15 P–B4ch K–R3 16 PxPch K–N2 17 R–R7ch K–N1

And so Black's King is back home after devouring two pieces. White's attack does remain strong, yet with accurate defensive play Black can parry it.

18 0–0–0 B–N2! 19 QR–R1 Q–B3 20 PxPch RxP! 21 P–KN4!? PxP

Subsequently Spassky showed that the defensive 21 . . . N–Q2! was more accurate.

22 P–N5 Q–K3! and Black has successfully parried the attack.

In the game the less accurate 22 . . . Q–B4?! gave White new attacking chances with 23 RxBch! KxR 24 Q–R2 R–B1 25 P–N6!. (Spassky did win the game on Move 78.)

When, in spite of very few moves having been made, the position is inherently closer to an endgame than to anything else, then there should be no qualms at all about activating the King. In L. Merenyi–J. R. Capablanca, Budapest 1928, White handled the Sicilian Defense very passively in the apparent hope of better chances for a *draw:* 1 P–K4 P–QB4 2 N–KB3 P–KN3 3 P–B3 P–Q4 4 B–N5ch?! B–Q2 5 BxBch QxB 6 PxP QxP 7 P–Q4 PxP 8

QxP QxQ 9 NxQ P–K4!. Black already has a slight edge because of the central pressure exerted by the KP. After a reasonable Knight retreat, however, (10 N–N3, 10 N–B2, 10 N–B3) White's problems would be minor. Nevertheless, after his previous docility he decides that without Queens it's safe to become active:

10 N–N5? K–Q2! 11 K–K2 K–B3!

If Black had been forced to misplace the QN with 10 . . . N–QR3, White's Knight sally would have had some point. As is, the rapid King development stamps the White Knight as misplaced while leading to a quick mobilization of forces by Black. It is not difficult to see that Black's King must be quite safe—there is almost nothing that White can use for attacking it (the already exchanged KB could have been effective!).

12 P–QR4 N–Q2 13 B–K3 P–QR3 14 R–Q1 KN–B3 15 N–Q2?!

Better is 15 P–QB4, to allow the exposed Knight to retreat to the good QB3 square.

15 . . . R–Q1 16 N–R3 N–Q4 17 N/2–B4 P–N3! 18 R–Q2 BxN! 19 RxB KR–K1!

Black's creative play has given him a marked edge in the center, development and piece activity. Perhaps a perfect defense would have held for White. As played, Capablanca wins with relative ease:

20 N–Q6?! R–K2! 21 P–QB4 NxB 22 PxN?! N–B4 23 N–K4 RxRch 24 NxR P–QR4! 25 N–N1 R–Q2 26 N–Q2 P–K5 27 N–N3 N–Q6 28 N–Q4ch K–B4 29 P–QN3 P–B4 30 R–R1 RxN! 31 PxRch KxP 32 P–N3 P–KN4! 33 P–QN4 P–B5! 34 P–B5 P–B6ch 35 K–B1 P–K6 36 R–K1 NPxP 37 RxP KxR 38 PxRP P–B5 White resigns

CHAPTER 7

King Moves to Prevent Threats

In the opening, most of the threats where the King has a role to play involve the King himself. As discussed earlier, the most common and effective King move on behalf of King safety is castling. Examples abound. For instance, let us consider two widely disparate variations for Black in the Sicilian Defense. The first one involves an idea by Larsen in the Nimzovitch Variation: 1 P–K4 P–QB4 2 N–KB3 N–KB3 3 P–K5 N–Q4 4 N–B3 P–K3 5 NxN PxN 6 P–Q4 N–B3! (Larsen) 7 PxP BxP 8 QxP Q–N3! 9 B–QB4! BxPch 10 K–K2. The best way to protect the KBP is the simple 10 . . . 0–0, with Black obtaining about equal chances in some very complicated play. The second variation, with White going for sharpness, runs as follows: 1 P–K4 P–QB4 2 N–KB3 N–QB3 3 P–Q4 PxP 4 NxP N–B3 5 N–QB3 P–Q3 6 B–K3!? N–KN5 7 B–QN5 NxB 8 PxN B–Q2 9 0–0 P–K3 10 BxN PxB 11 P–K5!? B–K2! 12 Q–R5. Again the best defense is 12 . . . 0–0, with Black's position being fully defensible.

There are times, however, when the King must be ready and willing to take an unconventional step to help his cause. It is so important *always* to keep the King in mind as a potential defender—if the other pieces can't do the job. The following game was played when Spassky was just 11 and Korchnoi 17 years old: V. Korchnoi–B. Spassky, Leningrad 1948, Sicilian Defense: 1 P–K4 P–QB4 2 N–KB3 P–Q3 3 P–Q4 PxP 4 NxP N–KB3 5 N–QB3 P–KN3 6 P–B4 B–N5?! 7 B–N5ch QN–Q2 8 BxNch QxB 9 Q–Q3 P–K4 10 N–B3 BxN 11 QxB Q–N5?

12 N–Q5!, and Black resigned. The reason for Black's resignation seems clear: Black has no "normal" way to prevent the threatened 13 NxNch which would win at least the Knight (12 ... B–N2?? 13 NxNch BxN 14 QxQ; 12 ... QxQ? 13 NxNch! K–K2 14 N–Q5ch, followed by 15 PxQ; 12 ... Q–K3?? 13 N–B7ch; 12 ... 0–0–0?? 13 Q–B3ch). Yet there is a simple "King-move way": 12 ... K–Q1!, as Korchnoi pointed out after the game. Then 13 NxN (without check!) is met by the *zwischenzug* 13 ... Q–R5ch, followed by 14 ... QxN. White, therefore, would probably head for the endgame with 13 QxQ NxQ 14 P–KR3! N–R3 15 PxP! PxP 16 B–N5ch K–B1 17 B–B6 R–KN1 18 BxP. Such an endgame is of course cheerless for Black, but you can be sure that had Black noticed the possibility of 12 ... K–Q1!, he wouldn't have resigned on move 12!

Another illustration of a King move parrying a threat occurred in V. Korchnoi–J. Timman, Match Game No. 4, 1976, English Opening: 1 P–QB4 P–KN3 2 P–K4 P–K4 3 P–Q4 N–KB3 4 PxP NxP 5 B–Q3! B–N5ch 6 N–Q2 P–Q4 7 PxPe.p. N–B4 8 B–B2 QxP 9 P–QR3! BxNch 10 QxB N–B3?! 11 P–QN4! N–Q5?! 12 PxN Q–K4ch—see Diagram 26. Black wasn't interested in defending an inferior endgame and preferred to search for complications by sacrificing a piece. Black's primary threat in the diagram position is to take the Bishop with *check*. Therefore the obvious 13 N–K2? is wrong: 13 ... NxBch 14 QxN QxR 15 0–0 (15 N–B3 B–B4 16 Q–Q2 B–Q6! is also good for Black) 15 ... B–B4 16 Q–N3 Q–K4!, and Black either keeps his material advantage or, after 17 B–N2 QxN 18 BxR 0–0–0!, obtains a clear positional plus. The correct solution to the problem is a "safe" King move:

13 K–B1! B–K3

An attempt to continue the attack. Now 13 ... NxB is harmless: 14 R–R2! B–B4 (14 ... N–Q5 15 B–N2 and the Knight is lost) 15 B–N2 B–Q6ch 16 N–K2 Q–K5 17 BxR 0–0–0 18 B–B3, and White will consolidate his position while keeping a decisive material advantage.

14 B–N2 0–0–0 15 N–K2! BxP 16 B–Q3 N–N6 17 BxQ NxQch 18 K–K1 KR–K1 19 BxB NxB 20 B–B4

DIAGRAM 26

BLACK

WHITE

Korchnoi–Timman
Game #4, 1976
after Black's 12th

White is still a piece up and Black doesn't have enough wood to generate anything of significance. Korchnoi won as follows:

20 . . . R–Q5 21 P–N3 R–Q6 22 P–QR4 R–N6 23 K–B1! R–N7 24 N–B1 P–KB3 25 P–R4 P–KR3 26 BxRP R–R1 27 B–N7 R–Q1 28 N–K2! N–Q7ch 29 K–N2 N–K5 30 KR–K1 R/1–Q7 31 K–B3 NxQBP 32 BxP R/N–B7 33 KR–Q1! N–N6 34 RxR NxRch 35 K–K3 Black resigns

Big threats are not always the only ones to worry about. Often a King move can also be effective in coping with smaller threats. In O. Castro–L. Evans, Sao Paulo 1978, Black had sacrificed a pawn early on to reach the position shown in Diagram 27. It turns out that none of the normal moves are playable for White. Castling loses immediately because of 1 . . . P–QN4 2 B–N3 P–N5, and Black wins the Knight as it can't move because of 3 . . . N–K7ch. Also not satisfactory is 1 P–Q3?! because of 1 . . . P–QN4! 2 B–N3 P–Q3, and Black regains the pawn with advantage (Evans). Yet there is a fine multi-purpose move for White:

DIAGRAM 27

BLACK

WHITE

Castro–Evans
Sao Paulo 1978
White to move

The King gets off the K-file so that a potential . . . P–Q3, is no threat while at the same time freeing K1 for the KR. Additionally, any Knight fork tactics are prevented, and the QBP is given additional protection. The King is safe enough on Q1 because White's position is sound, and with his development incomplete Black is in no position for a sharp attack.

1 . . . 0–0 2 P–Q3 R–K1 3 B–K3!

3 R–K1?! would allow 3 . . . P–Q3!, giving Black the chance to strengthen the center with 4 . . . PxP. With the text White gives back the pawn to consolidate his position.

3 . . . QxP 4 QxQ RxQ, with equal endgame chances.

Neither side has any particular strengths or weaknesses and the pawn formations are symmetrical. With reasonable play a draw should and did result.

CHAPTER 8

King Moves to Prepare Action

The best move that the King can make to prepare future action is to castle. The next question, however, is whether the King should move again *after* castling. This requires a closer look at both types of castling: Kingside and Queenside.

SECTION 1.
King Moves Beyond Kingside Castling

The King castled Kingside has a normal safe location on KN1 and there is generally little need to move it further out to KR1. In many openings, however, there is a need to set the KBP in motion to achieve certain central or Kingside attacking objectives. In such cases, the King position on KN1 may give the opponent various possibilities for a counterattack. When the KBP is to be moved up two squares, the King is generally better placed on KR1 than on KN1. Therefore, for such situations, the move K–KR1 is desirable in principle; the disadvantage is that it costs one whole tempo. Therefore it is important not to make this move automatically, but only when "there is nothing better to do." For White, positions arising from the Sicilian Defense offer many possibilities of demonstrating the value of a preparatory K–KR1. Most of the time the primary benefit of having the King on KR1 is that checks or pins along White's KN1–QR7 diagonal are preempted. Periodically, though, an additional benefit appears: the KN1 square is usable by White's pieces, in particular the QB. For instance, in the Closed Sicilian of V. Raicevic–S. Martinović, Vrnjacka Banja 1978, note White's piece placement: 1 P–K4 P–QB4   2 N–QB3 N–QB3   3 P–KN3 P–KN3   4 B–N2 B–N2   5 P–Q3 P–Q3   6 P–B4 P–B4   7 N–B3 N–B3   8 0–0 0–0   9 K–R1! K–R1   10 B–K3 B–K3   11 B–N1! (The Bishop here is safe from Black's . . . N–KN5 and supports White's central P–Q4 advance.) 11 . . . Q–Q2 (Black can't follow suit since 11 . . . B–N1?   12 PxP! PxP   13 P–Q4! leads to a line opening favorable to White.) 12 PxP BxBP   13 P–Q4! P–N3!, with only a slight advantage for White. With his last move Black has ensured good central presence and can look forward to eventual equality.

Even in open positions the QB can be well placed on KN1. Witness D. Bronstein–V. Korchnoi, Hastings 1975/6, Sicilian Dragon: 1 P–K4 P–QB4   2 N–KB3 P–Q3   3 P–Q4 PxP   4 NxP N–KB3   5 N–QB3 P–KN3   6 B–K2 B–N2   7 B–K3 0–0   8 N–N3 N–B3   9 0–0 B–K3   10 P–B4 Q–B1   11 K–R1 R–Q1   12 B–N1! (Again: safe, and controlling key central squares.) 12 . . . P–N3   13 Q–K1 N–QN5   14 R–B1 B–B5   15 BxB QxB   16 N–Q2 Q–B1   17 P–QR3 N–B3   18 N–B3. White has more space in the center and therefore a slight but pleasant advantage. (Bronstein won in 78.)

Mainly, though, we don't want to be bothered by pins and checks. J. Kaplan–A. Karpov, Madrid 1973 opened as follows: 1 P–K4 P–QB4   2 N–KB3 P–K3   3 P–Q4 PxP   4 NxP N–QB3   5 N–QB3 P–QR3   6 B–K2 Q–B2   7 0–0 N–B3   8 K–R1! (By removing his King from the KN1–QR7 diagonal White threatens an early P–KB4, to be followed by P–K5. Now with 8 . . . B–K2   9 P–B4 P–Q3 Black could have entered the type of Scheveningen Variation demonstrated in the next example.) 8 . . . B–N5   9 NxN! NPxN   10 Q–Q4! (Gaining time for protecting the KP by attacking the Bishop. White now is ready to play P–K5, e.g. 10 . . . B–K2?! 11 P–K5!. Karpov finds the best defense.) 10 . . . P–B4!   11 Q–K3 P–Q3. Now instead of 12 Q–N3 (still with some advantage to White though he lost in 52), the awkward position of Black's KB could have been best exploited by the developmental 12 P–QN3! and 13 B–N2.

A properly timed K–KR1 in the Scheveningen Variation was shown in E. Mednis–V. Jansa, Budapest 1978: 1 P–K4 P–QB4   2 N–KB3 P–Q3   3 P–Q4 PxP   4 NxP N–KB3   5 N–QB3 P–K3   6 B–K2 B–K2   7 0–0 N–B3   8 B–K3 0–0   9 P–B4 Q–B2   10 K–R1! (There is no way Black can take advantage of the tempo loss here: 10 . . . NxN allows the centralizing 11 QxN! and 10 . . . B–Q2 the discreet retreat 11 N–N3.) 10 . . . P–QR3   11 Q–K1 NxN   12 BxN P–QN4 (Quite inferior is 12 . . . P–K4?!   13 PxP PxP   14 Q–N3!.) 13 P–QR3 B–N2   14 Q–N3! B–B3   15 QR–K1 Q–N2   16 B–Q3, with a slight advantage to White because of his Kingside attacking chances. (White won in 35.)

Make no mistake about it: the potential pins or checks can be annoying. Follow the course of another Scheveningen variation, E. Mednis–J. Grefe, U.S. Championship 1975: 1 P–K4 P–QB4   2 N–KB3 P–K3   3 P–Q4 PxP   4 NxP N–KB3   5 N–QB3 P–Q3   6 B–K2 B–K2   7 0–0 0–0   8 P–B4 N–B3   9 B–K3 P–QR3   10 P–QR4?! Q–B2   11 Q–K1 NxN!   12 BxN P–K4   13 PxP PxP   14 Q–N3 B–QB4!. White's QB is pinned and thus he has nothing but

15 BxB QxBch   16 K–R1 K–R1!   17 RxN!

Black has cleared the air by exchanging off some potential attackers and is ready to complete his consolidation, after which he can even look forward to having the superior Bishop. White therefore selects a forcing equalizing line.

17 . . . PxR   18 Q–R4 R–KN1!

Black sees no point in 18 . . . Q–B3?!, as after 19 N–Q5! White has at least a certain draw.

19 QxBPch R–N2   20 Q–Q8ch R–KN1 Draw

The game B. Spassky–L. Ljubojevic, Bugojno 1978, a Closed Sicilian, illustrates the importance of the check. Diagram 28 was reached after 1 P–K4 P–QB4   2 N–QB3 N–QB3   3 P–KN3 R–N1!?   4 P–B4 P–KN3   5 N–B3 B–N2   6 B–N2 P–QN4!   7 P–QR3 Q–R4   8 0–0 P–N5   9 N–K2 P–B5!. Spassky now overrates his prospects:

10 P–Q4?

Imperative was 10 K–R1! N–B3 (10 . . . P–N6?!   11 PxP RxP   12 P–Q4! is good only for White.) 11 P–K5 (inferior is 11 P–Q3?!

DIAGRAM 28

BLACK

WHITE

Spassky–Ljubojevic
Bugojno 1978
after Black's 9th

P–N6! 12 QPxP NxP 13 PxP Q–N3!) 11 . . . N–Q4 12 P–Q4 PxPe.p. 13 BPxP, with approximate equality after either 13 . . . P–Q3 or 13 . . . 0–0 (Ljubojevic).

10 . . . PxPe.p. 11 BPxP Q–N3ch! 12 K–R1

12 P–Q4 B–QR3 13 B–K3 N–B3 is equally unattractive for White.

12 . . . PxP! 13 RxP BxP 14 BxB QxB 15 Q–R1 N–B3 16 N/2–Q4 NxN 17 NxN P–QR3!, with a sound extra pawn for Black.

The check has led to the win of a pawn and Ljubojevic realized this material advantage with little difficulty, winning on Move 39.

Similar considerations—but even more pronounced—apply when looking at plans from Black's side of the board. Since Black can afford less outright activity early in the game than White, it follows that Black must prepare more carefully than White. This refers to both an early . . . P–KB4 as well as other plans. A preparatory . . . K–KR1 can well come in very handy. A multi-purpose utilization of that move is beautifully demonstrated by the Ruy Lopez, H. Löwenfisch–A. Alekhine, Vilnus 1912: 1 P–K4 P–K4 2 N–KB3 N–QB3 3 B–N5 P–QR3 4 B–R4 N–B3 5 Q–K2 B–K2

6 P–B3 P–Q3   7 P–KR3?! B–Q2   8 P–Q3?! 0–0   9 B–B2?!. White has played the opening very timidly (to put it charitably) and this gives Black the chance to already formulate a plan for the attack:

9 . . . K–R1!   10 0–0 N–KN1!

In his excellent book *My Best Games of Chess 1908–1923* Alekhine makes some trenchant observations regarding Black's opening play. After this move he says: "Played, apparently, in order to continue with . . . P–KB4. White prepares for this eventuality by placing his Rook on K1 so as to obtain compensation in the center by P–Q4."

11 R–K1 Q–K1!   12 P–Q4 P–B3!

Alekhine: "In accordance with the principle that an advance on the wings is only possible after the position in the center is stabilized."

13 QN–Q2 P–KN4!

Alekhine: "The logical reaction against 7 P–KR3. The opening of the KN file after the (threatened) 14 . . . P–N5   15 PxNP BxP would evidently be to Black's advantage. To avoid this threat White is compelled to weaken the position of his King still more."

14 P–Q5 N–Q1   15 P–KN4 P–KR4!   16 N–R2 N–R3   17 N/Q–B1 P–B3!

By adding pressure against White's center to go with that on the Kingside, Black makes it much more difficult for White to defend his weaknesses.

18 N–N3 BPxP   19 KPxP Q–B2!   20 N–B5

After 20 P–QB4 PxP   21 PxP P–B4! Black advantageously opens the KB file. With the text White prevents this but at the cost of a new pawn weakness.

20 . . . NxN   21 BxN BxB   22 PxB Q–R2!   23 Q–K4 N–B2   24 N–B1 N–R3   25 N–K3 R–KN1!

Note how safe Black's King is tucked away in the corner. Meanwhile, the freeing of the KN1 square has first enabled Black's KN to be successfully redeployed and now the KR finds it very useful. The rest of the game is also excellently played by Alekhine; as it is beyond our basic theme, however, I shall make no further comments.

26 K–N2 B–Q1! 27 P–QR4 P–R4 28 P–N4 PxP 29 PxP B–N3 30 N–B4!? B–Q5 31 B–N2 QR–QB1! 32 QR–B1 RxN 33 RxR BxB 34 Q–B2 NxP!! 35 R–B7 Q–N3 36 R–B8 P–N5! 37 RxRch KxR 38 QxB PxPdbl ch 39 KxP Q–N5ch 40 K–R2 N–R5 41 P–B4 N–B6ch 42 K–R1 Q–R6ch 43 Q–R2 QxQmate

SECTION 2.
King Moves Beyond Queenside Castling

The King castled Queenside generally finds itself less safe on QB1 than the Kingside–castled King is on KN1. Since the QP usually has moved, the King is fairly often exposed to a Queen check; often also the QB file is at least semi-open and this gives ready–made opportunities for an attack along it against the King. These factors suggest that the King is much safer on QN1 than on QB1; additionally, from QN1 it protects the QRP. Therefore an early King move to QN1 is very often in order prior to attempting active play, and this is of even greater importance for Black. Nevertheless, the move does cost a tempo, and therefore should not be done automatically, and particularly not where the position is of such sharpness that the ultimate success of an attack may hinge on a single tempo.

We shall look at three examples of a useful K–QN1 from White's side; the even greater need for Black to prepare his active play by placing his King "out of the way" should be readily apparent to all. Being a move behind, Black can never afford as much activity in the opening as can White.

Often there is a specific reason for moving the King to go with the general one. Diagram 29 resulted after some passive play by Black in a Queen's Gambit Declined (1 P–Q4 P–Q4 2 P–QB4 P–K3 3 N–QB3 N–KB3 4 B–N5 B–K2 5 N–B3 QN–Q2 6 P–K3 0–0 7 Q–B2 P–QN3?! 8 PxP PxP 9 B–Q3 B–N2 10 P–KR4! P–B4 11 0–0–0 PxP 12 KNxP R–K1?!) in A. Alekhine–F. D. Yates, Hamburg 1910. White seems to be attacking aggressively, yet he now plays:

DIAGRAM 29

BLACK

WHITE

Alekhine–Yates
Hamburg 1910
after Black's 10th

13 K–N1!

The immediate 13 P–KN4?! is embarassed by 13 . . . N–K4, as 14 BxN is foiled by the *zwischenzug* 14 . . . NxBch. By preventing the capture of his KB with check White makes ready for 14 P–KN4. Additionally, by removing his King from the open QB file, White minimizes any potential counterplay by Black along that file.

13 . . . P–QR3   14 P–KN4! P–N4   15 BxN! NxB   16 P–N5 N–K5 17 NxN PxN   18 BxKP BxB   19 QxB BxP   20 N–K6! Q–K2   21 PxB P–R3

After 21 . . . P–N3?! Alekhine demonstrates the following win: 22 RxP! QxN!? 23 Q–KR4 Q–K5ch 24 QxQ RxQ 25 QR–R1. After the text White achieves a R and P endgame a pawn up, which he realizes with excellent technique.

22 PxP QxN   23 Q–Q4! Q–K5ch   24 QxQ RxQ   25 PxP KxP   26 QR–N1ch K–B3   27 R–R6ch K–K2   28 R–QB1 R–R2   29 R/1–QB6! P–R4   30 R–R6 RxR   31 RxR P–R5   32 R–QN6 R–K4 33 K–B2 R–B4ch   34 K–Q3 K–Q2   35 P–R3 R–B4   36 P–B4 K–B2   37 R–KR6 R–Q4ch   38 K–B3 P–B4   39 R–K6! K–Q2   40 R–K5! RxR   41 PxR K–K2   42 K–Q3 K–Q2   43 P–K4 P–B5   44 K–K2 K–K3   45 K–B2! Black resigns

In J. Timman–A. Karpov, Bugojno 1978 (Diagram 30) after Black's 11th move, the QB file is half open. Again White effectively minimizes Black's counterplay by putting his King on QN1. In certain respects the opening play is similar to that of the previous game: in a Queen's Gambit Declined Black employed a passive set-up. After 1 P–QB4 P–K3 2 N–QB3 P–Q4 3 P–Q4 B–K2 4 PxP PxP 5 B–B4 N–KB3 6 P–K3 0-0 7 Q–B2 P–B3?! 8 B–Q3 R–K1 9 N–B3 QN–Q2 10 0-0-0 N–B1 11 P–KR3 B–K3, the position in the diagram was reached. White has excellent attacking chances against Black's Kingside; whatever chances Black has must come from a . . . P–QB4 advance. Therefore prior to starting his attack, White removes his King from the QB file:

12 K–N1! R–B1 13 N–N5! P–N4?!

DIAGRAM 30

BLACK

WHITE

Timman–Karpov
Bugojno 1978
after Black's 11th

A move with no positive purpose (nothing is done to further the indicated . . . P–QB4 advance) but with negative aspects (the exchange of Black's QB weakens the King position and the advanced QNP will be more weak than useful). Timman recommends 13 . . . B–Q2! 14 B–K5 P–KR3 15 N–B3 P–QB4!, with White being only slightly better.

14 B–K5 P–KR3 15 NxB NxN 16 P–KN4 N–Q2 17 P–KR4! P–N5?!

Just chasing the N to a superior square. The immediate 17 . . .
BxP would have allowed better defensive prospects.

18 N–K2 BxP   19 P–B4 P–QB4

Black is ready to sacrifice the Exchange to brake White's attack,
yet it turns out to be only a short term pallative.

20 B–R6 B–K2   21 BxR QxB   22 N–N3! P–B3   23 RxP!!

Note how safe White's King is on QN1, while Black's King
position is being ripped open by force. The Rook is taboo: 23 . . .
PxR   24 Q–N6ch K–B1   25 N–B5, with mate to follow.

**23 . . . N/3–B1   24 R–R3 P–B5   25 N–B5 PxB   26 BPxP Q–B3
27 QR–R1 N–N3**

At essentially no cost in material White has achieved a powerful
attack. Timman now played 28 N–Q6 and won easily enough on
Move 46. Subsequently he demonstrated the following, immediately decisive, combination:

**28 NxP! KxN   29 R–R7ch K–N1   30 R–R8ch!! NxR   31 Q–R7ch
K–B1   32 QxNch K–B2   33 R–R7ch K–K3   34 QxR and wins**

In closed positions too the King is more comfortable on QN1. A
QP opening led to the following position in V. Korchnoi–A.
Karpov, Hastings 1971–2: 1 P–Q4 N–KB3   2 N–KB3 P–K3   3
B–N5 P–QN3?!   4 P–K4! P–KR3   5 BxN QxB   6 B–Q3 B–N2   7
QN–Q2 P–QR3   8 Q–K2 P–Q3   9 0–0–0 N–Q2. White is ahead in
development and controls more space. Yet not much is happening
in this inherently closed position. So White takes time out for:

10 K–N1!

Korchnoi says here: "This move will later prove useful. White
waits to see which central pawn structure Black will choose, since
this will determine White's subsequent plan."

**10 . . . P–K4   11 P–B3 B–K2   12 N–B4 0–0   13 B–B2 KR–K1
14 P–Q5! P–B4?**

Korchnoi considers this the decisive error, as the move does
nothing for Kingside protection nor for Queenside counterplay.

For the former 14 . . . B–KB1! was in order; for the latter 14 . . .
P–B3 makes sense.

15 N–K3 B–KB1   16 P–KN4 Q–Q1!?   17 P–N5!

With a winning attack for White (17 . . . PxP?!   18 QR–N1 etc).
Subsequently neither side played as well as could have been expected. White should have won more easily, while Black made no use of the offered chances. While the rest of the game is interesting, I have decided to make my only comments via the !/? symbols. Do note that White's King remains in safety on QN1 all the way through.

17 . . . P–KR4   18 P–N6! PxP   19 KR–N1 Q–B3   20 N–N5 B–K2
21 N–K6 N–B1!?   22 N–B7 Q–B2   23 QR–KB1?! P–QN4   24
NxR/R8 BxN?!   25 P–QB4 R–N1   26 B–Q3?! Q–K1?!   27 R–B1
B–KB3   28 R–N2 R–N3?   29 QR–N1 R–N1   30 Q–B1 P–N5   31
B–K2! P–R5   32 RxP! QxR   33 RxQ NxR   34 B–N4 N–B5   35
Q–Q1 P–N6   36 PxP B–N2   37 N–N2! B–B1   38 BxB RxB   39
Q–N4 R–K1   40 NxN PxN   41 QxBP B–K4   42 QxP R–KB1   43
P–N4! B–Q5   44 PxP Black resigns

CHAPTER 9

Correct and Incorrect King Moves

What to do when early on the King must move, yet has a choice of squares? Are there some basic principles that we can use to help arrive at the correct decision? Some of the time there is nothing else to do than mechanically to check out each of the alternatives. For instance in Diagram 31, V. Smyslov–D.

DIAGRAM 31

BLACK

WHITE

*Smyslov–Bronstein
1951 USSR
Championship
after Black's 13th*

Bronstein, 1951 USSR Championship (a Closed Sicilian which started 1 P–K4 P–QB4 2 N–QB3 N–QB3 3 P–KN3 P–KN3 4 B–N2 B–N2 5 P–Q3 P–Q3 6 B–K3 N–R3 7 Q–B1 N–KN5 8 B–Q2 N–Q5 9 P–KR3 N–K4 10 QN–K2 Q–N3 11 P–KB4 NxBPch?! 12 QxN QxP 13 QxQ NxPch) White's King must move either to Q1 or KB1. Let's check out 14 K–Q1: Black plays 14 . . . NxQch 15 K–B2 N–B5, and has gained three pawns for the piece and has an active attacking position with White's King exposed on QB2 and Black's Knight active on QB5. A particular disadvantage of 14 K–Q1? is that Black gains a tempo by capturing the Queen with check. Smyslov went through a similar analysis for 14 K–B1 and came up with the conclusion that it has no defects. Therefore he played:

14 K–B1! BxQ

Or 14 . . . NxQ 15 B–B3!, with a slight advantage for White.

15 R–N1 B–K3 16 B–QB3! BxQRP?!

Black should have played 16 . . . BxB 17 NxB B–B5 18 KN–K2 0–0–0, though after 19 B–B3 and 20 K–N2 White has completed his development and remains with the better chances (Smyslov). This position is of the middlegame type where the piece is stronger than 3 non-threatening pawns.

17 RxB NxR 18 BxN!

Rather than going for maximum material advantage with 18 BxR P–B3, White prefers to have his pieces in active play. Subsequently the 3 nimble minor pieces prove to be more effective than Black's Rook and 4 pawns:

18 . . . R–KN1 19 K–B2 B–B5 20 N–KB3 BxN 21 KxB K–Q2 22 R–Q1! P–QR4 23 N–K5ch K–B2 24 NxBP P–R5 25 P–K5 P–R6 26 B–QR1 KR–K1 27 N–N5 R–R4 28 N–K6ch K–Q2 29 B–Q5 P–R7 30 P–N4! R–QB1 31 N–N5 R–B1 32 P–B5! PxBP 33 PxBP P–R3 34 B–K6ch K–B2 35 PxPch PxP 36 N–K4 R–R6 37 NxQP RxRP 38 B–K5 R–QR1 39 N–B4ch **Black resigns**

Most of the time valid benchmarks exist either regarding the strategic requirements of the position or principles of King play. A

position of strategic significance in the French Defense results after
1 P–K4 P–K3 2 P–Q4 P–Q4 3 N–Q2 N–KB3 4 P–K5 KN–Q2 5
P–KB4 P–QB4 6 P–B3 N–QB3 7 QN–B3 B–K2 8 B–Q3 Q–R4!?.
Black's strategic idea is to take advantage of the pin of the QBP by
preventing White from recapturing with the QBP after 9 . . . PxP.
In this way Black would lessen White's central influence. The
natural 9 B–Q2 has the disadvantage that after 9 . . . Q–N3 Black
threatens both the QNP and QP. Therefore, in order to keep
maximum central strength, White should unpin the QBP by
moving the King. Since 9 K–K2? is clearly inappropriate, because
the King is needlessly left in the center, White is left with two
reasonable moves: (1) **9 K–B2?!**. With the logical plan of completing development with 10 N–K2 and then castling by hand
(P–KN3, K–N2). The move is careless however, because it allows
Black to establish a new pin with 9 . . . Q–N3!. After 10 N–K2
P–B3! it is already Black who is better. In Doda–W. Uhlmann,
Poland–East Germany 1974, White tried to minimize his difficulties by exchanging Queens with 11 Q–N3 QxQ 12 PxQ PxQP
13 PxQP 0–0 14 B–Q2, but after 14 . . . P–KN4!! found himself
still subject to a strong attack (Black won in 33). Even so 11 Q–N3
was better than 11 KPxP?! BxP 12 R–K1 because after 12 . . . PxP
13 PxP P–K4! 14 BPxP N/2xP! (note the pin on the QP!) Black rips
open the position and starts going after White's King. Therefore,
correct for White is the safe: (2) **9 K–B1!**. Black now has no concrete counterplay and after 9 . . . PxP (9 . . . P–QN4!? 10 PxP
P–N5 needs checking in master play) 10 PxP P–QN3 11 B–Q2
B–N5 12 B–K3 B–R3 13 N–K2, M. Botvinnik–W. Uhlmann,
Varna Olympiad 1962, White's superior center gave him the
advantage.

Keeping in mind general principles of King play can be of
significant help most of the time. Thus it is useful to state that:
"The King should not voluntarily head out into the open." In
Nordijk–Landau, Rotterdam 1927, an early example of Alekhine's
Defense, White ventured an unsound piece sacrifice: 1 P–K4
N–KB3 2 P–K5 N–Q4 3 N–KB3 P–Q3 4 B–B4 N–N3 5 BxPch?
KxB 6 N–N5ch. Black's King has three possible moves:

1. **6 . . . K–N3?** The game continuation, and quite wrong.
Why venture out when there is no clear need for it? 7 Q–B3!

KxN (or 7 . . . Q–K1   8 P–K6!) 8 Q–B7! P–N3   9 P–Q4ch
K–R4   10 Q–KB4 P–KR3   11 P–KR3 P–N4   12 Q–B7ch
K–R5   13 P–N3mate.

2. **6 . . . K–K1?!** Better than 6 . . . K–N3? but not best because White has at least a draw after 7 Q–B3.

3. **6 . . . K–N1!** As pointed out by Shamkovich this is the correct move. The King is safer here than on KN3 and, unlike the situation after 6 . . . K–K1?!, Black can guard his KB2 square. White now has nothing for the piece. A likely continuation would be: 7 Q–B3 Q–K1   8 P–K6 P–N3!   9 P–Q4 N–B3   10 P–B3 N–Q1, with Black being safe and sound.

Recalling the earlier discussion on castling, the following principle can be stated: "In open positions the King is better placed (and safer) on the side of the board (e.g. KN1) than in the center (e.g. K1)." Theory has known for a long time that in the Two Knights' Defense (1 P–K4 P–K4   2 N–KB3 N–QB3   3 B–B4 N–B3) 4 N–B3?! is harmless because of 4 . . . NxP!, and 5 BxPch? is counterproductive because after 5 . . . KxB   6 NxN P–Q4!   7 N/4–N5ch K–N1! Black's King is safe enough and the strong center plus the two–Bishop advantage give Black a clear positional edge. Let us see how to apply the above principles in deciding on Black's correct King move in the following variation of the Smith–Morra Gambit in the Sicilian Defense: 1 P–K4 P–QB4   2 P–Q4?! PxP   3 P–QB3 PxP   4 NxP N–QB3   5 N–B3 P–KN3   6 B–QB4 B–N2   7 0–0 N–B3! (Books on opening theory including the *Encyclopedia of Chess Openings* (1st edition) call this move an error. As we shall see, this judgment is incorrect. Why should such a sound developing move be wrong?) 8 P–K5?! N–KN5   9 BxPch?! KxB   10 N–N5ch. White's play has a superficial point: he recovers the piece while opening up the position to get at Black's King. Yet there are also other concrete factors to be considered, such as White's development being incomplete and the KP loose. Now 10 . . . K–B1?! is rather pointless (though not necessarily the worst move!) so that we'll consider only the "consistent" possibilities:

1. **10 . . . K–K1?.** The move was uncritically accepted by theory as the "only" move for over 20 years. Yet at the very

least it should have raised much suspicion. Why should the King want to remain in the center in an open position? 11 QxN NxP 12 Q-QR4!, with a very strong attack for White (he threatens, e.g. 13 N-K6!). White was soon victorious in M. Matulovic–Del Pezzo, Italy 1954.

2. **10 . . . K-N1!** Yes, of course! In J. Tompa–Z. Ribli, 1976 Hungarian Championship, Black had no difficulty in consolidating his pawn advantage: 11 QxN NxP 12 Q-K4 P-K3! 13 B-B4 P-Q4 14 QR-Q1 P-KR3! 15 N-B3 Q-B1! 16 Q-K3 NxNch 17 PxN B-Q2 18 N-K2 R-K1 19 B-N3 K-R2. Black is not only up a pawn, but has the center, two Bishops and the superior pawn formation. He won easily on Move 36.

Part II
THE MIDDLEGAME

The real action starts in the middlegame. Optimum coordination of pieces is what Capablanca considers to be the most important principle of middlegame play. Regarding the King, Capablanca differentiates between attacking it or defending one's own. For defending the King, use as few pieces as can do the job (so that the others are free for attacking functions elsewhere); but when attacking the opponent's King, bring forward all the pieces that can be mustered (to ensure attaining the goal).

The primary overriding objective of middlegame play is to mate the opponent's King. Since this is often impossible in a direct way, a substitute objective is to win material so that either thanks to the material advantage a direct Kingside attack then becomes feasible, or the material advantage is realized slowly and surely in an endgame.

The role of the King in the middlegame is somewhat paradoxical. On the one hand it must be sheltered from attacks. On the other—as we shall see—it has a meaningful role to play in various offensive and defensive activities.

CHAPTER 10
The Contained King

SECTION 1. The Handicap of the Contained King

We do want to safeguard our King; we never want to immobilize him. The King can be contained either temporarily or "permanently." Both conditions can be serious, though the temporary condition can be corrected *given sufficient time.* Where such time is not available, the end can be immediate and drastic. Perhaps the most common occurrence is the back rank mate. If we look at Diagram 32, G. Füster–Balogh, 1945 Hungarian Championship, Black to move, everything *looks* O.K. for White. And if White's KN or KR pawns were advanced just a bit, White would be fine. Temporarily, however, White's King is contained on the first rank. Even so, Black can't exploit this in a purely routine fashion, i.e. 1 . . . KR–R1?? leads to a back rank mate win for *White:* 2 QxRch! RxQ 3 RxRch, followed by mate. Yet there is a non-routine win for Black:

1 . . . Q–N7!!, and White resigned.

Why? Because there is no defense to the threatened 2 . . . RxR. If 2 RxQ, 2 . . . RxRch leads to a back rank mate; 2 Q–Q1 leads to a prosaic mate after 2 . . . QxPch etc.

The King can also be temporarily contained by having too many of his own pieces around him. Thus in Diagram 33, Murray—Gilbert, USA 1946, Black on move played simply: 1 . . . N–N6mate! Note that White's KNP and, particularly, the clumsy position of the KN, take away flight squares from the King. Most of the time things are not that easy, however, and

DIAGRAM 32

BLACK

WHITE

Füster–Balogh
1945 Hungarian
Championship
Black to move

DIAGRAM 33

BLACK

WHITE

Murray–Gilbert
USA 1946
Black to move

the victor must think up a way to force the defender's pieces to "self-contain" the King. A simple, typical example is shown in Diagram 34, P. Morphy–Amateur, New York 1857, White to move:

DIAGRAM 34

BLACK

WHITE

P. Morphy–Amateur
New York 1857
White to move

1 R–B8ch!! QxR   2 RxQch RxR   3 QxP Mate

Note how both of Black's Rooks take away flight squares from the King and White's single remaining piece can administer mate.

In the above cases the losing side, if it had time to just make one move, could have easily prevented damage. Where the King containment is "permanent," so is the damage. All the advice that can be given is to strive very hard *not* to land in such a position. Let's consider the position arising in A. Karpov–E. Torre, Manila 1976, after White's 30th move. White: K—b1 Q—d1 N—g4 P—a3, b2, d3, e4, g2, g3 Black: K—e8 Q—d4 B—g5 P—a4, b3, d6, e6 f7. A brief evaluation shows that White's King is in a permanent box. Black's KB ensures that no fleeing via QB1 is possible; Black's QNP (made "permanent" by being protected by the QRP) prevents the King from getting out via QR2 and QB2; *White's* QNP makes sure that the King can't have QN2. Looked at from the standpoint of prior exchanges having taken place, the initial position could perhaps be considered an endgame with White even up a pawn. Yet the overriding feature is the White King's unsafe situation—inherently a middlegame factor. It can even be said that with more material on the board White would be better off: he would have more defenders and could hope possibly to generate some counterplay. As is, Black's Queen just walks all over White's position:

30 . . . P–Q4! 31 PxP QxQP/4 32 N–B2 QxNP 33 N–K4 B–K6! 34 N–B3 Q–B3 35 P–Q4 Q–B5 36 P–Q5 P–K4! 37 Q–R1 Q–Q6ch 38 K–R1 B–Q5 39 Q–R8ch K–Q2 40 Q–R8 Q–B8ch 41 N–N1 Q–QB5

The boxed–in nature of the White King allowed Black an immediate mating combination: 41 . . . BxPch! 42 KxB Q–B7ch!: 43 K–B3 Q–Q5mate; 43 K–B1 Q–B7mate; 43 K–R1 Q–QR7mate. The text move threatens the same combination while still keeping the bind. White is still helpless.

42 Q–N7ch K–Q3 43 Q–N8ch KxP 44 Q–Q8ch K–K3 45 Q–K8ch K–B4 46 Q–Q7ch K–N3 47 Q–N4ch K–B3 48 N–B3 Q–B8ch White resigns

The absence of Queens does not necessarily lighten the load of the side with the contained King. The course of play from Diagram 35, A. Whiteley–E. Mednis, London–New York Telex Match 1976, after White's 28th move, demonstrates this very well. From a strictly materialistic endgame point of view White is not too badly off. He has a Rook and a passed QRP to counter Black's two minor pieces, and Black's Kingside pawn formation is, according to "the book," quite poor. Black can create a noose around White's King, however, and completely change the complexion of the position:

28 . . . B–R6!!

Now 29 RxN? runs into a back–rank mate combination: 29 . . . B–N7ch 30 K–N1 N–K7ch! 31 NxN R–Q8mate. And the attempt to consolidate with 29 R–N7 is refuted by 29 . . . N–R5!!: 30 NxN allows a "contained King mate" after 30 . . . B–N7ch 31 K–N1 N–K7, while 30 R–N8 is met simply by 30 . . . RxR! 31 RxRch B–KB1, and to prevent mate to his contained King, White will have to absorb heavy material loss by playing 32 BxP. White therefore tries to minimize Black's attacking power by an alternate way of exchanging off his Rook.

DIAGRAM 35

BLACK

WHITE

Whiteley–Mednis
Telex Match 1976
after White's 28th

29 R–R8 RxR   30 BxR N–Q6!   31 R–N8ch B–KB1

White can't protect his KBP, as either 32 K–N1? N–K7ch   33 NxN PxN or 32 N–Q1? B–N7ch   33 K–N1 N–K7mate lead to an immediate end.

32 R–K8!?

The only move, as Black's . . . N–K7 must be prevented. But now Black's forward KBP will become a powerful passed pawn, cost White a piece and lead to a prosaic win for Black.

32 . . . NxPch   33 K–N1 N–N5   34 K–R1!? N–B7ch   35 K–N1 N–N5   36 K–R1 P–B7   37 B–N2 P–B8 = –Qch   38 BxQ BxB   39 P–QR4 K–N2   40 R–K1 B–KR6 White resigns

Even where the contained King is in no immediate danger, the fact that it is contained is a severe handicap. A contained King not only can't help his side but generally even interferes with the maneuvering of his own pieces. This is well shown from Diagram 36, T. Petrosian–H. Mecking, Wijk aan Zee 1971, after Black's 36th move. The closed nature of the position (helped also by the absence of Queens) means that Black's King is temporarily safe, yet

DIAGRAM 36

BLACK

WHITE

Petrosian–Mecking
Wijk aan Zee 1971
after Black's 36th

the coming course of events show that Black is playing with at least one arm tied behind his back:

37 R–R1! K–N1

The threat was 38 RxPch, but now Black's KR is also in a sorry situation. The next step in White's plan is to establish a complete grip on the position. Thereafter White will prepare a decisive line opening.

38 N–B3! N–Q3   39 N–K5 B–K1   40 B–Q3 R–B1   41 K–B3 B–B3 42 R–KR2 B–K1   43 K–K3 R–B2   44 K–Q4! N–N2   45 P–QN4! N–Q1   46 R–R4 N–N2   47 R–QR2 N–Q3   48 R–KR1 N–N2   49 P–N5

Fixing Black's QNP as a weakness and showing that he has decided on P–QB4 as the ultimate line–opening method.

49 . . . N–B4   50 B–B2 N–Q2   51 R–QR3 N–B4   52 P–B4!

After some of his typical cat-and-mouse tactics, Petrosian opens up the game. Note that throughout Black's K and KR have been "disinterested" spectators.

52 . . . N–Q2　53 R–QB3 NxN　54 KxN PxP　55 B–K4! R–B1　56 K–Q6! R–B4　57 KR–QB1! Black resigns

The game was adjourned here and Black had in fact sealed the only move: 57 . . . P–R5. Subsequently he resigned without continuing. Ivkov supplies the following possible continuation: 58 RxP RxR　59 RxR PxP　60 R–B8 K–R2　61 R–B3! K–N1　62 K–K7! K–R2　63 RxP. Black is in a complete bind and must start losing decisive material.

Section 2. Creating "Air" for the King

The back–rank mate is the most common lethal threat against the castled King. It can be negated by the simple expedient of giving the King "air" by playing either P–KR3 or P–KN3. Isn't it always a good idea, therefore, to do this as early as possible in the game? No—it would be so only if back rank mates were the overriding strategic and tactical elements of chess. Since this is not so, the actual requirements and priorities of a position must be established. Make "air" for the King under the following conditions:

1.　When a back rank mate is threatened, or
2.　When there is nothing else of greater importance to do.

One should be particularly reluctant to play an early P–KN3 or P–KR3. As discussed in Chapter 1, Section 3, these moves create an inherent weakening of the King position and are particularly risky when the opponent is ready to launch a pawn storm there. Additionally, the time lost can be of significance someplace else on the board.

How does one choose between P–KN3 and P–KR3? In general P–KR3 is the preferred move, because it causes less weakening of the Kingside, but it may not be satisfactory if the opponent still has a KB ready to attack the Kingside. Under such circumstances P–KN3 is indicated. Again, as a general concept, with minor pieces on the board P–KN3 is the riskier move since it weakens both the KB3 and KR3 squares. It is usually played if the QB and Knights are gone. If the position is close to an endgame or if an endgame can shortly be anticipated, then P–KB3 is often good to get the King closer to the center for endgame play.

Now for some examples of positions where "making air" is in order. Diagram 37, V. Jansa–Cebalo, Smederevska Palanka 1978, after Black's 21st move, shows White with a significant strategic advantage. White has pressure along the Q-file and, more importantly, can ruin Black's Queenside pawn formation at will with BxN. Yet for tactical reasons the immediate attempt to win a pawn with 22 RxRch?! RxR 23 RxRch QxR 24 BxN?? allows a back-ranker starting with 24 . . . Q–Q8ch. Therefore in order is:

22 P–N3!

DIAGRAM 37

BLACK

WHITE

Jansa–Cebalo
S. Palanka 1978
after Black's 21st

Of course, 22 P–R3 would also be perfectly safe. Yet White prefers the text move (equally safe here) because, with a possible endgame in view, the King at KN2 will be closer to the center than it would be on KR2. Here too "open" is 22 P–KB3?! because after 22 . . . RxR! 23 RxR R–Q1 24 RxRch QxR 25 BxN? Q–Q8ch 26 K–B2 Black has the *zwischenzug* 26 . . . QxQBPch.

22 . . . RxR 23 RxR P–R4 24 P–R4 K–R2 25 R–Q3! R–KN1 26 R–B3

This direct attack wins a pawn and with it the game. Yet considering the helpless position of Black's pieces, the preparatory 26 K–N2! would have been even simpler. There is nothing Black could have done about the coming 27 R–B3. As played, Black gets a bit of counterplay:

26 . . . R–Q1!? 27 BxN PxB 28 RxP R–Q5 29 RxBP Q–N2 30 R–B3 RxKP 31 Q–B3 R–K8ch 32 K–N2 Q–KB2 33 R–B5! K–R3 34 Q–Q5 Q–K2 35 RxP R–QN8 36 R–R8 Q–N5 37 Q–B3 P–N3 38 Q–K3ch Black resigns

Consider now the crazy situation arising in L. Spassov–N. Krogius, Sochi 1977, after Black's 30th move. White: K—g1 Q—b1 B—e6 P—f2, g2, h2 Black: K—g7 R—d2 N—c6 P—a5, b2, h6. White is up a Queen for a Rook, but Black does have a strong passed QNP and White's Queen is awkwardly caught on the first rank. Watch how quickly White loses this position:

31 K–B1?

The King is not safe on the first rank! Correct was to get it off by playing 31 P–R4! (or 31 P–R3) followed by 32 K–R2. White would then have every expectation of winning.

31 . . . N–Q5 32 B–R2 R–B7

White's in trouble now, but with the consistent 33 K–K1! he could reach a drawn endgame after 33 . . . R–B8ch 34 K–Q2 RxQ 35 BxR. Instead . . .

33 Q–Q1?? R–B8 34 K–K1 N–B7ch! 35 K–Q2 RxQch 36 KxR N–R6 White resigns

From a Queen up to an endgame with a piece down (after the imminent 37 . . . P–N8 = Q), all within seven moves! And this because of the failure to provide air for the King when required. (White actually played on a bit before resigning: 37 K–Q2 K–B3 38 K–B3 P–N8 = Q 39 BxQ NxBch 40 K–B2 N–R6ch 41 K–N3 N–N4 42 K–R4 N–B6ch 43 KxP N–Q8 44 P–B4, and without awaiting Black's reply, White resigned.)

Finally, an example of an air move as a luxury. Diagram 38 is G. Lebredo–T. Petrosian, Vilnus 1978, after White's 26th move.

DIAGRAM 38

BLACK

WHITE

Lebredo–Petrosian
Vilnus 1978
after White's 26th

Black has a considerable space advantage and the more active R and N. First Petrosian activates his Queen:

26 . . . Q–Q3   27 N–N3 Q–Q6!   28 Q–B2 Q–K7   29 P–R3 R–KB1!   30 K–R2 P–KR3!

Black's position does look overwhelming but there is no immediate win. Therefore Black takes time out to prevent any future back rank mates and also gives White the chance to worsen his position. This occurs immediately:

31 N–B1?! Q–K8   32 P–Q4 N–N5ch!   33 PxN R–B8 White resigns

Mate can not be prevented.

CHAPTER 11

King Moves to Prepare for Action

The part the King plays in preparing for middlegame action can be generally (except for the methods of Section 4) thought of as a negative sort. That is, the King gingerly gets out of the way and lets the "big boys" take over. Nevertheless, the principles and methods of this activity warrant close study.

SECTION 1. Unpinning: King, Pieces and Pawns

A piece caught in a pin can not be used during the course of the pin and thus is lost both as an attacker and a defender. This loss is absolute if the pin involves the King. To return the piece to action it must be unpinned, and the two ways of doing this are by either using piece (including pawn) movements or by a move of the King itself.

Inherently the more difficult case is where the King can't do the unpinning itself, either because it's impossible or because there is no time for it. Consider the following position—the conclusion of a 1977 study by Korányi. White: K—h1 Q—c6 B—f1 P—a6, c3 Black: K—a7 Q—a1 B—b8, c8 P—d5. Black is up a piece, yet the very clumsy position of his King means that White would have an elementary win if White's KB could participate in the attack. But it is pinned, and there is no time for unpinning it by a King move. Therefore the unpinning must be done without loss of time. This is how:

110

1 Q–B5ch K–R1 2 QxPch K–R2 3 Q–Q4ch! K–R1 4
Q–K4ch K–R2 5 Q–K3ch K–R1 6 Q–B3ch K–R2 7 Q–B2ch
K–R1 8 Q–N2ch K–R2 9 Q–N1ch K–R1 10 B–N2ch B–N2
11 BxBmate

A farfetched study of no importance to practical play? Not at
all! In fact the "stepwise" unpinning method is very important
for the execution of combinations. I wish that I had been
familiar with it in my youth. The game E. Mednis–J.W. Collins,
New York State Championship, 1954, still sticks in my mind. It
is a game that I had played very well, and, despite missing
several easier wins ("not playing them" is really a more accurate
description of what I was doing) I had reached the position
shown in Diagram 39. But by now I wasn't confident of my
position any more and decided to play a brilliant combination
for the draw:

33 RxPch!! KxR 34 Q–R4ch K–N3 35 Q–N4ch

DIAGRAM 39

BLACK

WHITE

Mednis–Collins
New York State 1954
after Black's 32nd

White would have an elementary mate if he could utilize his
Rook. But he can't—the Rook is very definitely pinned.
Therefore I agreed to a draw (???) here. Later on I showed the
game and combination to International Master Al Horowitz. He

looked a few moments at this position, said "You played a brilliant combination for the *win*," and quickly ran off the next moves:

35 . . . K–R2   36 Q–R3ch K–N3   37 Q–N2ch! K–R2   38 R–R3mate

Simple and obvious—if you know it!

Expectations based on a pin which a "simple" King move can break are ephemeral in nature and should not be regarded as of much significance. Diagram 40 shows a complicated middlegame without Queens (R. Spielmann—A. Alekhine, Stockholm 1912, after White's 21st move). White has been throwing his Kingside pawns forward in the expectation that—in view of the pin on Black's Knight—it is quite safe to do so. Alekhine shows it to be otherwise:

21 . . . K–K1!

DIAGRAM 40

BLACK

WHITE

Spielmann–Alekhine
Stockholm 1912
after White's 21st

Both attacking the KNP and making possible 22 . . . N–Q4, which will protect the KP while attacking the KBP. Black's advantage is close to decisive.

22 P–KR3 N–Q4   23 P–B5

Not wishing to defend the horrible position after 23 BxP NxKBP 24 BxN RxB, Spielmann selects a sacrificial continuation. Because of Alekhine's sharp play, it only serves to accelerate the end, but from a practical standpoint can not be criticized.

23 . . . BxN   24 PxB BxP   25 BxRP N–B5!

And not 25 . . . N–K2? because of 26 QR–Q1! BxR   27 R–Q7 B–N5   28 BxN BxB   29 B–N6ch, which is what, according to Alekhine, Spielmann had hoped for.

26 QR–Q1 BxR   27 R–Q7 B–N5! White resigns

In the above example, the King move released a piece from a pin. Equally easy is to free a pawn. In J. Grefe–Y. Seirawan, California 1978, after Black's 37th move: White: K—h2 Q—g5 R—e3 B—g2 P—a5, d4, f4, g4 Black: K—g8 Q—d6 R—d1 B—g6 P—a7, d5, e6, f7. Black has just played his Queen to Q3 to inhibit White's P–KB5. Yet relief is only temporary:

38 K–R3!

The King is safe here, and the threatened 39 P–B5 devastating.

38 . . . K–B1   39 P–B5 B–R2   40 Q–R6ch K–N1   41 Q–N5ch K–B1   42 R–QB3! Black resigns

There is no defense against the coming 43 R–B8ch, as 42 . . . Q–Q2   43 Q–R6ch K–N1 leads to mate after 44 P–B6.

Section 2. Mobilizing Pieces

The need for the King is absolute, yet all too often it seems that he is in the way of his own pieces, either taking away a useful square as a result of sitting on it or interfering with the coordination of a number of pieces. What is required in such cases is gently to move the King away to some safe location out of harm's way. There are an almost infinite number of ways a King can interfere, but the most important situation involves the action of major pieces along the ranks, i.e. the Queen and Rooks attempting to perform long distance work. It is this that we shall explore in a consistent way.

A basic case is shown in Diagram 41, V. Korchnoi–O. Nedeljkovic, 1957 European Team Championship, after Black's 24th move. Clearly Black is in serious trouble: his pieces have no scope, while White has a space advantage all across the board. In particular White's Q, KB and N are well placed for an attack against Black's Kingside. What is still lacking is a meaningful role for White's Rook. Remembering that a Rook is most dangerous along open lines and that the KN file is open on White's side, it becomes clear that that is where the Rook should be. Therefore:

25 K–R1! B–N1   26 R–N1 R–B2   27 B–K1!

DIAGRAM 41

BLACK

WHITE

Korchnoi–Nedeljkovic
European Team
Championship 1957
after Black's 24th

Mobilizing White's last inactive piece. Note that if White's King had gone to KB2, not only would it have been less safe but it also would have interfered with the QB's mobilization.

27 . . . B–N4   28 B–R4 Q–Q2   29 NxB PxN   30 Q–R5 P–KN3

There is no choice, but now the KN file is ripped completely open, with decisive effect.

**31 BxKNP! PxB   32 RxPch R–N2   33 B–B6 N–K1   34 R–R6!
K–B1   35 R–R8ch R–N1   36 RxRch KxR   37 Q–R8ch Black resigns**

He loses the Queen: 37 . . . K–B2   38 Q–R7ch.

Now look at the position arising in A. Kotov–H. Steiner, 1955
USSR–USA Match, after Black's 26th move. White: K—g1 Q—c2
R—c1, f3 B—g6 P—a2, b2, d4, e3, f4, g4, h3 Black: K—g8 Q—c7
R—e7, f8 N—d6 P—a5, b7, c6, d5, e6, g7, h6. As in the previous
example, Black is cramped and without counterplay, while White
has a large space advantage. How should White proceed to
capitalize on these factors? One strategic point stands out: Black's
KRP has been forced forward and therefore is vulnerable to a
line–opening P–KN5 advance by White. Thus White's plan is as
follows: mobilize major pieces along the KN file and then advance
the KNP.

27 K–R1!

Objectively, 27 K–R2 is equivalent, but White didn't want to
put the King on the same diagonal as Black's Queen.

**27 . . . K–R1   28 R–KN1 Q–Q1   29 R/3–N3! R–Q2   30 P–N5!
N–B4   31 BxN PxB   32 PxP PxP   33 Q–N2!**

The KN file is completely open and White has tripled on it.
There is no defense.

33 . . . R/2–KB2   34 R–N6! Q–K2

After 34 . . . R–R2 the fastest win is 35 R–N7!.

35 R–N8ch Black resigns

If the King is still in the center, the chances that he will be in
the way of major–piece mobilization are very high. In such cases
it is often required to move him aggressively out of the way. In
A. Bisguier–S. Reshevsky, U.S. Championship 1957–58, after
White's 31st move, Black has a twofold advantage: a material
advantage of the Exchange for a pawn, and, even more important, excellent attacking prospects against White's weakened
King position. Yet at present Black is attacking without using his
QR; thus getting it into the game is the next order of business:
White K—g2 Q—f1 R—c1 B—d3, f4 N—a4 P—a2, b3, c4, e4,
g3 Black: K—e8 Q—d4 R—b8, f6 B—e7, g4 P—a5, c6, d6, f7

31 . . . K–Q2! 32 B–K2 BxB 33 QxB RxB!

With the QR ready to join the action, the situation is ripe for ripping open White's King position. Reshevsky describes the text as "forceful and irrefutable." Amen!

34 PxR R–N1ch 35 K–B3 B–R5! White resigns

There is no defense to the mate threat starting with 36 . . . R–N6ch.

In the above example, the King cleared the way for the Rook to reach the KN file along the first rank. The same approach goes for activating the Queen for long range action. Diagram 42 shows Ladisic–Roos, Bagneux 1976, after White's 20th move. Black has an obvious strategic advantage—the superior pawn formation, as a result of having a passed QRP. Additionally, he has a tactical possibility: . . . N–N6ch. But for this to become feasible, he needs more firepower along the KR file. His plan is therefore clear:

20 . . . K–Q2! 21 N–Q2??

DIAGRAM 42

BLACK

WHITE

Ladisic–Roos
Bagneux 1976
after White's 20th

White is oblivious to Black's threat. Mandatory was 21 BxN KB5.

**21 . . . N–N6ch! 22 PxN PxPch 23 K–N1 Q–B1! 24 B–B6!?
Q–KN1! 25 KR–N1 R–R8ch! 26 KxR Q–R2ch 27 K–N1
Q–R7ch 28 K–B1 Q–R8mate**

Actually White didn't want to be mated and thus resigned after
Black's 23rd move.

So far the piece mobilization we have examined was of a rather
heavy handed type. For a more sophisticated version, consider the
play resulting from Diagram 43, M. Najdorf–S. Reshevsky, 1952
Match, Game 3, after White's 26th move. The position is approximately even, with White's good extra Q-side pawn balancing
Black's good extra central pawn and neither side having any
particular weaknesses. It is logical for Black to mobilize his Rook,
and the open QB file is the place for it to be. Yet the immediate 26
. . . R–B1?! suffers from a tactical deficiency: after 27 NxP! PxN
28 BxPch, followed by 29 BxR, White has a Rook and 2 pawns in a
good position for two pieces. Therefore Black prepares the Rook
move with:

26 . . . K–R1! 27 Q–K3?!

DIAGRAM 43

BLACK

WHITE

*Najdorf–Reshevsky
1952 Match, Game #3
after White's 26th*

With this move White starts a plan which is not positionally workable. As Reshevsky points out, correct was 27 R–QB1! R–B1 28 Q–Q2, with an even endgame in the offing.

27 . . . R–B1 28 N–K2 K–R2!

Preparing to mobilize the Knight. An immediate Knight move (e.g. 28 . . . N–B5??) loses to 29 QxRPch. After the text move, Black's QNP is "poisoned," as shown in the following analysis by Reshevsky: 29 QxNP? N–B5 30 BxN RxB 31 N–B3 (31 P–R5 P–Q4!) 31 . . . P–Q4! 32 Q–B2 P–Q5 33 N–K2 P–K4!, with a winning position for Black, since White's Q-side will be lost.

29 N–N3 Q–R4 30 P–B4?

Weakening his position, with disastrous results. After 30 R–QB1! White would have fair drawing chances (Reshevsky).

30 . . . N–B5 31 BxN RxB 32 Q–Q3 QxRP 33 P–K5ch K–N1! 34 PxP B–Q1

White's achievement of a passed QP is a Pyrrhic victory: the pawn is easily blockaded and the holes in White's position are gigantic.

35 N–R5 R–B7 36 R–Q2 RxR 37 QxR P–B3! 38 Q–K2 Q–K5! 39 QxQ BxQ 40 P–N4 K–B2 White resigns

White actually played 41 K–B2 and then resigned without awaiting Black's reply. After 41 . . . B–Q6 Black would immediately win the QNP and then in due course the unsupportable QP, thereby emerging two pawns up.

Section 3. Pawn Advances: Opening Lines and Other Goals

Advancing a pawn is a sensitive operation because the locality from which the pawn advanced is opened up, and can't ever be closed by retreating the pawn when it would be convenient to do so. This means that pawn advances which would tend to weaken the King position must be executed carefully. This is doubly so when an attack is contemplated by throwing forward at least one of the pawns providing the King–cover. Preparations for mobilizing the KBP were discussed in connection with the Opening (in Chapter 8, Section 1). Opening of the KN or KR files generally requires that the King be moved off the file to be opened. There is a twofold reason for this. First, the King may not be safe enough and, secondly, it may interfere with the proper mobilization of the pieces. A model example of an attack along the KN file is provided by the game A. Rubinstein–A. Alekhine, Dresden 1926: 1 P–Q4 N–KB3 2 N–KB3 P–K3 3 B–B4 P–QN3 4 P–KR3 B–N2 5 QN–Q2 B–Q3! 6 BxB PxB 7 P–K3 0–0 8 B–K2 P–Q4 9 0–0 N–B3 10 P–B3 N–K5! 11 NxN PxN 12 N–Q2 P–B4 13 P–KB4 P–KN4! 14 N–B4 P–Q4 15 N–K5 NxN 16 QPxN. Black has already set his KNP into motion, yet it is obvious that without heavy firepower along the KN–file his prospects for a successful attack are slim. Therefore Alekhine played:

16 . . . K–R1! 17 P–QR4?!

According to Alekhine, it was imperative to organize resistance along the KN file with 17 P–KN3! R–KN1 18 K–R2!, followed by R–KN1.

17 . . . R–KN1 18 Q–Q2 PxP!

Forcing White to recapture with the Rook and thereby accept an inferior pawn formation, since 19 PxP?! Q–R5 leaves White defenseless to the dual threats 20 . . . QxRP and 20 . . . RxPch! (20 Q–K3 is met by 20 . . . R–N6, followed by 21 . . . QxRP).

19 RxP Q–N4 20 B–B1 Q–N6! 21 K–R1 Q–N2! 22 Q–Q4 B–R3! 23 R–B2 Q–N6 24 R–B2 BxB 25 RxB QR–QB1! 26 P–N3 R–B2 27 R–K2 QR–KN2 28 R–B4 R–N3!

There is no defense to the threats along the KN and KR files. White decides to sacrifice the KRP in order to exchange off a pair of Rooks, but Black spurns that to go after bigger game.

29 Q–N4 R–R3 30 P–R4 Q–N2! 31 P–B4

In response to 31 Q–Q6 Alekhine gives the following line: 31 . . . R–N3 32 R/4–B2 P–B5! 33 PxP P–K6.

31 . . . R–N3!   32 Q–Q2 R–N6!   33 Q–K1?!

Speeds up the inevitable. Black was threatening 33 . . . R–R6ch 34 K–N1 Q–N6 etc., and the immediate 33 K–N1 loses to 33 . . . P–Q5!   34 PxP P–K6!   35 Q–B2 R–R6, followed by 36 . . . Q–N6 (Alekhine).

33 . . . RxNP White resigns

Of course, most of the time in practical chess the possibilities are not so clearly oriented towards a single goal. Consider Diagram 44, M. Chiburdanidze–N. Gaprindashvili, 1978 Women's World Championship Match, Game 3, after Black's 20th move. White has a clear advantage because of her superior pawn formation, with Black's QP in particular being a chronic weakness. As compensation Black hopes to get open lines for her Bishop pair, and as a defensive resource hopes to have available a properly timed . . . N–Q5 to close off the Q-file. White, for her part, doesn't want to play 21 QxQ, as after 21 . . . PxQ Black's forward KBP would be significantly strengthened. To try to exploit the pressure along the Q-file White would do best to open another theater of action so that Black would be kept busy on several fronts. Her next move serves several functions admirably:

21 K–R1!

DIAGRAM 44

BLACK

WHITE

Chiburdanidze–Gaprindashvili
1978 Match, Game #3
after Black's 20th

Threatens to open the KN file, while also preventing the capture of the KB with check in the potential variation 21 . . . N–Q5   22 QxQ! PxQ   23 N–K7ch K–R2   24 NxN PxN   25 N–B6, with advantage for White. Black also doesn't get sufficient compensation for lost material after 21 . . . P–B4   22 N–B7 B–B2   23 QxQ PxQ 24 RxP N–Q5   25 NxN PxN   26 KPxP B–K4   27 R–QB6 QR–B1 28 N–Q5!.

21 . . . QxQ?!

Afraid of the prospective opening of the KN file, Black seeks salvation in an endgame a pawn down. This is inherently a poor bargain. As Soviet GM Razuvaev has suggested, the gutsy 21 . . . K–R2!? offered better practical chances.

22 BxQ P–B4   23 N–B7 B–B2   24 BxBch RxB   25 N–N5 PxKP 26 NxP R–Q2   27 NxKP, and White has won a pawn and has excellent winning chances.

Black actually succeeded in gaining a draw on Move 55, but only because White's technique was insufficient. In this case 21 K–R1! served as a "bluff" to scare Black from allowing the opening of the KN file.

After Kingside castling, King movement is usually required for action along the KN file that involves advancing the KNP. It is even more necessary when planning the opening and utilization of the KR file. Without King movement, the KR would have to go through considerable contortions to get back to "its" file. An excellent example of the strategies involved in opening the file, mobilizing forces along it and exploiting it for decisive attacks, is shown from Diagram 45, I. Csom–V. Liberzon, Bad Lauterberg 1977, after Black's 24th move. White has a considerable space advantage, while Black is without counterplay. However, Black's only chronic weakness—the backward QBP—is sufficiently protected so that White can't expect success by just sitting on the QB file. What is required is opening of action along another front, a front where Black is low in defenders. The Kingside in general and the KR file in particular come to mind:

25 P–KR4! N–N2   26 P–R5!

DIAGRAM 45

BLACK

WHITE

Csom–Liberzon
Bad Lauterberg 1977
after Black's 24th

Since Black is in no position to menace White's King, White can advance the KRP without any "King preparation."

26 . . . R–R1   27 B–QR1 R–R4   28 B–R3! R/1–R1   29 K–N2!

Allowing the mobilization of the KR along the to-be-opened KR file. White decides that there is no need to spend time in protecting the QRP.

29 . . . RxP   30 B–N2! B–B1   31 PxP RPxP   32 R–KR1! Q–Q1 33 B–N4! R/7–R4   34 Q–B1!

Mobilization along the KR file proceeds apace, with the Queen heading for KR2. Note how well out of the way the King is on KN2.

34 . . . R–B1   35 Q–KN1 B–N2   36 Q–R2 P–QB4   37 B–B1!

Bringing the QB into the game. Black has no time now for 37 . . . PxP? because of 38 RxR QxR   39 B–N5!, and there is no defense to the threatened combination 40 Q–R7ch K–B1   41 QxBch!! KxQ   42 B–B6ch K–B1   43 R–R8mate.

37 . . . K–B1   38 B–Q2! B–N4   39 N–B4 R–R3   40 Q–R7 Q–Q2 41 KR–QB1!

The Rook's immediate work on the KR file is done, and so it swings over for action on the QB file. The immediate threat is 42 BxNP!.

41 . . . R/3–B3   43 R–R2! Q–K2?

Allowing the Rook's penetration leads to an immediate catastrophe. Mandatory was 42 . . . R–R3 (Csom), though after 43 RxR BxR   44 PxP White has a significant advantage.

43 R–R7! Q–B2

Or 43 . . . R/3–B2   44 BxKP! PxB   45 NxNPch; or 43 . . . R/1–B2   44 R–R8ch R–B1   45 RxRch RxR   46 BxKP! (Csom).

44 NxNPch! PxN   45 B–R6! BxB   46 QxBch K–K1   47 QxPch K–Q1   48 Q–B6ch K–Q2   49 RxN! Black resigns

With Kings castled Queenside, opening of and action along the QB file often becomes important. These motifs, coupled with a pin, are well illustrated in the play from Diagram 46, E. Haag–W. Golz, Zinnowitz 1966, after Black's 17th move. White has a slight edge in development and an actively placed QB and K5 Knight.

DIAGRAM 46

BLACK

WHITE

Haag–Golz
Zinnowitz 1966
after Black's 17th

Yet his key maneuver is the freeing of his QBP, achieved by sacrificing his QP. Of course, an immediate 18 P–B5?? is purposeless because of 18 . . . QxPch. A little "King preparation" changes everything, though:

18 K–N1! B–Q3

Ignoring the threat is no defense. The blockading 18 . . . B–B4 is also useless because of 19 P–N4!. The best try is 18 . . . K–N1!?, even though after White's preparatory 19 R–QB1! Black still lacks a satisfactory way of coping with the threatened 20 P–B5.

19 P–B5!! BxN

After 19 . . . BxP,   20 R–QB1 is a murderous pin: 20 . . . K–N1 21 P–N4 etc.

20 PxN PxP   21 R–QB1 Black resigns

His compensation for the lost Queen is inadequate, e.g. 21 . . . PxB?   22 QxB! or 21 . . . BxN   22 BxP! etc.

For some central pawn advances the King is also best "out of the way." In the position after White's 22nd move in M. Euwe–A. Alekhine, 1937 World Championship Match, Game 21 (1 P–Q4 N–KB3   2 P–QB4 P–K3   3 N–KB3 P–QN3   4 P–KN3 B–N2   5 B–N2 B–N5ch   6 B–Q2 B–K2   7 N–B3 N–K5   8 0–0 0–0   9 P–Q5 NxB   10 QxN B–KB3   11 QR–Q1 P–Q3   12 PxB PxNP   13 N–Q4 BxB 14 KxB Q–B1   15 Q–K3 BxN   16 RxB N–B3   17 R–K4 R–B3 18 P–B4 Q–Q2   19 P–KN4 R/1–KB1!   20 P–N5 R–B4   21 P–KR4 Q–B2   22 R–B3) it is easy to see that White has an overextended Kingside pawn formation. According to classic strategy, this is best countered by a pawn advance in the center. At the moment, though, both possible advances carry certain disadvantages with them. Thus after 22 . . . P–Q4?! Alekhine feels that White gets too many practical chances with 23 RxP P–Q5   24 Q–K4 PxN   25 PxP! N–Q1   26 R–K7, while 22 . . . P–K4?! suffers from the following tactical deficiency: 23 N–Q5 N–Q5   24 N–K7ch! QxN   25 RxN, and White's defensive load has been significantly decreased. But Black can prepare central action by first playing

22 . . . K–R1!

This gets the King out of any pins along White's QR2–KN8 diagonal, as well as preventing the above N–K7ch. Black now is ready to choose his advance. Of course, 23 RxP?! is met by 23 . . . N–K4!, winning the Exchange.

23 Q–Q3 P–Q4!   24 RxP

Positionally hopeless is 24 PxP PxP   25 R–R4 P–Q5. Therefore White is ready to sacrifice the Exchange, but Black wants to accept it only on the most advantageous terms.

24 . . . N–N5!   25 Q–K3 N–B7!   26 Q–Q2 QxR   27 PxP Q–B2 28 QxN?!

A better try was 28 K–N3! (with the threat 29 P–K4!), after which Alekhine gives the following line: 28 . . . N–K8!   29 R–B2 N–N7!   30 P–K3 NxRP   31 KxN P–KR3! "with decisive threats."

28 . . . RxBP   29 Q–Q3 Q–R4   30 RxR RxR   31 Q–R3 R–N5ch 32 K–B2 P–KR3! White resigns

As the last example I give a demonstration of the King achieving a more active defensive role prior to the execution of a decisive pawn advance. White: K—g1 Q—e3 R—e1 B—c3, c4 P—a2, b3, f4, g4, h3 Black: K—h7 Q—h4 R—a8, f8 B—g6 P—a7, b7, f7, h6. In the position after Black's 30th move in V. Smyslov–P. Trifunovic, Zagreb 1955 White has sacrificed an Exchange but has more than sufficient compensation: a pawn, the Bishop pair, and strong attacking chances against Black's weakened Kingside. White also has a particular prosaic plan: the winning of Black's Bishop with P–B5. As a matter of fact, during the previous two moves White has been sending his KB and KN pawns forward for just this purpose. Because of the resultant weakening of his Kingside, however, White can't proceed with the immediate 31 P–B5?, because of 31 . . . QR–K1! (31 . . . BxP? 32 Q–K5!, and White wins) 32 PxBch PxP   33 B–K5 RxB!   34 QxR Q–B7ch   35 K–R1 Q–B6ch, with perpetual check. Therefore White first protects his KN3 square and KRP with

31 K–N2!   R–KN1

31 . . . QR–K1 is refuted by 32 QxR! RxQ   33 RxR P–B3   34 R–K7ch and 35 B–K1.

32 Q–K7! QxQ   33 RxQ QR–K1

There is no satisfactory move, e.g. 33 . . . QR–KB1   34 K–B2! and there is nothing to be done about the coming 35 P–B5. After the text White gains two pieces for the Rook and the rest is relatively simple technique for Smyslov.

34 RxR RxR   35 P–B5 P–R3   36 K–B3 R–QB1   37 B–Q4 P–N4 38 B–Q3 R–B8   39 PxBch PxP   40 P–KR4 R–Q8   41 K–K2 R–KR8 42 P–R5 R–R7ch   43 B–KB2 K–N2   44 PxP P–KR4   45 PxP RxP 46 B–Q4ch K–N1   47 B–K4 P–R4   48 K–B3 Black resigns

Section 4. Offering Exchanges

Exchanging (or *offering* to exchange) pieces is one of the key operations throughout a game. The exchanging can be done for any one of a number of good reasons, including: removing a dangerous attacker, simplifying a position into an endgame to realize a material advantage, aiming for a draw by means of a routine exchange of all the pieces. It is well accepted that in the endgame the King has a significant role in this operation. Yet there also should be no reluctance to involve the King in middlegame "exchangings." The King can participate in two kinds of exchange operations: where he remains in place with the piece brought over to be protected by him, and where he moves to be supportive of the coming exchange attempt. The first case is quite routine and there should be no reluctance at all for the King to participate. In Diagram 47, J. Kupper–A. Dückstein, Zurich 1959, after White's 24th move, White plans to build up a Kingside attack along the KR file with 25 K–K2 and 26 R–R1, followed by doubling Rooks and/or a timely N–N5. Black, on move, puts an immediate stop to all of this with

24 . . . Q–KN2!   25 QxQch

The Queen has no attractive retreat square, but after the exchange White's chances for an attack are non-existent.

25 . . . KxQ   26 K–K2 B–K2   27 N–Q2 KR–QN1   28 P–KB4 B–QB1   29 KR–QN1 P–N5   30 B–Q3 B–K3   31 N–N3 R–N3   32 K–K3 K–B2   33 N–Q2 R–Q1

DIAGRAM 47

BLACK

WHITE

Kupper–Dückstein
Zurich 1959
after White's 24th

The position is in dynamic balance and neither side sees a way to make progress. The break 33 . . . P–B4 leads to no advantage after 34 QPxP BxPch 35 K–K2 PxP 36 PxP QR–QN1 37 RxR RxR 38 B–N5 (Barcza).

34 N–N3 R–QR1 35 N–Q2 R–Q1 36 N–N3 R–QR1 37 N–Q2 Draw

Obviously no one should ever exchange Queens automatically, even when it seems safe. After all, the position on the rest of the board must also be taken into account! The greatest danger of acting that way is when in time pressure. Witness the drastic conclusion in Diagram 48, E. Walther–A. Dückstein, Zurich 1959, after White's 40th move. Black has a number of reasonable moves, ranging from the attacking 40 . . . R–B5 and 40 . . . N–B5 to the defensive 40 . . . R/B–Q2 and 40 . . . Q–K3. But with one move to go before time control and under the psychological handicap of having been exposed to a truly strong attack *earlier* in the game, he reasons "why not offer the exchange of Queens?" with

40 . . . Q–B3?? 41 QxQch Black resigns

After 41 . . . KxQ 42 N–N8ch he loses the Exchange and lands in a hopeless endgame.

DIAGRAM 48

BLACK

WHITE

Walther–Dückstein
Zurich 1959
after White's 40th

Now back to good exchanging. Take note of the situation after Black's 25th move in L. Szabo–B. Larsen, Portoroz Interzonal 1958: White: K—b1 Q—a7 R—g1 B—b7 P—a2, b2, e3, f4, h3 Black: K—g8 R—c7, f2 B—e7 N—d7 P—e6, f7, g7, h6. Black has sacrificed his Queen for R and N and an attacking position. The immediate threat is 26 . . . B–B3, and the B can also be brought into action via QB4. White obviously wants to repulse the attack, and the standard method is to try to exchange off as many attackers as possible. Therefore:

26 R–QB1! RxRch

Black has little choice, as after either 26 . . . B–B4 or 26 . . . N–B4 that piece would be pinned, whereas White's Queen liberates itself with 27 Q–R8ch.

27 KxR B–B4   28 Q–R8ch K–R2   29 K–N1! BxP   30 P–QR4 P–B4   31 B–B8?

Chasing the Knight where it wants to go. Winning was 31 P–N4!, which prevents Black's next move, while getting the connected passed pawns going.

31 . . . N–B4   32 P–N4 R–B8ch!   33 K–R2

It is also difficult to visualize a White win after 33 K–B2 R–B8ch 34 K–N2 NxPch ˙ 35 QxN RxB.

33 . . . R–B7ch   34 K–N1 R–B8ch   35 K–R2 R–B7ch   36 K–N1 Draw

In the next examples the King has to do more work in furthering exchanges. An instructive situation is shown in R. Fischer–M. Tal, Portoroz Interzonal 1958, after White's 23rd move (1 P–K4 P–K4 2 N–KB3 N–QB3 3 B–N5 P–QR3 4 B–R4 N–B3 5 0–0 B–K2 6 R–K1 P–QN4 7 B–N3 0–0 8 P–KR3 P–Q3 9 P–B3 N–Q2 10 P–Q4 N–N3 11 PxP NxP 12 NxN PxN 13 Q–R5 Q–Q3 14 N–Q2 B–K3 15 N–B3 BxB 16 PxB N–Q2 17 P–QN4 KR–Q1 18 B–N5 P–KB3 19 B–K3 Q–K3 20 KR–Q1 P–QB4 21 N–R4 B–B1 22 N–B5 P–N3   23 Q–N4). White seems to have an attractive attacking position. The immediate threat is 24 N–R6ch, winning the Queen, while 23 . . . K–R1? leads to great difficulties after 24 N–Q6!. Yet with an active King move, Black not only prevents all threats but even achieves a Queen exchange under favorable conditions:

23 . . . K–B2!   24 N–R6ch BxN   25 QxQch KxQ   26 BxB PxP 27 PxP KR–QB1

The open QB file yields a slight initiative to Black. Not wanting to defend passively, Fischer goes for sharp counterplay which in the end is exactly sufficient for the draw.

28 B–K3!? R–B5   29 R–Q2 RxNP 30 QR–Q1 N–B1   31 R–Q6ch K–B2   32 R–N6! RxNP   33 R/1–Q6 P–QR4   34 R–N7ch K–N1 35 RxBP R–K1   36 R/6–B7 N–K3   37 RxRP P–R5   38 R–R7 R–R1 39 R/KR7–N7ch K–R1   40 R–R7ch K–N1   41 R/KR7–N7ch Draw

Up to now the King has helped in the exchange of major pieces. It is equally capable of helping out the minor pieces. Diagram 49 is from A. Karpov–I. Radulov, 1973 Leningrad Interzonal, after White's 17th move. White has a slight advantage, because his Bishop—as a natural result of the existing pawn formation—has more scope than Black's. The position is rather closed, however, and this enables Black to make good use of his King to make the coming Bishop exchange offer:

17 . . . P–KR4!   18 B–Q2 K–R2!   19 P–QN4 B–R3!   20 KPxP RxP   21 BxB

DIAGRAM 49

BLACK

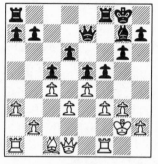

WHITE

Karpov–Radulov
Leningrad 1973
after White's 17th

There is no logic in avoiding the exchange, as after either 21 B–B3?! or 21 B–K1?! it would be Black's Bishop which has more scope.

21 . . . KxB   22 Q–Q2ch K–N2   23 PxP PxP   24 QR–K1 R–Q1

With the Bishop exchanged, Black's remaining pieces are as good as White's, and the chances are approximately equal. Karpov keeps making some tries but Black is not to be denied his draw.

25 R–K3 R–Q5   26 Q–K2 Q–Q3   27 R–QN1 R–B2   28 P–QR4 P–N3   29 R–K1 R–Q2   30 P–R4 RxQP   31 RxR QxR   32 QxPch K–R2   33 Q–K6 Q–B4   34 QxQ PxQ   35 K–B2 K–N2   36 P–R5 R–Q5   37 PxP PxP   38 R–K6 RxBP   39 RxP P–B5 Draw

SECTION 5. Preventing Possible Counterplay

A key requirement for practical chess success is the ability to win superior ("won") positions. To enhance one's success in this, it is of utmost importance to prevent all "unnecessary" counterplay. The most effective counterplay is that based on the opponent's King location and thus it follows that a proper positioning of the King

can prevent such counterplay. What can be considered as a classic
example is shown in Diagram 50, M. Tal–K. Darga, USSR–West
Germany match, 1960, after Black's 23rd move. With some
previous sharp play, Tal has both won a pawn and established a
strong attacking formation. The position must be considered as
"won," but at the moment there is nothing decisive, and White's
King does look somewhat open. The great attacking master now
plays:

DIAGRAM 50

BLACK

WHITE

Tal–Darga
USSR–West Germany 1960
after Black's 23rd

24 K–R1!!

Tal's own description of the thinking behind this move: "This is
the simplest way of demonstrating the hopelessness of Black's
position. White moves his King away from a square on which it
could be checked [i.e. by the Queen from QB4 or QN3—EM], and
plans to strengthen his position decisively. Black's attempt to
obtain counterplay [and reestablish material equality—EM]
merely hastens the end."

24 . . . RxNP 25 R–K6!

Threatening 26 R–Q6. Note that 25 . . . Q–B4 (without check!)
is pointless because of 26 QxN.

25 . . . R/7–N1   26 R–Q6 R/N–Q1   27 R–Q1! Black resigns

Black has no useful move left and is defenseless against the threatened 28 B–B3, winning the pinned Knight.

Quite a different kind of "won" position is shown in Diagram 51, D. Bronstein–W. Uhlmann, Tallin 1977, after White's 25th move. With a piece sacrifice Black has laid bare White's King position and, having gained three pawns for the piece, even has full material equivalent. With all five of Black's remaining pieces ready to swarm over White's King, it is clear that in the long run White's King position is indefensible. His only practical chance is to try to create some play against Black's King, by virtue of having a Rook on the QN file and playing the Knight to Q6 with check. Therefore, before continuing with his attack, Black plays the "preparatory"

DIAGRAM 51

BLACK

WHITE

Bronstein–Uhlmann
Tallin 1977
after White's 25th

25 . . . K–B2!   26 K–B2 R–R4!

Not 26 . . . Q–Q4?, which allows the forking 27 N–B6.

27 R–B3 Q–KN1!   28 B–KB4 NxR   29 QxR

White is absolutely without counterplay, even as he starts losing material. After 29 QxN Black has the pleasant choice between 29 . . . RxB and 29 . . . R–B4.

29 . . . RxB   30 Q–R6 N–N4ch White resigns

There are times when the best way of preventing counterplay is to delay executing the indicated plan until it is demonstrably safe to do so. A good example of such a tactic is given in this position, M. Tal–Y. Averbakh, 1974 USSR Team Championship, after Black's 15th move. White: K—e1 R—a1, h1 B—d2, f1 N—g3 P—a3, b2, f2, g2, h2 Black: K—e8 R—a8, h8 B—a5, e6 N—c3 P—a7, b7, c6, d4, f7, g7, h7. Black's Knight is caught in a pin and must be lost. On a material basis Black will get 3 pawns for the piece, but the doubled QBPs that result devalue the material equivalence considerably. The immediate capture 16 PxN?! is very dangerous, as White is too far behind in development, whereas the try for an elegant castling method has a tactical hole in it: 16 B–Q3?! 0–0–0 17 0–0? N–K7ch!. Tal fashions a King maneuver that has no disadvantages:

16 P–B3! 0–0–0   17 K–B2! B–N3   18 PxN PxPch   19 B–K3

White's piece configuration is smooth enough that Black has no particular counterplay, e.g. 19 . . . R–Q7ch is of no consequence after 20 B–K2.

19 . . . BxBch   20 KxB KR–K1   21 N–K4! B–Q4

The only way to prevent immediate loss of the QBP. After 21 . . . P–KB4? 22 NxP! White laughs at Black's possible discovered checks.

22 P–N4 BxN   23 PxB R–Q4   24 R–B1 P–KN3   25 B–N2, with a won endgame for White.

After the imminent capture of the forward QBP, White's material advantage is sufficient for the win. However, subsequently White played carelessly and won only because Black, in a drawn position, overstepped the time limit on Move 40.

Perhaps a most sophisticated type of King move to prevent counterplay is the so-called "quiet" King move in the middle of a violent attack. Diagram 51 showed something of this sort. An even more thematic demonstration—in fact two separate "quiet" moves—arises from Diagram 52, Y. Balashov–F. Gheorghiu, Leningrad 1977, after White's 17th move. White has just sacrificed a Knight on his KB5 to rip open Black's position. It is something like a long range strategic investment: White feels that the holes in Black's position, the generally disorganized Black pieces, the King in the center in an open position—all these factors will in due course allow White to build up decisive pressure against Black's position. The immediate threat is to Black's KB, and Black must react to it:

17 . . . B–KB1

DIAGRAM 52

BLACK

WHITE

Balashov–Gheorghiu
Leningrad 1977
after White's 17th

Clearly inadequate is 17 . . . 0–0? because after 18 NxB KxN 19 B–Q4 the pinned Knight will be lost. The serious alternative is 17 . . . R–KN1. Then premature is 18 NxBch? RxN 19 B–Q4 R–N3 20 KR–B1 because with 20 . . . Q–B2*ch* Black protects his KBP and then retreats the Knight to KN1. The correct approach for White—similar to the game—is 18 K–N1!, followed by B–Q4, KR–KB1 etc.

18 KR–B1 Q–Q2 19 B–Q4 Q–K3 20 K–N1!

Haste makes waste of a great attacking position here: 20 P–N5? NxP! 21 BxR R–B1ch 22 K–N1 N–B6ch, and Black wins. The preparatory text safeguards the QRP and prevents time–gaining checks on the QB file. White can now look forward to a strengthening of his pressure, and after e.g. 20 . . . R–KN1, the tactical 21 BxN QxB 22 NxPch QxN 23 QxPch K–Q1 24 QxR is sufficient (Minic and Sindik). Black tries a countercombination, but it meets convincing refutation.

20 . . . NxKP   21 Q–B4!

Of course, not 21 PxN?? because of 21 . . . BxPch, while Black, for his part, was threatening 21 . . . N–B6ch or 21 . . . N–Q7ch. But after the text everything is clear—with the opening of the King file signalling the death of Black's Knight.

21 . . . R–KN1   22 KR–K1 0–0–0   23 PxN

White has recovered his piece and has material equality, while the holes in Black's position remain, and his King is only marginally safer on the Queenside.

23 . . . P–B3   24 P–KR3 R–K1   25 K–R1!

Making sure that Black can't capture the KP with *check*. Now 25 . . . BxP?! 26 N–N3 P–Q4 27 R–B1ch leads to an immediate catastrophe. In any case, Black can't protect all of his weaknesses.

25 . . . P–KR4   26 B–B2 PxP   27 PxP BxP   28 NxPch BxN   29 RxB QxP   30 R–B1ch K–N2   31 R–N6ch Black resigns

SECTION 6. Preparing Specific Continuations and Combinations

How many times have you played a "winning" combination, only ruefully to find out that it doesn't win because your opponent has a defense based on the fact that your King is on exactly the wrong square? Such things happen to all of us now and then, and the point of this section is to assist the reader to minimize the number of times in the future he will be unpleasantly surprised.

As mentioned at the beginning of the chapter, most King action will tend to be negative, i.e., to remove it out of the way of potential harm. Nevertheless, part of the time the King itself can be an integral part of a direct or indirect action. Diagram 53, V. Korchnoi–R. Hübner, Wijk aan Zee 1971, after Black's 34th move, offers a good illustration. A superficial look at the diagram can easily give an erroneous impression. Black seems to be in fine shape: he has the superior pawn formation (i.e., a passed QRP), the two Bishops, an active Bishop on KR6, the possibility of playing his KB to QN3. Yet White's next move shows that there also are negatives in Black's position:

35 K–R1!

DIAGRAM 53

BLACK

WHITE

Korchnoi–Hübner
Wijk aan Zee 1971
after Black's 34th move

This not only prevents counterplay along the KN1–QR7 diagonal, but prepares a concrete plan aimed against Black's QB.

35 . . . R–B1　36 N–B4 R–R1

Black has no other reasonable move since 36 . . . QxP? loses to 37 NxQP.

37 R–KN1! QxP

Going for counterplay is the best way of ensuring the draw.

38 P–N4! QxNP??

But required here is the active 38 . . . P–R6! 39 QxB P–R7. An exhaustive analysis by Hübner has shown that the game should then end a draw. The main line is 40 R–R1 QxNP 41 Q–Q3 P–N4 42 N–Q2 Q–N7 43 N–N3 R–R6 44 QxP RxN 45 Q–K8ch K–N2 46 Q–Q7ch K–N3 47 Q–K8ch etc.

39 QxB K–N2 40 Q–KB3 B–K2 41 N–K3 Black resigns

Generally what the attacking side wants to prevent is a defense based on a check to the attacker's King. Such a check very often enables the defender to gain the necessary tempo to set up a defensible position. A relatively simple example is shown in the position in S. Reshevsky–D. Byrne, 1957 Match, Game 7, after Black's 31st move. White: K—g1 Q—f4 R—f1 B—c2, h2 P—a4, b2, d5, g4 Black: K—h8 Q—d7 R—a8 B—e7 N—e8 P—a6, c4, d6, h7. White has ripped open Black's King position and, with his Q, R, and 2Bs well placed, is in great shape to start decisive action against Black's King. Yet a necessary consequence of having opened up Black's King is that his own is also somewhat exposed. In particular, the immediate attempts at a *coup de grace* with 32 Q–R6? or 32 Q–B7? fail to 32 . . . QxNPch 33 K–R1 Q–N2. But note that only thanks to the check can Black's Queen get to the defensive KN2 square. Now, without the check . . .

32 K–R1! N–B3

The threats were 33 Q–B7 or 33 Q–R6. Moving the KB loses as follows: 32 . . . B–B3 33 P–N5 B–N2 34 Q–K4 BxP 35 R–B8ch K–N2 36 QxPch KxR 37 QxQ.

33 P–N5 R–KB1

Equivalent to resignation. In reply to the only reasonable move, 33 . . . N–R4, Reshevsky gives the following pretty line: 34 Q–Q4ch! N–N2 (34 . . . K–N1 35 B–B5, followed by 36 B–K6ch) 35 R–B7 R–KN1 36 Q–R4 P–KR4 37 QxPch! NxQ 38 R–R7mate.

34 PxN BxP 35 QxQP Q–KN2 36 R–KN1 Q–R3 37 Q–B4 QxQ 38 BxQ BxP 39 B–KN3 R–K1 40 R–K1 R–KN1 41 K–R2 R–Q1 42 P–Q6 Black resigns

In the previous example, the check that was to be prevented was an immediate one. In our next example, Diagram 54, A. Alekhine–A. West, Portsmouth 1923, after Black's 21st move, the check is a bit further down the road. The diagram position is easy to evaluate: White must have a significant advantage. The reasons also are easy to see: excellent piece placement, while Black's Queenside is as yet undeveloped, various weaknesses in Black's Kingside, the chronic weakness of Black's KP. Nevertheless, the game must still be won. In general, Alekhine's discussions of a particular position show the deepest strategic and tactical insights. This is what he has to say here: "White must win the game if he can attain the formation: N at KR5, Q at KN4. But this plan is at present impracticable, for after 22 P–K5 N–Q4, Black threatens 23 . . . N–K6. On the other hand, the White Queen when played to KR5 would no longer defend the Knight on Q4, which Black would threaten to capture with *check*."

DIAGRAM 54

BLACK

WHITE

Alekhine–West
Portsmouth 1923
after Black's 21st

Therefore White plays

22 K–R1!

Some additional comments by Alekhine in regard to this move are also of interest: (1) "This and the next move form the necessary preparation for the decisive attack, and (2) "The text move makes sure that Black can never capture the Q4 Knight with check and the next move prevents a potential . . . N–K6."

22 . . . P–QR4   23 R–QB3! Q–N3   24 P–K5 N–Q4   25 N–R5! R–K2

After 25 . . . NxR White wins as follows: 26 Q–N4 P–N4 27 N–B6ch K–B1 28 PxN, and Black is defenseless against the various threats.

26 R–N3 N–R1   27 Q–Q3 Q–B2   28 BxN! KPxB   29 N–B6ch Black resigns

After 29 . . . K–B1 White wins with 30 Q–R7 and after 29 . . . K–B2, 30 RxPch! is the fastest win. It is misleading to think that White's attack won "effortlessly." This became so *only* because of Alekhine's preparatory 22 K–R1! and 23 R–QB3!.

A genuine combination is prepared by White from Diagram 55, A. Jusupov–E. Magerramov, USSR 1977, after Black's 30th move.

DIAGRAM 55

BLACK

WHITE

Jusupov–Magerramov
USSR 1977
after Black's 30th

The position on the board is most dynamic, with White having a strong Kingside attack and Black trying to win with his two passed

Queenside pawns. Who will come first? White on move spies an attractive winning combination, but also sees that unfortunately the position is not yet quite ripe for it. After his next preparatory move, however, it will be ripe:

31 K–R2! P–QR4?

Oblivious of White's plan, Black continues "doing his thing." Of course, White's threat had to be prevented; perhaps by 31 . . . Q–R1 so that 32 NxP? can be foiled by the Knight recapture 32 . . . NxN.

32 NxP!! PxN

The threat was 33 NxN, and 32 . . . NxN? is not feasible, so there was no choice. But now White grabs the KN file with

33 Q–N4 N–N3

To prevent mate on his KN1, Black's Knight must move. The "normal" square seems 33 . . . N–Q2, but that is refuted by 34 R–K1!!, and Black is defenseless against the threat 35 RxR and 36 Q–N7mate. The point of White's 31st move is now clear: Black can't play 34 . . . RxR *with check,* and thus White's Rook on K1 is both inviolate and winning. Of course, after the text White's win is equally easy as he wins back the piece and maintains a killing attack.

34 PxN Q–Q2   35 Q–B3 Q–K3   36 N–B7ch RxN   37 PxR QxP 38 P–R5 P–N6   39 P–R6 P–R5   40 R–N7 Q–K3   41 Q–N3 Black resigns

The dual threats are 42 QxRch and 42 RxPch, with 41 . . . R–KN1 losing to 42 R–K1 Q–B1   43 RxRch QxR   44 R–K8!.

Make no mistake about it, having the King on the wrong square can bring much woe to everyone, including grandmasters—as demonstrated by the next two examples. The first is from B. Parma–E. Bukic, 1978 Yugoslav Championship, after Black's 43rd move: White: K—a2 Q—g2 N—d5 P—a4, b2, c4, f6 Black: K—b8 Q—f5 B—g3 P—a6, b7, e5, h2, h6. White's prospects seem nil: not only is he a pawn down, but Black's forward KRP is only an eyelash from queening, whereas White's KBP is securely contained by Black's Queen. With an air of philosophic desparation White pushed his KBP:

44 P–B7! QxP?

It's true that Black has a win, but not this easily! As Parma himself pointed out after the game, correct was to place the King "out of the way" with 44 . . . K–R1!, after which White has no satisfactory move, e.g. 45 QxB P–R8 = Q   46 Q–N8ch K–R2   47 P–B8 = Q   Q/B–QN8ch!   48   K–R3   Q–R8ch   49   K–N3 Q/KR8–Q8ch, and Black, having been the one to start checking, is the one who mates first; or 45 P–R5 QxP!   46 QxB P–R8 = Q   47 QxP Q–KN1, and White's "attack" is over.

45 QxB!! P–R8 = Q   46 QxPch

This move comes *with check*, and this tempo makes all the difference.

46 . . . K–R2

The really frustrating thing for Black is that after 46 . . . K–B1 47 N–N6ch K–Q1   48 Q–Q6ch K–K1   49 N–Q5!, the most that he has is equality.

47 Q–Q4ch K–N1   48 Q–R8ch Draw

There is no way Black can escape perpetual check.

What happens to the side with the advantage in the following position, W. Uhlmann–S. Gligoric, Leningrad Interzonal 1973, after Black's 52nd move is not much better. White: K—g3 Q—a7 R—e2, g7 P—c4, e4, h3 Black: K—f6 Q—e8 R—h4, h5 P—d6. White is two pawns ahead and Black's King is more exposed than White's. White thinks the position is ready for a combination, but pays insufficient attention to the location of his own King.

53 P–K5 ch?

Instead, 53 K–N2! makes the King safe by preventing a . . . RxRP *with check*. If then 53 . . . RxRP, 54 P–K5ch! does win.

53 . . . PxP   54 R–KB2ch R–KB5   55 R–N4?!

Part of the combination started with White's 53rd move, but erroneous because of Black's (unexpected!) reply. Even so it's doubtful if White any longer has winning chances—after all, he has thrown away a valuable pawn.

55 . . . RxPch! 56 KxR Q-R4ch

Ouch!

57 K-N2 QxRch 58 K-B1 K-N3 59 Q-R6ch K-R4 60 RxR PxR 61 Q-R5ch Draw

CHAPTER 12
King Moves to Mark Time

You have a position where your opponent has no particular immediate threats. On the other hand, your own pieces stand as well as possible, so that moving any one of them is inadvisable. The clock shows that you have little time left. You must make a move, but what to do? How about a pawn push? Such a scenario has taken place countless times in tournament play, with generally disastrous results for the "pawn pusher." The only correct answer to the question: "How about a pawn push?" is a resounding "No!." Pawn moves always change the inherent status of a position, often lead to a weakening of the pawn formation and/or general position *and* can never be reversed. Pawns should only be pushed if this is good for either offense or defense. Never, never move a pawn if nothing *positive* comes from it. Pawn moves should always be the *last* choice when attempting to maintain the status quo—yet often (particularly in time pressure) they become the first choice!

There is one ideal method of marking time and it's called moving the King. In the kind of positions where direct attacks on the King are not occuring, it is usually unimportant exactly which one of the squares in "his corner" the King sits on. Thus a dipsy-doodle dance by the King within a small area upsets nothing and "kills time," either to make the time control, get ready for adjournment or conserve thinking time for decisive action later.

A simple example of a "nothing" King move occurs in Diagram 56, S. Reshevsky–R. Byrne, New York 1951, after Black's 35th move. A quick look suffices to see that Black is in a

DIAGRAM 56

BLACK

WHITE

Reshevsky–R. Byrne
New York 1951
after Black's 35th

very bad way. Not only is he without prospects for active play, but also he can't improve his defensive formation. White has a general bind on the position, a ready–made infiltration route along the QR file and control of the KB file. With all these pluses, what does White now play but

36 K–N2!

Reshevsky calls this "a waiting move." The reason for its choice is strictly practical. White has 5 moves to complete before the time control; by playing this move quickly he has more *thinking* time for his next four moves. Such a strategy works here because Black can't do anything to improve his situation.

36 . . . Q–Q2   37 R/1–QR1

Time for chess again.

37 . . . P–R4   38 R–R8 RxR

38 . . . Q–Q1 allows 39 NxP.

39 RxR BxN   40 KPxB K–R2   41 Q–QB3 R–N1   42 Q–B6 P–N5

Black is defenseless: 42 . . . B–B2 loses to 43 RxR, and after 42 . . . B–N3 White has the pretty 43 Q–R8ch! RxQ 44 RxRmate.

43 R–Q8 PxPch 44 K–R2 Black resigns

After 44 . . . Q–KB2 the simplest win is 45 QxQch BxQ 46 RxR KxR 47 P–Q7.

Since King moves are excellent for marking time, they also serve perfectly for positions where the opponent is in *zugzwang*. Opportunities for both uses of marking time will be found in the course of play, D. Bronstein–G. Stahlberg, Zurich Candidates Tournament 1953, after White's 37th move. White: K—a2, Q—d5 R—e1 P—a3, b2, e6, g3 Black: K—h7 Q—f6 R—e7 P—a7, b7, f5, g5, h5. It is difficult to be both quick *and* correct in evaluating such a position. Black is up a pawn, yet White's KP is clearly a power. Black is in time trouble and needs to form a viable plan for getting to Move 40 in good shape. His Q and R stand well enough, and starting to play with the pawns is inadvisable without substantial concrete thinking—therefore Black's first move should be

37 . . . K–N3!

Coming closer to his pawns is both good and safe.

38 Q–Q8 K–N2! 39 Q–Q6 K–N3! 40 Q–Q8 K–R3! 41 Q–Q5 P–B5!

The last three King moves were made to preserve the status quo until the time control. With this successfully accomplished, Black again has sufficient thinking time to fashion a definite plan (in fact, the game was adjourned here). Analysis showed that the creation of connected passed pawns should give Black a theoretically winning position.

42 PxP QxBP 43 R–K5 Q–B3 44 Q–K4 P–N4! 45 Q–K2 P–R3 46 P–R4!

The only try—Black must be prevented from playing . . . Q–QB5ch at some later stage.

46 . . . PxP 47 Q–K3 P–R5 48 R–K4 K–N3! 49 Q–K2 P–KR6 50 R–K3 K–N2! 51 Q–R2 R–N2! 52 Q–K2 R–K2?!

Again short of time (the time control was on Move 56), Black plays a "safe" move. Subsequently, Bronstein demonstrated that with the paradoxical–looking 52 . . . K–B1!! Black would not only stop the KP but put White in something like *zugzwang*! Then either 53 R–KB3 or 53 RxP are met by 53 . . . RxPch!, while Black himself is threatening to win the endgame after 53 . . . QxNPch! 54 QxQ RxQch 55 KxR P–N5!.

53 Q–R2 P–R6! 54 KxP RxP?

White now retains sufficient chances against Black's weakened Kingside, where Black will be left with only one pawn. According to Stahlberg he could have retained excellent winning chances by 54 . . . Q–B5!, as even after best play for White (55 R–KN3! RxP 56 QxP R–K4) Black has quite an active and secure position.

55 Q–B7ch Q–B2 56 Q–B3ch! R–B3 57 RxP Q–K2ch 58 K–R2 Q–K3ch 59 K–R1 K–N1 60 R–R1 Q–B3 61 Q–KR3

White now has a strong attacking formation and Black decides to force the draw.

61 . . . Q–R5ch 62 K–N1 Q–K5ch 63 K–R1 Draw

Of course, *zugzwang* positions in the middlegame are rather uncommon, but when they do occur they are apt to be in "purer" form than the case above. A perfect example is Diagram 57, K.R. Jones–J. Hanken, 1978 U.S. Open Championship, after White's 29th move. A careful investigation shows that none of White's pieces can move! A Rook move either leaves the QRP hanging or allows . . . Q–B8ch, a Knight move allows . . . NxQP!, a Queen move at the very least loses the QP, and a King move allows the devastating . . . Q–B7. Therefore, as soon as White's pawn moves are exhausted . . . Black sits back and waits for just this:

29 . . . K–R1! 30 P–N5 K–N2! 31 N–K2?!

Instantly hopeless. White had to try 31 P–R4 K–R1! 32 N–R3!? even though 32 . . . NxRP! must win, e.g. 33 RxN Q–B8ch 34 K–R2 R–B6 35 Q–N4 Q–K7ch 36 Q–N2 QxQP, and Black's attack will be decisive.

DIAGRAM 57

BLACK

WHITE

Jones–Hanken
1978 US Championship
after White's 29th

31 . . . NxRP

Good enough, but immediately killing was 31 . . . NxQP!, e.g. 32 QxN Q–B7ch 33 K–R1 R–B6.

32 P–R4

32 RxN Q–B8ch 33 K–R2 R–B7ch is worse, but the text also offers no long–range hope. The remaining moves were:

32 . . . N–B4 33 R–KN1 N–K3 34 Q–N4 Q–B7ch 35 K–R1 Q–B6ch 36 K–R2 QxQ 37 RxQ R–B7ch 38 R–N2 RxRch 39 KxR N–B4 40 N–B1 P–R3 41 K–B3 PxP 42 PxP N–K3 43 K–N4 N–B5 44 K–B3 P–R5 45 N–R2 NxP White resigns

CHAPTER 13
To Be or Not to Be Afraid

One of the key factors involved in middlegame play is King safety, and this will be covered from several sides. One of the important questions always is: is my King safe or unsafe? Or to phrase it in more human terms, encompassing psychological aspects: should I be *afraid* for my King's safety? This chapter will consider the correct way to look at this question.

We are not concerned with the perenially scared type of player who, no matter how secure the King's bastion, always conjures up possible spooks. But we are interested in differentiating between the situations where there is a genuine need to worry about King safety and those where the King can take care of itself. For the enemy to do real damage to your King, he will need more than a single piece in the attack. Thus a check is by itself no cause for alarm, unless there is a definitive follow-up. If you yourself are on the warpath against the enemy King, then the need to worry about uncoordinated checks is particularly small. If we look at Diagram 58, B. Ivanovic–M. Vukic, 1978 Yugoslav Championship, after Black's 35th move, we see that White has doubled his Rooks on the seventh rank and has his Queen actively placed. All that is needed is for the Knight to come into action and White's control of the position will be absolute:

36 N–K5!

The threat of 37 NxPch is so strong that Black's attack on the QN file can be ignored as inconsequential.

36 . . . RxPch   37 K–B1 Black resigns!

DIAGRAM 58

BLACK

WHITE

Ivanovic–Vukic
1978 Yugoslav
Championship
after Black's 35th

There is no defense. 37 . . . Q–QB1 loses simply to 38 QxQch KxQ 39 R–B8ch and 37 . . . R–N8ch 38 QxR RxQch 39 KxR Q–QB1 loses to the slightly more complicated 40 NxPch! QxN 41 R–B8ch.

When a clearly unstoppable attack is in the works, more dangerous–looking threats can also be withstood without undue fear. White, though a Rook down, has a very strong attacking formation in Diagram 59, D. Bronstein–L. Ljubojevic, Petropolis Interzonal 1973, after Black's 21st move. Black's Kingside is weak on the dark squares, particularly KB3. White's plan is therefore clear:

22 RxB! NxR   23 N–B6ch K–R1   24 Q–KR4!

White is on the verge of achieving imminent mate and thus doesn't worry about what Black can do to his King. At the moment Black can only mobilize his Queen and a Knight for the attack. Given sufficient time this could be sufficient strength, but White sees that time is what Black won't have.

24 . . . Q–N4ch   25 K–K3!! P–KR4   26 NxP! Q–Q6ch

DIAGRAM 59

BLACK

WHITE

Bronstein–Ljubojevic
Petropolis 1973
after Black's 21st

Instead, 26 . . . PxN allows mate after 27 QxPch K–N1   28
Q–N6ch! K–R1   29 B–B6. In the game Black didn't want to be
mated and played the defeatist 26 . . . QxBch?!, resigning after
27 PxQ N–Q4ch   28 K–Q4! N–K3ch   29 KxN NxB   30 N–B6ch
K–N2   31 QxN KR–Q1   32 P–K6 PxPch   33 KxP R–KB1   34
P–Q7 P–R4   35 N–N4 R–R3ch   36 K–K5 R–B4ch   37 QxR PxQ
38 P–Q8 = Q PxN   39 Q–Q7ch K–R3   40 QxQNP R–KN3   41
P–B4. The text move is the main line that White had to consider.

**27 K–B2 N–K5ch   28 PxN Q–Q5ch   29 K–N2 QxNPch   30
K–R3 Q–B6ch   31 N–N3ch K–N1   32 B–B6 White wins**

Mate on KR8 follows.

Fear starts raising its head—often without an objective basis—
when the side with the imperiled King lacks the opportunity
for immediately aggressive play. Consider the position in A.
Karpov–V. Korchnoi, 1974 Match, Game 8, after White's 36th
move. White: K—g2 Q—d1 R—d2 N—f3 P—a2, b3, c4, f2, g4,
h3 Black: K—g7 Q—e4 R—d6 B—b6 P—a6, b7, d5, f7, g6, h6.
Karpov has succeeded in undermining Black's isolated QP and is
on the verge of winning it, since 36 . . . P–Q5? is bad because of

37 P–N4! followed by 38 P–B5. Therefore Korchnoi tries the only counterchance left:

36 . . . P–KR4!   37 PxRP!

This suggestion of R. Byrne's is the only fruitful try at winning. In the game Karpov chose the "super-safe" 37 RxQP?! but after 37 . . . RxR   38 QxR QxQ   39 PxQ PxP   40 PxP K–B3 Black's King was close enough to the QP and the game drawn after 41 K–B1 K–K2   42 N–Q2 B–B2!   43 N–K4 P–B4   44 PxP PxP   45 N–B5 K–Q3   46 NxNPch KxP   47 P–N4 (otherwise the Knight is lost after 47 . . . K–B3) 47 . . . K–B5   48 N–B5 B–N3 49 NxP K–N4   50 N–B5 KxP   51 N–N3 K–R6.

37 . . . PxRP   38 RxP R–N3ch

Here 38 . . . RxR?! 39 QxR QxQ   40 PxQ gives White excellent winning chances because of the weakness of Black's KRP.

39 K–B1, with winning chances for White.

White is a pawn up and Black must prove that his counterchances are adequate. In this regard, the looseness of Black's King position also becomes a factor. Thus, for instance, after 39 . . . R–KB3, White retains the advantage with 40 R–N5ch K–B1 41 P–B5!.

Perhaps the most important point to be made in discussing fear is: never, never be afraid on "principle." In other words, just because you can't prove to your 100% satisfaction that your King is safe, don't assume that *therefore* the King is unsafe. The sound, practical *positive* attitude is that if you don't see a decisive attack hitting your King, consider that the King is safe and act accordingly. For a deeper look into both the practical and psychological aspects of this question, consider the situation in Diagram 60, L. Vadasz–A. Adorjan, Hungary 1978, after Black's 15th move. No, Dear Reader, there are not two typographical errors in the diagram. That is a *White* Knight next to Black's King and a *Black* Bishop in front of White's King. No question that the position is a crazy one, with the only certainty being that at the moment White has the material advantage of one minor piece plus two pawns. What will

DIAGRAM 60

BLACK

WHITE

Vadasz–Adorjan
Hungary 1978
after Black's 15th

happen in the future is unclear, but is there much doubt about White's next move?

16 Q–R4

Why not? The Queen is attacked and White retreats it to the most useful defensive square. Yet Vadasz didn't play thus: instead he played 16 QxR??, allowing Black to have a clear advantage in playing material, and Black went on to win without undue difficulty on Move 36. The explanation for Vadasz's incomprehensible action is "fear out of principle." He simply wasn't sure that White's position would be defensible after 16 Q–R4. Yet how can his course—committing suicide by giving up the Queen for insufficient compensation—ever be the correct approach? In the play that follows I've utilized some of GM Adorjan's excellent analysis.

16 . . . B–Q6 17 P–B6! KxN! 18 PxB Q–K2ch 19 N–K4 QxNch 20 B–K3 KxP 21 0–0–0

The position has clarified a lot, with White having completed his development and still retaining a material (one pawn!) advantage. If Black tries to gain it back by 21 . . . QxBPch 22 QxQ BxQ,

White plays 23 P–QN3 B–R3 24 BxP R–N4 25 B–Q4ch P–B3 26 KR–K1, and can look forward to a slight, trouble-free, endgame advantage. This is hardly something to be afraid of! Alternatively, Black can again head for complications with:

21 . . . RxP!? 22 KxR Q–K4ch 23 K–R3 R–QN1 24 Q–N3

The only move, but the Queen "sacrifice" here is fully motivated both for positional and material reasons. Black's attackers will only be Q and B, and White, with 2 Rooks for the Queen, even has a material advantage.

24 . . . RxQch 25 PxR Q–B6! 26 KR–K1! P–QB4! 27 B–Q2!

27 PxPe.p. Q–R4ch! 28 K–N2 Q–K4ch! leads to perpetual check.

27 . . . Q–B7 28 B–R5 BxP! 29 PxB QxQBP White is better, but Black has drawing chances.

The position is still unbalanced, yet White has a significant material advantage and it is clear that Black's Queen by itself won't be able to threaten any wins. The exposed nature of White's King, however, does give Black good drawing chances by utilizing perpetual check motifs.

No one could have anticipated this position when considering the situation of Diagram 60. Even so, one point is clear: White had no need to commit suicide on Move 16!

So far we have been discussing situations where there was no objective basis for being afraid for the safety of one's King. There are, of course, plenty of times when one has to be not only careful but definitely concerned ("afraid"). If the King position is inherently insecure and no immediate win is in sight anywhere else, then worry about King safety is definitely in order. The position in G. Kasparov–A. Roizman, USSR 1978, after White's 17th move, shows just such a case. White: K—g1 Q—f2 R—a1, f1 B—f4 N—e4 P—a2, b2, c2, d3, g2, h2 Black: K—f7 Q—d5 R—a8, g6 B—e7, g4 P—a7, b7, c6, d4, f6, h7. Black's King is within striking distance of almost all of White's pieces and is sheltered only by a sickly, weak KBP. As Botvinnik suggests, the order of the day for Black was first to safeguard his King by 17 . . . K–N2!, followed by 18 . . . K–R1!. Then Black could start to carry out his plans for the KN file. Instead Black is only concerned with "doing his thing:"

17 . . . QR–KN1? 18 QR–K1! P–KR4?! 19 B–N5! Q–Q1

19 . . . RxB?! loses to 20 NxP. Yet now too White is able to pour it on.

20 Q–B4 B–K3 21 P–KR4! B–Q4 22 P–KN4!

Black had to worry about King safety on Move 17; White has no such need here because he has Black in a complete bind. If now 22 . . . PxP, 23 P–R5. Therefore Black decides to flee with his King—but much too late for real safety.

22 . . . K–N2 23 PxP PxB 24 Q–K5ch K–R3 25 PxR PxP 26 R–B5! RxPch 27 K–R2 Black resigns

White's King is still safe, but Black's will go under after 28 R–R5ch, etc.

There are positions which cry out "Extreme Danger—Do Not Enter." Those who do not pay heed are drastically punished. As a typical illustration, look at the course from Diagram 61, M. Taimanov–F. Gheorghiu, Leningrad 1977, after White's 27th move. Black has built up an active attacking formation and in spite of being in great time trouble he goes to work:

27 . . . NxNP!? 28 KxN B–R6ch!

The only sensible move now is 29 K–N1, and after 29 . . . Q–B6, 30 N–K3. Black has definite compensation for the piece and can continue with, e.g. 30 . . . P–N6 or 30 . . . R–N2 or 30 . . . RxP, with the ultimate outcome uncertain. Even from the practical standpoint 29 K–N1 was logical because Gheorghiu was so short of time that it was questionable whether he could physically complete the required moves through the time control at Move 40. Yet White, with lots of time on his clock, with hardly any thinking responded . . .

29 KxB??

Heading for the edge of the board, with almost no defenders around and with enemy pieces swarming about must be considered

DIAGRAM 61

BLACK

WHITE

Taimanov–Gheorghiu
Leningrad 1977
after White's 27th

an act of self-immolation. The text move is of the type that can only be played after considerable calculation proves that it's safe. On any and all *general* principles, it must be considered unsafe.

29 . . . Q–B6ch   30 B–N3

With lightning speed came Black's move:

30 . . . B–B3!!   White resigns

The devastating threat of . . . P–N5mate can not be prevented, and only slightly postponed by 31 N–K3 P–R4 etc. Black's moves require only a second or so on the clock and *that much time* Black still had remaining.

CHAPTER 14

King Moves to Prevent Threats

In this and the next two chapters the King's usefulness as a defender will be demonstrated. In the middlegame the King can and should be used as a normal piece in the defense of his sector. Chapters 15 and 16 will consider various aspects of defensive strategy; here we'll take up the subject of coping with immediate threats.

Some threats are direct and prosaic and the required King move is equally direct and simple. Diagram 62 is U. Andersson–H. Westerinen, Geneva 1977, after Black's 22nd move. Black is in a complete mess on the Queenside and the first rank and is about to lose at least one piece because of the unstoppable threat of RxP. But at the moment Black has a threat of his own: 23 . . . Q–R6, followed by 24 . . . R–B8ch. White therefore plays:

23 K–N2! Black resigns

Black's threat has been prevented, while White's remains unpreventable, e.g. 23 . . . P–QB3 24 RxP PxN 25 RxN, etc.

In the next, though still simple example, the King has to watch for both strategic and tactical threats. Diagram 63 is

DIAGRAM 62

BLACK

WHITE

Andersson–Westerinen
Geneva 1977
after Black's 22nd

DIAGRAM 63

BLACK

WHITE

Aronson–Tal
1957 USSR
Championship
after White's 21st

Aronson–M. Tal, 1957 USSR Championship, after White's 21st move. Black's King is in check and none of the interpolations are satisfactory. Therefore the King should move, but where?

21 . . . K–R1!

Preventing the strategic threat, i.e. the exchange of Black's good Bishop, after 21 . . . K–R2?! 22 B–K4!.

22 P–B4?

According to Tal the decisive error. Also faulty was 22 B–N4? because of 22 . . . P–N4! 23 BxR RxB 24 R–K4 P–B3! 25 RxP PxB. After the indicated 22 P–B5! P–B3! the unbalanced position would contain equal chances.

22 . . . PxP   23 Q–Q2 Q–N3ch!   24 B–Q4 Q–N3   25 QxP K–R2!

Because of the pin on the KNP, White threatened 26 RxPch. Black's King move prevents this and Tal uses the newly opened lines for a vigorous attack of his own:

26 QxBP B–N8!!   27 B–K5 N–K3!   28 Q–Q6 Q–B4   29 B–B4 N–N4   30 Q–N4 B–K5   31 BxB RxB   32 R–KB1 R–K7   33 Q–Q6 RxQRP   34 Q–Q5 Q–B7   35 P–B5 R–Q1!   36 B–Q6 R–K1! White resigns

There is no defense to the threatened 37 . . . R–K8.

A more complicated version of King play to ward off tactical threats follows from this position, M. Vidmar–K. Opoccensky, Sliacč 1932, with White on move: White: K—g1 Q—b5 R—f2 B—f1, g3 P—a3, f3, g2, h2 Black: K—h8 Q—e3 R—d1, d3 P—a7, b7, f7, g7, h7. White has a slight material advantage, but Black's strong attacking position contains an immediate threat: 1 . . . RxBch! 2 KxR (White's Rook is pinned!) 2 . . . R–Q8mate. This threat is best prevented by unpinning the Rook:

1 K–R1! Q–K7!

Black's Queen must remain on the King file as otherwise White mates Black with Q–K8ch. Black now threatens 2 . . . RxBch; of course, 2 RxQ?? allows instant mate. Yet White's King can again do its defensive work:

2 K–N1! Q–K6! 3 K–R1! Draw

White can't avoid the draw; Black, because he is down material, doesn't want to avoid it.

In H. Mecking–V. Korchnoi. 1974 Match, Game 4, after White's 24th move, Black, with a King move, points up the difference between a sham and a real threat. White: K—g1 Q—e5 R—c1 N—b1 P—b2, f2, g2, h2 Black: K–g8 Q—a8 R—b8 B—c6 P—c7, e6, g7, h6. White threatens 25 QxKPch followed by 26 QxB. Black can't move his Bishop (e.g. 24 . . . BxP?? 25 RxP, followed by mate on KN7) and after the passive 24 . . . R–K1?! White is clearly better after either 25 QxBP or 25 P–B3. Black, however, has an effective King move:

24 . . . K–R2! 25 P–B3

It turns out that White's threat was not so much to capture the KP, but to do so with *check*. With that prevented, 25 QxKP?! RxP is more than fine for Black.

25 . . . R–N4! 26 QxKP RxP 27 QxB QxQ 28 RxQ RxNch 29 K–B2 R–N2

The endgame is only cosmetically better for White. True, he succeeds in winning Black's backward QBP, but the resulting R + 3P vs R + 2P endgame with the pawns on the same side of the board is a well known book draw.

30 K–N3 K–N1 31 P–B4 K–B1 32 K–N4 R–N7 33 K–R3 R–N2 34 P–N4 K–B2 35 P–B5 R–R2 36 K–R4 R–R6! 37 RxPch K–B3 38 R–B6ch K–B2 39 P–R3 R–QN6 40 R–B2 P–N4ch Draw

Of course, many threats involving the King are considerably sneakier and more complicated. Consider Diagram 64, Novopashin–V. Korchnoi, 1962 USSR Championship, after White's 20th move. Black is ahead a significant amount of material and has a strong grip on the center. There is a certain looseness in Black's King position, however, and this, coupled with the White Rook's location on the 7th rank, means that Black should be careful. In fact, White has a diabolical threat which shows itself after a "normal" move such as 20 . . . B–Q3??: 21 N–N5!! QxQ 22 N–R7ch K–N1 23 NxPch, and Black gets mated after 23 . . .

DIAGRAM 64

BLACK

WHITE

*Novopashin–Korchnoi
1962 USSR
Championship
after White's 20th*

K–R1 by 24 R–R7 and after 23 . . . K–B1 by 24 BxP. Korchnoi puts an end to White's dreams by:

20 . . . K–N1!! 21 NxKP

Now 21 N–N5?? is pointless, and, seeing no concrete attacking prospects, White wins back a good central pawn by acquiescing to a lost endgame. This is hardly a promising practical approach— but good advice cannot be offered in such positions.

21 . . . QxQ 22 NxQ R–K1! 23 BxP R–K8 ch 24 N–B1 P–B4!

In the game Korchnoi played 24 . . . B–B4?! and followed it up with another inaccuracy on Move 28, winning only by a hair on Move 42. The text move is his recommendation for a swift and sure win.

25 P–N4 P–B5 26 K–N2 R–K7ch 27 K–B3 RxBP, with the passed central pawns guaranteeing an easy win for Black.

How sophisticated a threat–preventing King move can be is illustrated by the play arising from the position in Tchigorin and Ponce–Steinitz and Gavilon, Consultation Game 1889, Black to move. White: K—g1 Q—d1 R—a1, f1 B—f3 P—a2, c3, e4, f2, g2, h2 Black: K—h8 Q—f6 R—a8, f4 B—b6 P—a7, b7, c7, e5, g5, h7. Though material is equal, Black unquestionably has a strong attacking position on the Kingside, and with his next move he gets ready for the execution of his attack:

1 . . . R–KN1

With the threat 2 . . . P–N5 3 B–K2 P–N6 4 RPxP BxPch (4 . . . RxBP also wins) 5 K–R2 R–R5ch! (or "brilliantly" 5 . . . Q–R5ch) 6 PxR QxPmate. What is the best way of coping?

2 K–R1!!

This way! The key is not so much to hold on to the KBP, but to prevent the ripping open of the King position as occurred in the above note. In the game White chose the routine—and Kingside—weakening—2 P–KR3? and lost as follows: 2 . . . P–N5! 3 PxP (Immediately losing is 3 BxP?! R/1xB! 4 PxR RxBP 5 RxR QxRch 6 K–R2 Q–R5mate.) 3 . . . P–KR4! 4 P–N5 (4 . . . PxP followed by 5 . . . P–N6 was threatened; 4 PxP? allows 4 . . . RxB) 4 . . . RxNP 5 K–R2 R–R5ch 6 K–N1 Q–B5 7 R–K1 RxPch! White resigns.

Analysis after the game by Lasker and Steinitz showed that 2 K–R1! was indicated and should have held the game:

2 . . . P–N5 3 B–K2 BxP

Other moves offer no more: if 3 . . . RxBP 4 RxR QxR 5 BxP, while the position after 3 . . . RxKP 4 P–B3! also looks defensible.

4 P–N3! Q–KR3!

Clearly 4 . . . RxP? fails to 5 K–N2. After the text move 5 PxR? loses to 5 . . . P–N6, but Steinitz worked out the following draw:

5 Q–Q5! BxP 6 QxKPch R–N2 7 Q–K8ch Draw

White has perpetual check. The reason why 2 K–R1! worked is that it prevented the decisive weakening of White's Kingside.

When a King move not only prevents a threat, but also serves a positive purpose, then necessarily the move gains in value and power. Diagram 65 shows the situation in V. Smyslov–Ilivitsky,

DIAGRAM 65

BLACK

WHITE

Smyslov–Ilivitsky
1955 USSR Championship
after White's 17th

1955 USSR Championship, after White's 17th move. White seems to have a very clear threat: 18 QxPch. Yet note how easily Black parries it:

17 . . . K–B2!!

As long as it can't be taken by check, Black's KRP is quite safe (18 QxP?? R–R1). With the center closed, Black's King is sufficiently safe on KB2. And, by vacating the KN1 square, Black enables his K2 Knight to enter action via KN1 and KB3. It has suddenly become clear that White's heavy artillery is whistling in the wind along the KR file.

18 N–Q2 NxN 19 BxN N–N1! 20 P–B4!?

A reasonable try at complications, with such variations as 20 . . . BxPch 21 K–R1 BxP? 22 QxPch B–N2 23 B–QB3 N–B3 24 BxN KxB 25 R–KN3 Q–B2 26 Q–R4ch (Soltis) in view.

It is understandable that White has no interest in 20 QxP N–B3 21 Q–R4 R–R1 22 Q–N3 N–K5 23 Q–K3 RxR 24 PxR, and White's extra KRP is valueless, while he himself is in a straight-jacket.

20 . . . QR–B1! 21 PxP?

Underestimating Black's planned sacrifice. Unpleasant defense with 21 B–K3 was the best White had.

21 . . . QxRch! 22 BxQ RxBch 23 K–B2 BxPch 24 K–B3 PxP 25 QxPch B–N2 26 R–N3?

Leads to loss of the Rook. But even after the better 26 Q–R4 N–B3 White's disorganized forces would be no match for Black's army.

26 . . . N–K2 27 RxP

Otherwise 27 . . . R–KR1 traps the Queen. Black now gets a decisive material advantage and wins routinely.

27 . . . NxR 28 Q–R5 BxP 29 B–Q3 K–N2 30 P–N3 R–B6 31 K–K2 R–QB3 32 P–KR4 R–K1ch 33 K–B1 R–K6 34 QxP N–K2 35 Q–R7ch K–B1 36 P–N4 B–N2 37 K–B2 P–Q5 38 P–N5 R–QB6 39 B–K2 R–B4 40 P–R5 R–B4 41 P–R6 RxPch 42 K–K1 B–K4 White resigns

CHAPTER 15

Performing Various Defensive Tasks

SECTION 1. Protecting Material

The King is often a fine natural defender of nearby pawns and pieces. There is no reason why the King shouldn't do some work—absolutely nothing is gained by having a "prima donna" King who refuses to dirty its hands with menial work.

The course of play from the next three positions demonstrates some straightforward examples of such work. Diagram 66 is W. Browne–K. Frey, Lone Pine (Calif.) 1977, after Black's 19th move. In positions of this type, White's slight advantage is derived from the pressure he is able to exert against Black's isolated QP. Therefore, Black's immediate threat is 20 . . . NxB, since 21 QxN leaves the KP hanging and 21 PxN blocks the Q-file. The KP needs protecting, yet 20 R–K1?! is illogical because the Rook should be used for action along either the half-open QB or Q files. A perfectly sound defender is the King:

20 K–B2! QR–Q1   21 KR–B1! P–B3   22 R/5–B3 N–K4   23 K–N1 N–B3   24 B–B1!

As a way of getting his KB onto a more active diagonal, White has had a slight change of plan for his King. The advanced doubled Rook will temporarily guard the KP, while the King will take over the function of protecting the KBP.

24 . . . Q–B4   25 K–N2! R–K3?!

DIAGRAM 66

BLACK

WHITE

Browne–Frey
Lone Pine 1977
after Black's 19th

Black's position on the Queenside is starting to be unpleasant; 25 . . . R–K2 seems like the best defensive plan.

26 P–QN4! P–QR3

Here and on the next move the QNP is taboo because of R–B8!.

27 P–QR4 R/1–K1?

Leading to an unpleasant pin. The minor evil was 27 . . . R–R1 (Browne).

28 P–N5 PxP 29 BxNP! R–QB1?! 30 P–R5! B–K1 31 B–Q3 Q–R4 32 P–N4 Q–B2 33 B–KB5 R–R1 34 BxR, and White wins

Black has no compensation for the lost Exchange and White won routinely on Move 45. White's King remained on KN2, safe and sound.

Somewhat different in nature but equally simple in application is the pawn protection mode of the following position, M. Chiburdanidze–N. Gaprindashvili, Women's World Championship Match 1978, Game 7, after Black's 30th move.

White: K—g1 Q—b6 R—d1 N—f3 P—a4, b3, e4, f2, g2, h3
Black: K—g8 Q—c3 R—e8 N—f4 P—a5, b7, c6, f7, g6, h7.
Black has the mild tactical threat of taking off the KRP, e.g. 31
QxNP? NxRPch, with advantage to Black because of the
weakening of White's Kingside. The simplest way of protecting
the KRP (while also negating any trouble from checks on the
first rank) is

31 K–R2!

Now 31 . . . NxRP?? loses to 32 KxN. Instead, in the game
White played the inaccurate 31 R–Q8?!, committed another
error on Move 34 and resigned after Move 40. The text is a
suggestion of Soviet GM Holmov, with the following variation
also given by him:

31 . . . RxP?

Black's King will now be the weaker of the two. Therefore
correct is 31 . . . Q–N5 [Mednis] with equality.

32 QxNP Q–B7?

Even after the better 32 . . . R–N5 33 R–Q8ch K–N2 34
Q–K7 White has strong pressure.

**33 R–Q8ch! K–N2 34 R–Q7, with a winning attack for
White.**

In Diagram 67, A. Karpov–G. Kuzmin, Leningrad 1977, after
Black's 17th move, White has a slight edge because of Black's
isolated QP. Even though White has three attackers on it, 18
NxP?? is not possible because Black has . . . RxRch, drawing off
White's other Rook from the Q-file. Karpov solves this problem
simply by having his King protect the KR:

18 K–B1! Q–B2 19 B–N3 Q–N3 20 P–N4 P–R3 21 N–B4!

The QP is still not ripe for plucking because Black would get
White's QBP in return. Therefore White first seeks to gain space
by exchanging a pair of Rooks. Exchanging both pairs would
also be fine for White, as Black's counterplay would thereby
vanish: 21 . . . RxRch?! 22 RxR R–K1 23 RxRch NxR 24
N–Q5 Q–Q1 25 Q–B5, with advantage to White.

DIAGRAM 67

BLACK

WHITE

Karpov–Kuzmin
Leningrad 1977
after Black's 17th

21 . . . R/3–K1   22 RxRch RxR   23 N–K2 R–Q1?

White's King is well situated on KB1, helping with piece protection and guarding the first rank, thus making 24 NxP a threat. The routine protection of the QP with the text move leads to a most unpleasant pin on the KN. Correct was the active 23 . . . R–QB1!, aiming for counterplay as the best method of protecting the QP. Black then has good chances for eventual equality.

24 B–R4! N–K4

24 . . . P–N4 would seriously weaken the Kingside; yet the text move is also unsatisfactory.

25 Q–B5 P–Q6?!

Karpov parries this attempt at counterplay with ease. Unattractive, yet inescapable, was the endgame resulting after 25 . . . N–B5 26 BxN QxB 27 QxQ PxQ 28 RxP RxR 29 NxR NxP 30 K–K2 N–B5 31 N–B5 K–R2 32 K–Q3.

26 PxP N–B5   27 N–B3! NxP   28 N–K4 Q–K3   29 NxNch PxN 30 Q–B3 R–K1   31 BxP K–R2   32 P–Q4 Black resigns

A pawn down in a very bad position, Black has no interest in continuing.

Now we come to the part where the King has to exhibit more guts in his protection work. In the following position, A. Karpov–G. Kuzmin, Leningrad Interzonal 1973, after Black's 26th move, White: K—g2 Q—c2 R—e1, e2 B—d3 N—f3 P—a3, b2, c3, f4, g3 Black: K—f8 Q—b6 R—d8, h6 N—c6, d7 P—a7, b7, d5, f7, g7. White has a most harmonious development of forces, while Black's are scattered hither and yon. With his mobilization complete, Karpov starts decisive operations:

27 P–KN4!

Black's pieces will be pushed further back by the advancing pawns. White seems to be loosening his Kingside pawn formation, but Karpov has correctly seen that his King will be able to adequately guard the base pawn.

27 . . . Q–B2   28 P–N5 R–KR1   29 K–N3! N–B4   30 B–B5 P–KN3?!   31 P–N4! N–K5ch

Giving up a pawn offers no chance, yet after 31 . . . PxB 32 PxN Q–Q2 33 N–Q4! NxN 34 PxN Black's Kingside is in shreds and he will lose the forward KBP. And 31 . . . N–Q2 is smashed by 32 BxP! PxB 33 QxP Q–B1 34 R–K6!.

32 BxN PxB   33 QxP K–N2   34 P–N5 N–R4   35 Q–K7! QxQ   36 RxQ R–Q6   37 R–B7 N–N6   38 K–N4!

A King move with the cautionary point of unpinning the Knight. Black now is defenseless against the coming doubling of Rooks on the 7th, reinforced, if necessary, by a N–K5.

38 . . . R–KB1   39 R/1–K7 Black resigns

Black's King and central pawn formation look somewhat shaky in Diagram 68, W. Uhlmann–B. Larsen, Leningrad Interzonal 1973, after White's 15th move. Larsen comes up with an instructive method of improving both:

15 . . . P–KR4!

To prevent a later P–KN4 by White, which would undermine Black's KB/K pawns.

DIAGRAM 68

BLACK

WHITE

Uhlmann–Larsen
Leningrad 1973
after White's 15th

16 QR–Q1 K–N3!!

With the primary idea of providing additional support for the KBP. The King is sufficiently safe, and, by attacking the QB, it arrives with a gain of tempo.

17 P–R4 Q–Q3 18 R–B4?!

Here and in the further course of the game, White plays against the KBP, but this turns out to be an exercise in futility. Hindsight tells us that better was 18 B–B4 Q–N5, with approximate equality.

18 . . . KR–QB1 19 B–R3 RxN! 20 PxR N–Q4 21 BxB QxB 22 R/1–KB1 NxR 23 RxN Q–QB2 24 P–Q5 B–Q2 25 Q–N4 R–K1 26 R–B1 P–N3 27 K–R2 K–B3!

With material having been substantially reduced, the King is safe here and this placement allows Black's next move, thereby completely securing his Kingside pawns.

28 P–B4 P–N3! 29 P–K3 R–QB1 30 R–B1 Q–K4 31 B–B1 R–B4 32 Q–R3 P–KN4! 33 QxP?

Although in time pressure, White nevertheless decides to go for stray pawns. Mandatory was 33 PxPch KxP 34 Q–B3 QxQ 35 RxQ P–N4 with Black only slightly better (Larsen).

33 . . . Q–Q3! 34 R–N1 P–N4! 35 RPxPch KxP 36 K–N2 P–R5!

Larsen's use of the King is exemplary: first for defense and now as an active part of the offense.

37 PxRPch KxP 38 K–B2 PxP White resigns

As White was playing 39 Q–N8 his flag fell and he was forfeited. The endgame after 39 . . . QxQ 40 RxQ P–B6 would be hopeless for him, anyway,

Diagram 69, V. Smyslov–V. Makagonov, 1944 USSR Championship, after Black's 46th move, shows a tense situation. White has the slight material advantage of the Exchange for a pawn, but the pawn is a strong protected passed QRP. One of White's Rooks has effectively penetrated Black's position, but the other is very passively placed. Black, for his part, threatens to capture White's QBP and thereby penetrate with his Queen. To secure winning chances White must also activate his Queen. Smyslov correctly foresees that his King can be counted on to provide crucial defensive support and plays:

47 QxRP! QxP 48 QxPch R–Q2 49 K–B2!

The King, though feeling somewhat uncomfortable, does satisfactorily protect the QB on K3 and thus prevents any immediate invasion by Black. Black's Queen now must head back to protect its King.

49 . . . Q–R4 50 Q–K6! Q–B2 51 P–B5 K–N2 52 R–N6 K–B1 53 QxKP Q–N2 54 R–QB6ch K–N1 55 P–Q5 N–R4 56 Q–K5ch K–R1 57 Q–K6 K–N1 58 R–N2!

Deflecting the Knight from its defensive position. After 58 . . . P–R6 Smyslov was planning 59 RxNP! QxR!4 60 QxR NxR 61 PxN, winning.

58 . . . N–N6 59 B–B4ch K–R2 60 R–R6ch Black resigns

DIAGRAM 69

BLACK

WHITE
Smyslov–Makagonov
1944 USSR
Championship
after Black's 46th

After 60 . . . QxR 61 QxRch Black's Bishop is lost.

Often, of course, the protection of material is part of a larger objective. A look at Diagram 70, W. Uhlmann–B. Spassky, Moscow 1967, after White's 16th move, shows that White has been furiously shoving his Kingside pawns at Black's King. The particular object of attack is Black's KN3 pawn, yet the ultimate interest is Black's KN3 *square*. Black's correct plan can only be:

16 . . . K–N2!

The point/pawn must be protected. The greedy, careless 16 . . . P–N5? loses to 17 PxP PxN 18 P–N7!, as in Bobotsov–Lehmann, Zevenaar 1961.

17 PxP?!

This clearing of the Kingside pawn formation turns out fine for Black. Hort suggests 17 B–N5, and rates the position "unclear."

17 . . . PxP 18 B–N5 P–N5! 19 Q–Q2?

The piece sacrifice is completely unsound. Required was 19 BxN, followed by a KN move. Black would be somewhat better since the

DIAGRAM 70

BLACK

WHITE

Uhlmann–Spassky
Moscow 1967
after White's 16th

opening of the KB file gives him active play—something he wouldn't have if White hadn't played 17 PxP?!.

19 . . . PxN 20 Q–R6ch K–B2 21 Q–R7ch B–N2 22 R–R3 R–R1! White resigns

After 23 RxPch Q–B3! 24 RxQch KxR Black wins back the trapped Queen and remains a piece up in an endgame.

In Diagram 71, Schüssler–Y. Rantanen, Stockholm 1977/78, after Black's 23rd move, White has a solid advantage due to his greater space control. With the help of a really deft King move, he wins in short order:

24 K–B2!!

With the idea of protecting the KR—so Black thinks. True, that is one point of the move, but there are other points as well:
(1.) Black won't be able to capture White's Rook with check,
(2.) White's K1–K3 squares are protected, so that White threatens 25 RxR followed by 26 R–Q7,
(3.) The King is brought closer to the center for a potential endgame, and
(4.) White sets a devilish trap!

DIAGRAM 71

BLACK

WHITE

Schüssler–Rantanen
Stockholm 1977/78
after Black's 23rd

24 . . . R/1–K1?

. . . which Black promptly falls into! An unpleasant endgame after 24 . . . N–K4 25 BxN PxB 26 Q–K4 is the best that Black has (Minev).

25 R–Q7!!

Back–rank mate threats lead to substantial loss of material for Black, with 25 . . . N–K4? serving no function and losing a piece after 26 RxN!.

25 . . . N–R3 26 QxPch! KxQ 27 RxQ RxR/2 28 RxR P–B5 29 R–K6 N–N1 30 RxRP R–QB2 31 B–Q4 Black resigns

He's two pawns down and also stands worse.

SECTION 2. Protecting Territory

The King is perfectly capable of protecting nearby territory, and there should be no reluctance in using it for such purposes. Territory can mean a whole area or just a single important point. An example for the latter is the following position, A. Karpov–L.

Ljubojevic, Bugojno 1978, after Black's 33rd move. White: K—g2 Q—d2 R—b4, f3 N—c3, d4 P—a5, f4, g5, h2 Black: K—g8 Q—d7 R—c8, f8 B—g7 P—a6, b7, d6, f7, g6, h7. White has the material advantage of a piece for two pawns, but there is a certain looseness in his position which gives Black some swindling chances. In particular, the Black Queen has access to its KN5 square, and at some moment could give an unpleasant check there. Karpov decides that it's time for his King to do some work:

34 K–N3!

With the primary point of protecting the KN4 square. There are, however, also other advantages to the move: the KBP is protected some more and the King can feel generally safer on the third rather than second rank in this position.

34 . . . R–B4　35 N–N3 R–B4　36 N–Q5 P–R4　37 P–R3!

The KN4 square again needs strengthening. Yet note that White has achieved a lot by having Black's KRP move forward two squares: Black has forsaken chances for counterplay via a potential . . . P–KR3, and Black's KNP has been weakened and is now susceptible to a White P–KB5 break.

37 . . . R–K1　38 Q–Q3 Q–B3　39 N–K3 R–N4　40 RxR PxR 41 P–B5! R–K4　42 P–R4 K–R2　43 N–Q4 Q–B8　44 N–N2 P–N5 45 N–K2

White's Knights protect their King very well, and he can feel quite comfortable on the third rank. White now starts using his extra piece to go for Black's weak KN3 point/pawn and this means the beginning of the end for Black.

45 . . . Q–B3　46 PxPch PxP　47 N/K–B4 R–KB4　48 N–K3 RxN 49 RxR B–K4　50 Q–B4 Q–Q2　51 N–Q5 Q–KB2?!　52 N–B6ch K–N2　53 NxPch Black resigns

Covering larger stretches of territory is equally easy for a sufficiently protected King. Diagram 72 shows T. Petrosian–M. Botvinnik, 1963 World Championship Match, Game 19, after Black's 20th move. White has a considerable advantage because of greater space and superior piece placement (in particular Black's KB is seriously misplaced). Because of the exchange of the light

DIAGRAM 72

BLACK

WHITE

Petrosian–Botvinnik
1963 Match, Game #19
after Black's 20th

squared Bishops, squares have been weakened near White's King, and Black's KBP aims at White's KNP. Petrosian therefore takes time out from concrete action and plays a typical "Petrosian move:"

21 K–N2!

In one fell swoop steadying all the squares in the King's vicinity: KB3, KN3 (KNP), KR3. After this pause for defense, White returns to active play.

21 . . . P–R4   22 N–B3 Q–R4   23 B–R3 KR–K1

Passive and unattractive, yet after 23 . . . R–B2   24 Q–K4! the pressure along the Q-file would be very unpleasant.

24 R–Q4 N–N1   25 R/1–Q1 RxR   26 RxR PxP   27 RPxP Q–B2 28 Q–K4 P–N3   29 Q–R4!

The consistent way of taking advantage of the weaknesses on the K-side. In the game Petrosian went to the Queenside with 29 Q–N7?!, which gave Black a chance to resist (White still won on Move 66).

29 . . . K–N2

After either 29 . . . B–B1 or 29 . . . B–N2,   30 N–N5 is decisive.

30 R–Q1!, with a won position for White.

The coming 31 R–KR1! is irresistable. Note how well placed *White's* King is on KN2, from where it protects the key KB3 square (at the moment occupied by the Knight!).

It is well known that the Knight is the premier blockader. Yet, in fact the King is also an excellent blockader and is just a bit inferior to the Knight. The characteristics of the King—no long range power, but the ability to offer complete coverage of the immediate area—make it well suited to sit in the front of an enemy pawn. Blockading action can be either specific or territorial. A good example of the former is provided by the further play from the following position, M. Tal–V. Korchnoi, 1958 USSR Championship, after White's 22nd move. White: K—f1 Q—g4 R—h1 B—d3 P—a3, c2, f2, h2, h5 Black: K—e8, Q—b8 R—h8 B—d7 P—a7, c3, d5, e6, f6, g7. Tal has sacrificed a pawn for a sharp attacking position. Black's KNP is attacked so that his next move is routine:

22 . . . K–B1   23 R–N1 P–N4!!

The non-routine point of Black's routine 22nd move. Korchnoi feels that White should now have played 24 P–KR4!, and after 24 . . . Q–B5!   25 PxP an approximately even endgame would have resulted. But White's next move is so obvious and tempting!

24 PxPe.p.?! K–N2!

The final move in Black's strategy starting with his 22nd. The King blockades White's KNP securely and totally, and White's attacking chances have been considerably reduced.   Though material now is even, Black's center pawns are a potential great power and, now that Black's King is relatively safe, the shortcomings in White's King position will become readily apparent.

25 P–KR4 P–R4   26 R–N3 Q–N8ch   27 K–N2 Q–N2   28 P–R5 P–Q5ch   29 B–K4 B–B3?

After the exchange of Bishops, White's position is defensible.

According to Korchnoi, good winning chances were to be had with
29 . . . Q–N4! 30 R–R3 Q–N4!.

30 BxB QxBch 31 K–N1 Q–Q4 32 Q–B4 Q–K4

The chances are now in dynamic balance and the game could
have ended in a repetition of moves after 33 Q–B3! Q–Q4 34
Q–B4! Q–K4 etc. Instead, in his eagerness to win, Tal has a
horrible hallucination:

**33 P–R6ch?? RxP 34 QxRch?! KxQ 35 P–N7 QxRch White
resigns**

DIAGRAM 73

BLACK

WHITE

Byrne–Spassky
Bugojno 1978
after Black's 16th

What could be called territorial blockade is demonstrated from
Diagram 73, R. Byrne–B. Spassky, Bugojno 1978, after Black's
16th move. White has been precipitiously shoving his Kingside
pawns, whereas Black has been developing his Queenside, while
working to prevent any dangerous line opening on the Kingside.
White now has nothing better than his next move:

17 PxP K–R2!!

The crux of Black's defensive plan. The King has absolutely no
interest as such in White's forward KRP. But the King wants to sit
right in front of it, so that all of White's attacking prospects along
the KR file are obstructed. You may remember a similar defensive

set-up from Diagram 5, Reshevsky–Malich, Siegen Olympiad 1970.

18 N/3–K2 Q–B2   19 N–B4 R/K–B1   20 P–B3 P–N4

With Black's King protecting himself so effectively, his forces on the other side have sufficient time to start a thematic attack against White's King.

21 N–R3 P–N5   22 N–KN5ch K–R1

With the expenditure of 4 tempos, White's QN has been able to push back Black's King one square. Sometime soon White should play P–KR7–in the game he gets nowhere and Black soon blockades the KRP again.

23 B–KB4 B–K1!   24 NxN BxN   25 K–N1 P–R4   26 P–B4 B–K1 27 R–B1 P–R5   28 B–K2?!

Perhaps this is the moment for trying 28 P–R7!?. After the text, Black regroups his forces and breaks open the position with a central advance.

28 . . . P–N6!   29 P–QR3 Q–Q1!   30 N–B3 NxN   31 RxN K–R2!

Blockade!

32 B–N5 Q–R4   33 R–N3 P–Q4!   34 KPxP PxP   35 Q–B4 B–Q2 36 R/N–QB3 B–KB4ch   37 B–Q3?

Leading to an immediate collapse because of Black's response. Mandatory was 37 K–R1.

37 . . . RxP!   38 Q–Q2 RxR   39 PxR BxQRP   40 R–B1 BxBch 41 QxB B–B1 White resigns

Black's King is still paralyzing White's Kingside prospects, while White's Queenside is all Black's.

SECTION 3. Consolidating the Position

As used in "the trade," the expression "consolidating the position" usually means safeguarding the position by preventing any and all threats to it. Here we shall look only at those positions where King location and King play are an inherent part. Consolidation can aim at either of two ultimate goals: either achieving a draw or, after the necessary consolidating is accomplished, going on for a win. In the latter case, consolidation can involve the safe retaining of material advantage or the stopping of enemy action, so that one's own attacking plans can be brought to fruition.

A relatively clear case of consolidating the King position so as to proceed with one's own plans is illustrated in the further play from the following position, R. Byrne–V. Liberzon, Haifa Olympiad 1976, after Black's 43rd move. White: K—g2 Q—e3 B—e4 N—d4 P—a3, b4, h3 Black: K—h8 Q—e1 R—f1 P—a6, b6, g5, h6. White has a slight material advantage and both Kings are exposed. How should White go for a win, without incurring undue losing chances?

44 N–K2!!

Only so! The small number of pawns remaining means that the winning chances in the endgame after 44 QxQ?! are scant. White very correctly reasons that with three pieces his attacking prospects against Black's King are considerably better than those Black's two pieces can marshall against White's King. Correspondingly, White's three pieces can also provide greater protection for his King than Black's two pieces can for his King. Thus White has the best of both worlds: greater attacking prospects and a more secure defense. He expects, therefore, that he will be able to consolidate his King position and then will be able to start on a successful attack.

44 . . . R–B3

Black seeks to set up a firm defensive formation. The active 44 . . . R–N8ch would be parried as follows: 45 K–R2! R–B8 46 Q–Q4ch K–N1 47 B–Q5ch K–B1 48 Q–R8ch K–K2 49 Q–K5ch K–Q1 50 Q–Q6ch K–K1 51 Q–K6ch K–Q1 52 B–N2! R–B7 53 QxNPch etc.

45 B–B3!

Preventing 45 . . . Q–KB8ch.

45 . . . Q–QR8   46 N–Q4 Q–R7ch   47 K–N3!

Since White wants to use all his pieces for action, he doesn't want to interpolate any of them. The King is placed both more usefully (actively!) and safely on the third rank than on the first or second ranks.

47 . . . K–N2   48 Q–K7ch Q–B2   49 Q–K5! K–R1

Black should refrain from creating any new weaknesses. In the game Black played 49 . . . P–KR4?, and resigned after 50 B–Q5, in view of 50 . . . Q–N3   51 N–K6ch K–R3   52 B–K4! RxN   53 Q–R8ch.

50 B–Q5 Q–KN2   51 N–B5 Q–B1   52 N–K7 K–R2   53 B–K4ch K–N2   54 K–N2!!

Black's pieces are just barely able to defend the Kingside. White now uses his King to put Black in *zugzwang*, and thus forces him to disrupt the delicate coordination of his forces. Pawn moves on the Queenside are immaterial, and after. . .

54 . . . K–B2   55 B–Q5ch K–N2   56 N–N8, White wins

Purely defensive consolidation is illustrated by the further play from Diagram 74, V. Ciocaltea–M. Najdorf, Nice Olympiad 1974, after Black's 33rd move:

34 K–Q2!!

Truly a multi-purpose consolidating move: protecting the B and R, not allowing . . . QxP with check as in the game, getting the King off the awkward first rank, preventing the pinning . . . B–N5, and allowing the King to get to the third rank for both defensive and offensive purposes. It is an after-the-game recommendation by Ciocaltea—in the game itself he blundered with 34 BxB?? QxPch   35 R–Q3?! (somewhat better 35 K–K2) 35 . . . Q–R8ch   36 K–Q2 QxPch   37 K–B3 Q–QN7ch White resigns.

34 . . . B–N5

34 . . . R–B2 is parried by 35 Q–B4!, and 34 . . . RxR 35 QxR BxB is met by 36 KxB!, to be followed by heading for Black's QRP with K–B4 and K–N4.

35 Q–B4 Q–Q1   36 Q–B6 R–Q2   37 QxQch RxQ   38 K–B3!, with equal chances.

DIAGRAM 74

BLACK

WHITE

Ciocaltea–Najdorf
Nice 1974 Olympiad
after Black's 33rd

After winning the QRP, White will have an extra Q-side pawn to compensate for Black's Kingside majority. White's doubled QP is without significance.

A more involved strategic defensive plan is demonstrated from Diagram 75, T. Petrosian–I. Boleslavsky, 1949 USSR Championship, after Black's 23rd move. The position is unbalanced and unclear. Yet one aspect of it is certain: Black plans an attack along the KN file. Petrosian fashions a creative method of minimizing the threat, based on an active King:

24 K–R2! K–R1 25 PxP! PxP 26 K–N3!

This move makes clear the idea behind White's previous move. The King is to be used for blockading the KNP (and KN file), and the pawn exchange has robbed Black of the opportunity of playing . . . NPxP himself, thereby opening the KN file at his own convenience. Another point of the text move is that it frees the KR file for rapid mobilization of White's Rooks.

26 . . . R–B1 27 R–KR1 R–B4 28 R–R4 P–R4 29 R/1–KR1 B–B2 30 Q–B3

Faulty is 30 RxNP? because of 30 . . . RxKP!

DIAGRAM 75

BLACK

WHITE
Petrosian–Boleslavsky
1949 USSR
Championship
after Black's 23rd

30 . . . B–R3! 31 R–KB1

Both sides maneuver with precision and creativity, and the chances remain in balance. Again White can't win material, since 31 QxP? is met strongly by 31 . . . RxQP!!.

31 . . . Q–B2 32 Q–B2 P–K3 33 Q–B4 B–B1 34 R/1–KR1 K–N1! 35 Q–K2 BxN 36 PxB R–Q4

Black has a firm position and threatens to start operations along the Q-file. Therefore, Petrosian chooses an unexpected drawing combination.

37 QxPch!? Draw

After 37 . . . PxQ 38 R–R8ch K–N2 39 R/1–R7ch K–N3 40 R–R6ch K–N2 41 R/6–R7ch! White has perpetual check. It is worth pointing out again how well White's King on KN3 consolidated the position.

The following two examples show the defender juggling his forces in utmost precision so as to enable his position to hang by a thread. To be successful in consolidating complicated, tactical, wild and wooly positions, necessary are great care, good nerves, and the ability fully to utilize the King's defensive powers. We'll first consider the position of Diagram 76, V. Jansa–V. Raicevic, Vrnjaćka Banja 1978, after White's 26th move. White has sacrificed a piece for two pawns and aimed (erroneously!) for this position. His prospects seem bright: he threatens 27 NxR, and, if the Rook moves, he wins by 27 B–N5. Yet note how easily Black's King helps to consolidate his position:

DIAGRAM 76

BLACK

WHITE

Jansa–Raicevic
Vrnjaćka Banja 1978
after White's 26th

26 . . . K–K1!   27 NxR

Of course, 27 B–N5? fails to 27 . . . RxNPch. But with Black's KN protected, Black has little need to fear the text, since the weaknesses in White's King position give Black excellent attacking chances.

27 . . . QxN   28 B–K3 P–Q5   29 R–B7?!

Looks better than it is, since Black would have developed his QB in any case. The immediate 29 B–B4 gave better defensive prospects.

29 . . . B–Q2   30 B–B4 R–N1!   31 B–N3 Q–Q1!   32 R/K–QB1 B–N3!   33 Q–R8

Black has carefully consolidated the position and is ready to throw White back along a wide front, e.g. 33 R/7–B2 P–Q6 34 R–Q2 B–B3, followed by 35 . . . Q–Q4. White—in mutual time pressure—therefore tries a few tactical tricks but doesn't come close to achieving anything. Of course, 33 . . . BxR?? loses to 34 Q–R5ch, but Black's Queen now returns to activity, with decisive effect.

33 . . . Q–N4 34 P–KR4 QxNP 35 RxB KxR 36 Q–B6 Q–N3! 37 Q–B3 K–K1! 38 Q–N3 N–Q2

Black has fully consolidated his piece advantage and now wins in a walk.

39 P–R4 P–Q6 40 K–R2 P–Q7 41 R–Q1 B–R4 42 Q–B4 P–N4 43 PxP PxP 44 Q–R2 B–N5 45 Q–N3 Q–N5 46 Q–B2 K–Q1! 47 R–QR1 R–B1 48 Q–Q3 Q–QB5 49 Q–N6 Q–QB8 50 Q–N5ch B–K2 White resigns

Truly a marvelous performance of consolidation—and against the premier attacking player of our time—is demonstrated by Black from the following position, M. Tal–I. Platonov, 1969 USSR Championship, after White's 31st move. White: K—c1 Q—e3 R—d4 N—f4 P—b3, c2, e5, g5 Black: K—d8 Q—b6 R—g7 B—c8 N—d7 P—a6, d5, e6. Black is up a piece for a pawn, but his pieces seem in a complete bind. For ultimate success, Black must first prevent all of White's threats and then try to win thanks to his extra piece (i.e. the Bishop, which presently looks completely toothless and without scope). There are no shortages of land mines, as the following analysis by Reshevsky shows:

(1.) 31 . . . RxP? 32 NxKPch

(2.) 31 . . . N–B1? 32 RxPch

(3.) 31 . . . N–B4?! 32 NxQP! PxN 33 RxPch

(4.) 31 . . . K–K2?! 32 P–N6! N–B1 33 Q–QB3 NxP
      (if 33 . . .) B–Q2 34 RxP! Q–N8ch 35 R–Q1; if 33
      . . . B–N2 34 R–N4) 34 QxB QxR 35 Q–B7ch
      K–K1 36 Q–B8ch, with a perpetual check draw.

Platonov sidesteps the first set of mines by playing:

31 . . . K–K1! 32 N–R5 R–R2!

There is no win with 32 . . . RxP?! 33 QxR QxR 34 Q–N8ch K–K2 35 Q–N5ch! and White has again perpetual check—the second mine.

33 N–B6ch

33 P–N6? loses to 33 . . . RxN 34 P–N7 K–B2!—Black's King can reach the KNP.

33 . . . NxN 34 KPxN R–R8ch 35 K–N2 R–R5!

Thanks to neat tactics, Black forces White to weaken his King position. If now the "trappy" 36 P–B7ch?, 36 . . . K–B1! stops and soon wins the KBP.

36 P–B3 R–R7ch!

The present impotence of Black's Bishop means that there is no win in 36 . . . RxR?! 37 PxR K–B2 38 Q–R3! QxQPch 39 K–R2 Q–K5 40 Q–R8, and Black has nothing better than himself to give perpetual check.

37 K–R3 R–QB7! 38 Q–R3 Q–R4ch 39 R–QR4 Q–B4ch 40 R–QN4 P–R4!

Black can't let White mobilize his KNP; therefore only a draw results after 40 . . . QxP?! 41 QxQ RxQ 42 R–KR4! R–N6 43 R–R8ch K–B2 44 R–R7ch! K–N1 45 R–N7ch K–B1 46 P–N6! P–K4 47 R–B7ch K–N1 48 R–N7ch etc. (Reshevsky).

41 Q–R8ch K–Q2 42 Q–R7ch K–B3 43 QxR PxRch 44 K–R2 PxP 45 P–N6 P–K4!

Finally liberating the Bishop, yet obviously White's passed pawns must be treated with utmost respect.

46 P–B7 B–K3! 47 Q–Q3 Q–B7ch!

The last significant mine was 47 . . . P–B7?! 48 Q–R6ch K–B2 49 P–B8 = Q QxQ 50 Q–R7ch K–B3 51 Q–R6ch K–Q2 52 Q–N7ch K–K1 53 Q–N8ch K–K2 54 Q–N4ch! K–Q2 55 Q–N7ch, again with perpetual check (Reshevsky).

48 K–R3 Q–R2ch! 49 K–N4 Q–B4ch 50 K–R4 P–B7 51 P–B8 = Q Q–R2ch 52 K–N4 Q–N2ch 53 K–R4 P–B8 = Q

Thanks to having the Bishop, Black's King is safe, whereas the death of White's King is only a matter of time.

54 Q/B–B1 QxQ   55 QxQ Q–R2ch   56 K–N4 Q–B4ch   57 K–R4 K–N3! White resigns

Black's King move prepared mates by 58 . . . Q–R4 or 58 . . . B–Q2; after the forced 58 P–N4, mate also is imminent: 58 . . . Q–B7ch 59 K–R3 P–Q5 etc.

CHAPTER 16
Active in Defense

In the previous two chapters, the main function of the King was to protect something nearby. For this the King's activity had to be very accurate but in small steps. There come times, however, when the King must become very active—verily like a busy bee—to ensure that he or his army remain alive.

Sometimes—though, it must be stressed, not too often—the King can successfully attempt to challenge his attackers in broad daylight. This is illustrated by the play from the following position, I. Ramane–L.Fismane, USSR 1977, after White's 17th move. White: K—g1 Q—e5 R—a1, f5 B—c1 P—a2, b2, c2, d3, g2, h2 Black: K—f7 Q—d7 R—g8, h8 B—f6 P—a7, b7, c5, d5, e7, h6. White seems to have started a strong attack, yet his Queenside is undeveloped and the Q and KR loosely placed. Black can exploit these factors by the surprising and active

17 . . . K–N3!!

The unpinned Bishop now attacks the Queen, while the Rook is attacked twice. White can just barely achieve a draw.

In the game Black played the routine 17 . . . R–Q1?!, and after 18 R–B3 Q–N5, White could have retained an advantage with 19 Q–K2!. Instead she offered an equalizing exchange of Queens with 19 Q–B5?!, and won (in 52) only because Black seriously misplayed the adjourned position.

18 Q–N3ch!! KxR   19 Q–R3ch R–N5   20 Q–R5ch! B–N4

If 20 . . . R–N4, 21 Q–R3ch etc.

21 BxB RxB   22 Q–R3ch!

Only so, because it is important to keep Black's pieces on a string. After 22 R–KB1ch? K–K4 Black's King escapes to safety on the Queenside.

22 . . . R–N5   23 Q–R5ch! R–N4!

23 . . . K–B5? voluntarily runs into a mating net, while 23 . . . K–B3? allows a similar result after 24 R–KB1ch K–N2? 25 Q–B7. Of course, there is little logic in going into 23 . . . K–K3?! 24 QxRch.

24 Q–R3ch R–N5   25 Q–R5ch Draw

Most of the time, though, the King's activity is strictly defensive in nature. It is important to realize that an open type of King position, with defenders nearby and the King able to breathe, is often very much preferable to being caught in a safe–looking, passive box. Under such circumstances the expected safety is often illusory. These considerations come into view when considering the position in Diagram 77, Arnason–A. Miles, Reykjavik 1978, after White's 20th move. White has started a very dangerous pawn storm on the Kingside, and the danger to Black is obvious, e.g. 20 . . . PxP? 21 QxRP, and Black has no satisfactory move, since after 21 . . . N–B3, 22 P–N5 pushes the Knight back, while 21 . . . P–B3 is exceedingly passive. Only by either giving his King air or blockading White's Kingside avalanche can Black look forward to good prospects. Black has long–term strategic opportunities, (QB attacking White's KP, while White's KB is without scope)—but the immediate need is to survive in the short term! Black played:

20 . . . N–B3!!   21 PxP N–R2!   22 P–B6?

White overvalues his prospects. The opening of the position leads to more opportunities for Black than for White, and Black's King on the third rank will be more secure than White's on the first. Correct was 22 Q–K3!, and after 22 . . . Q–K2 White could either go for sharpness with 23 P–B6!? or solidity with 23 N–N3. In either case the chances would be in balance.

22 . . . NxNP!   23 PxP KxP   24 Q–K3 P–B3   25 N–N3 QR–Q1   26 N–R5 ch K–N3!

DIAGRAM 77

BLACK

WHITE

Arnason–Miles
Reykjavik 1978
after White's 20th

The King is safe here, giving important support to the KBP (and therefore also to the Knight), allowing Black potential play along the KR file—and even serving to undermine White's Knight position (see Move 34!).

27 RxR RxR   28 R-KB1 R-KB1   29 R-B5 N-R2!   30 R-B2 B-B1!   31 B-R4! Q-K2!   32 B-B6 N-N4   33 R-N2 BxP!   34 RxB KxN   35 Q-K2! Q-K3!

At the moment the active King should stand his ground since 35 . . . K-N3?! 36 R-R4 gives White definite attacking chances.

36 R-N3ch?

After this routine move, Black's King returns to safety and his material and positional superiority is soon decisive. Miles has analyzed as correct for White the fascinating sacrifice 36 Rx-Ndb1 ch!, with the likely continuation being 36 . . . KxR 37 Q-Q2ch! K-N3 38 Q-N2ch K-B2! 39 B-Q5 QxB 40 KPxQ! R-KN1 41 QxRch KxQ, with the K and P endgame leading to a superior—but not necessarily won—Q and P endgame for Black.

36 . . . K–N3 37 B–Q5 Q–B1 38 Q–N2 R–R1 39 R–B3 R–R5
40 R–B5 R–B5 41 B–B7ch KxB 42 QxN RxR 43 QxR QxQ 44
PxQ K–N2 45 K–B2 K–R3 46 K–B3 K–N4 47 K–K4 P–R4 48
P–N3 K–N5 49 K–Q5 K–B5! 50 KxP P–K5 White resigns

The most common *active* defensive maneuver for the King is
simply scampering away from danger to safety. This can take
place in many contexts. The easiest route is in your own
territory under reasonable shelter. Diagram 78, N. Bakos–E.
Mednis, Canadian Open 1956, after White's 23rd move,
provides a thematic illustration. White has sacrificed a piece to
open up Black's Kingside and gain an annoying pawn outpost on
KB6. Clearly Black is unsafe on the Kingside and he must head
back toward the center:

23 . . . K–B1! 24 R–K3 NxBP!

DIAGRAM 78

BLACK

WHITE

Bakos–Mednis
Canadian Open 1956
after White's 23rd

Black must use the extra piece to get counterplay; otherwise
White will build up a menacing attack.

25 R–QB3 Q–K4! 26 RxN QxB/7 27 P–B4 QxP! 28 P–B5
P–K4!

The position must be kept as closed as possible.

29 QxP K–K2!

The King is best sheltered behind the closed center, and, additionally, this allows both Rooks to be mobilized against White's Kingside.

30 BxP R–R1   31 Q–B3 QR–KN1   32 P–R3 K–B1   33 B–K4 R–R5   34 Q–K3 Q–N4   35 Q–R7 K–N2!

To activate his Queen, Black had to give up blockading the KBP. White therefore threatened 36 P–B6, followed by 37 Q–R8ch. An immediate 35 . . . RxB? is met by 36 Q–R8ch, followed by 37 QxR. Therefore, Black's King again scampers to safety. This is now on the Kingside, with Black's pieces there having completely supplanted White's.

36 P–B6ch K–R3!   37 K–R1?!

In a hopeless position White speeds up the loss by overlooking Black's major tactical threat.

37 . . . RxB White resigns

Successful King scurrying, under more open conditions, but still pretty much restricted to one's own side of the board, occurs in the play arising from the position, M. Tal–A. Suetin, 1958 USSR Championship, after White's 27th move. White: K—f2 Q—h6 R—b1, f3 B—e3 P—a3, c3, e4, g2, h2 Black: K—g8 Q—c7 R—d1, d8 B—c4 P—a7, b7, e7, f6, g6. Tal threatens 28 QxPch K–B1   29 B–R6mate, to which 27 . . . P–KN4? is no defense because of 28 Q–N6ch K–B1   29 BxNP. The passive 27 . . . B–B2? loses after 28 R–R3. Therefore Black's King has to take his life in its own hands:

27 . . . K–B2!

The King both protects the KNP and gives itself the opportunity to flee to K3.

28 Q–R7ch K–K3   29 Q–R3ch

Since White has no time for 29 RxR RxR   30 QxNP?? because of 30 . . . R–KB8mate, Tal tries a combination.

29 . . . K–B2   30 RxBPch! KxR

And not 30 . . . PxR?? because 31 Q–R7ch wins the Queen.

31 Q–B3ch K–K3!   32 RxR RxR   33 QxR QxP   34 Q–N4ch K–B2   35 BxP Q–Q3!

Black has kept up with White through all the bloodletting, and now recovers his pawn to reach full equality.

36 B–Q4 QxP   37 Q–B4ch K–K1   38 Q–N8ch K–B2   39 Q–B7 B–R3 Draw

The previous examples of King activity for defense were child's play compared to what Black's King has to go through in the play arising from Diagram 79, Karker–A. Andersson, Correspondence 1977, after White's 20th move. White has sacrificed a full piece to get at Black's King and his prospects look bright. How is Black to defend himself?

20 . . . K–Q2!

DIAGRAM 79

BLACK

WHITE

Karker–Andersson
Corr. 1977
after White's 20th

Black plans to consolidate his material superiority by King activity—but not King foolishness (20 . . . KxR?? loses the Queen to 21 B–N5ch)! Not only does Black's Queen now aim at White's Rook, but after the follow-up 21 . . . B–K2 Black would be quite safe. Therefore White must stoke the fire with more material.

21 RxQB! KxR   22 Q–N4ch K–Q4!

The Kingside is unsafe: 22 . . . K–B2   23 Q–R5ch! K–N1   24 Q–N4ch B–N2?? (24 . . . K–B2 is a draw) 25 Q–K6ch K–B1   26 R–KB1ch and White wins. Therefore Black tries to flee to the Queenside.

23 R–Q1ch K–B3   24 Q–QB4ch K–N2   25 QxNPch K–B1   26 R–Q3 Q–Q2   27 B–N5!

To prevent the King from fleeing via Q1.

27 . . . R–R2   28 B–B6 B–N2   29 BxB QxB   30 QxP P–K5!   31 R–QN3!

White is a whole Rook down, but the exposed position of Black's King gives White exactly enough play for perpetual check.

31 . . . R–N2   32 R–QB3ch R–QB2   33 QxPch K–N1   34 Q–QN6ch R–N2   35 Q–Q6ch K–R1   36 Q–QR6ch!

But not 36 R–QR3ch? R–R2   37 Q–B6ch Q–N2, and Black has successfully regrouped.

36 . . . K–N1

Not 36 . . . R–R2?? 37 R–B8ch RxR   38 QxR/8mate!

37 Q–Q6ch R–B2 Draw

After 38 Q–QN6ch K–B1   39 Q–QR6ch Black's King must go back to QN1 because 39 . . . K–Q1?? loses the Queen after 40 Q–R8ch! K–Q2   41 RxRch KxR   42 Q–R7ch.

CHAPTER 17
The King in the Open

Just as it was true in the opening, so also in the middlegame the King feels decidedly uncomfortable when in the open. But how inherently insecure is he? The next three sections will take a quantitative look at this.

SECTION 1. The King Is Unsafe

The King caught in the open in the middle of the board, with lots of attackers swarming over it and without at least a preponderance of defenders to assist it, is in the long run a sitting duck. The King will be lost unless the defending side has a material advantage to work with and/or strong attacking prospects someplace else. The latter situation will force the erstwhile attacker to put forth less than maximum effort, because part of his force is required for defensive work.

The dividing line between being safe or unsafe is always thin. Just a small misstep separates life from death. The type of situation that exists so often is illustrated by the following position, E. Mednis–D. Minic, Mannheim 1975, after White's 36th move. White: K—h1 Q—h6 R—f1, g3 P—a2, b3, c4, g2, h2 Black: K—f7 Q—d4 R—d2, e8 P—a6, b7, f5, g6. White has his Queen and two Rooks pointing at Black's King, which is just off the center and protected by the thin cover of two Black pawns. It should be clear that disaster can strike any moment. White also has an obvious threat in the position (37 QxPch). How should Black protect himself against it?

36 . . . R–K3?

Not this active, obvious way, because White also has another threat. Of course, 36 . . . Q–B3?? leaves a Rook hanging; therefore necessary was the passive looking 36 . . . R–KN1!. I was then planning 37 Q–N5 (reintroducing the threat 38 RxPch) 37 . . . R–N2 38 R–K3!. Black can improve however, with 37 . . . R–KB7! and retain excellent drawing chances. But after the text, the Black King's head will roll because White can open the position decisively.

37 RxBPch! PxR   38 Q–R7ch! Black resigns

The choice is between a routine mate after 38 . . . K–B1   39 R–N8, or a poetic one after 38 . . . K–B3   39 Q–N7.

It is not only in an open center that the King is unsafe; the edge of the board is almost equally bad. If the attacking side has a total grip on the position, then the King's chances are nil. Such a situation exists in Diagram 80, Rudenski–Sineljnikov, USSR 1978, after Black's 28th move. White's forces control the board (at no investment in material) and all that is required for victory is to open up Black's King position some more. Therefore:

29 P–KR4! PxP

DIAGRAM 80

BLACK

WHITE

Rudenski–Sineljnikov
USSR 1978
after Black's 28th

There is nothing else. If 29 . . . R–N1, 30 RxPch! (the threat in the position) 30 . . . QxR 31 PxPch KxP 32 QxQ; if 29 . . . P–N5 30 Q–K7 P–N4 31 RxPch! QxR 32 QxNPmate—note how exposed the King is on the edge.

30 Q–K7! P–N4 31 Q–K6ch K–R4 32 P–KN4ch!

Opening the position!

32 . . . PxPe.p. 33 Q–R3ch K–N3 34 Q–B5ch K–R3 35 R–Q7!

With the threat 36 RxQPch K–N2 37 Q–B6mate. Black loses the Queen after 35 . . . Q–N3 36 Q–R3ch Q–R4 37 RxKR-Pch!.

35 . . . R–KB1 36 RxQPch K–N2 37 Q–K5ch K–B2 38 Q–B6ch Black resigns

The King has been chased from an unsafe position on the edge to certain death in the center (38 . . . K–K1 39 R–Q8).

Even where the attacker's position is less overwhelming than in the previous example, unless the King can set up a line of defenders (pawns and pieces) he will be punished on an open edge. The following position arose in L. Evans–I. Dorfman, Sao Paulo 1978, after Black's 37th move. White: K—h1 Q—f3 R—c5 P—a3, b4, f4, g3, h2 Black: K—h7 Q—d7 R—d4 P—a6, e6, f7, g6, g7. His complete control of the Q-file means that Black is ready to head for White's insecure King. The center is too open for White's King to think of heading there, but Black will prove that the edge is also unsafe. To prolong the game White should have played 38 R–B1, though after 38 . . . R–Q6 Black wins the QRP for starters while remaining with the much superior position. As played, White will get mated:

38 R–B2?! R–Q6 39 Q–B6 R–Q8ch! 40 K–N2 Q–Q6

The threat is 41 . . . Q–B8mate, while 41 Q–B4? loses heavy material after 41 . . . R–Q7ch. To prevent immediate disaster White had to play 41 R–B2, though after 41 . . . QxRP Black does have a won position. White doesn't want to part with his material, yet the King will be shown to be hopelessly unsafe on the edge.

41 K–R3?! R–KN8! 42 Q–B5 Q–B8ch 43 K–R4 R–N7!!
White resigns

After 44 RxR QxR 45 P–R3 Q–B6! White's King is caught in
a mating net, the threat being 46 . . . P–B4! and 47 . . .
Q–R4mate. After 46 Q–KN5 Black first plays 46 . . . QxRP,
stopping White's Queenside hopes and then returns with his
Queen to the Kingside.

In the previous examples, the attacking side could get the
defender's King in the open at no material cost. This, of course,
is the ideal situation. The most important practical question
when attacking is how much material to give up to achieve
various levels of enemy King "exposure?" A proper answer is of
great importance for both sides, so that the attacker is not
overconfident in his actions, nor the defender too complacent in
organizing his defenses. These principles are brought out very
well in the course of play from Diagram 81, L. Pachman–T.
Petrosian, Portoroz Interzonal 1958, after White's 18th move.

DIAGRAM 81

BLACK

WHITE

Pachman–Petrosian
Portoroz 1958
after White's 18th

Black has sacrificed his Queen for R and N—materially insufficient compensation, yet not a major investment, either. For
his material inferiority, Black has certain positional com-

pensation: completed development, active piece placement, absence of readily vulnerable points, and White's King presently in the center along the open Q-file. Subsequent analysis has shown that Black in fact has the superior chances. However, White—under the impression that Black's Queen sacrifice was more necessary than strong—has the mistaken feeling that it is he who has the superior chances. Therefore, White pays insufficient attention to drawing opportunities because he thinks he should win!

18 . . . P–K5!

Opens the KB's diagonal and gains some space in White's territory, at the same time limiting the range of White's KB. White therefore tries to undermine this outpost, but at the cost of loosening his position.

19 P–B3 QR–Q1ch   20 K–K1

The King won't be safe here, but neither is it safe after 20 K–B1 N–Q5 21 BxN RxB, when Black's Rook will wind up with decisive effect on Q7.

20 . . . N–Q5

Perfectly O.K., yet even more unpleasant for White would have been 20 . . . KR–K1!, and if then 21 P–B4, 21 . . . N–Q5!.

21 BxN BxB   22 PxP NxP

Now White could have obtained fair drawing chances in the R and opposite–color Bishop endgame after 23 QxN! KR–K1 24 QxRch RxQch. White doesn't play thus because he erroneously thinks that he can consolidate his material advantage. Black, for his part, should not have given White the above opportunity and instead continued with 22 . . . KR–K1!.

23 B–K2? KR–K1   24 R–B1 R–K2   25 R–B3 R/1–K1   26 R–Q3 B–N8

We still have the same force equivalence as in the diagram, and, with White's King in the open, Black has a winning attack.

27 P–R3 B–B7ch!

The definitive winning line, as analyzed by Gligoric and Matanovic. The game course was 27 ... B–R7   28 B–B3! B–N6ch   29 K–Q1 N–B7ch   30 K–Q2 B–B5ch   31 K–B3 NxR   32 KxN R–K6ch   33 K–Q4 B–R3   34 P–B5 P–QN4!   35 BxP?? (After 35 P–B6! White has good chances for the draw since his King can escape mate threats.)   35 ... B–N2ch   36 K–Q5 R/1–K3!, and White overstepped the time limit searching in vain for a defense to 37 ... R/6–K4ch, to be followed by a devastating discovered check.

28 K–Q1

28 K–B1? N–N6ch leads to an endgame where White is a piece down.

28 ... B–R5!   29 B–B3

Black will now be a tempo ahead of the game continuation and this is sufficient to win. White's other tries (as given by Gligoric and Matanovic) are:

(1.) 29 K–B1 N–B7   30 B–Q1 NxRch   31 QxN R–K8   32 Q–Q4 B–N4ch   33 K–B2 R–Q1   34 Q–N4 R–Q7ch   35 K–N3 B–B3—Black wins

(2.) 29 R–KB3 R–Q2ch   30 B–Q3 R/1–Q1   31 K–K2 N–B4—Black wins

29 ... N–B7ch   30 K–Q2 B–N4ch   31 K–B3 NxR   32 KxN R–K6ch   33 K–Q4 B–B3ch   34 K–Q5 R–Q1mate

If, at the time we start active play, it is possible to get the enemy King out into the open, then often considerably more sacrificing is affordable. What can be considered a "typical Tal" position is shown below: M. Tal–Miagmarsuren, Nice Olympiad 1974, after Black's 22nd move. White: K—g1 Q—g7 R—a1 B—c1 N—f5 P—a3, c3, f2, g2, h2 Black: K—e6 Q—d8 R—a8, e8 B—b7 N—e5 P—a7, b6, h6. Black's development is essentially complete and his pieces do not stand particularly badly. Nevertheless, Tal felt little reluctance in sacrificing a whole Rook (for 2 pawns) to bring about this position. His benchmark was clear: Black's King is completely open (note that there are no pawns along either Q or K files). Black's King is shown to be unsafe as follows:

23 N–Q4ch K–Q3   24 B–B4!!

Bringing maximum attacking power against the King (while completing his development) is the consistent way to handle such a position. Tal admits that when he originally went into the combination he anticipated recovering the sacrificed material with 24 QxB, but now noted that after 24 . . . Q–Q2! he is forced to exchange Queens, because 25 Q–K4?? is refuted by 25 . . . N–B6ch.

24 . . . B–Q4   25 R–K1 K–B4!?   26 RxN!

White has gotten his piece anyway, and under favorable circumstances. After 26 . . . R–KN1   27 Q–N7! is very strong, so Black must exchange. Despite the lack of a Rook, White's Q and two minor pieces can exert sufficient threats against Black's open King.

26 . . . RxR   27 QxR Q–Q2   28 N–B2 R–K1   29 Q–Q4ch

Not clear is 29 B–K3ch K–N4   30 P–QB4ch?! KxP   31 Q–Q4ch K–N4   32 Q–Q3ch K–B3   33 N–N4ch K–N2   34 QxBch QxQ   35 NxQ R–Q1   36 N–B3 R–Q6 (Tal).

29 . . . K–B3   30 P–B4 B–K3   31 Q–K4ch! K–B4   32 P–R3!!

By making air for his King, White prevents back–rank mates and thereby any and all of Black's potential counterplay. Now Black's King will not be able to resist the coordinated attack of White's pieces.

32 . . . B–B4   33 B–K3ch K–Q3   34 Q–B4ch K–K2   35 N–Q4
Black resigns

After 35 . . . B–K3   36 Q–R4ch K–B2   37 QxP White has 3 pawns for the Exchange and an overwhelming position. Since Black saw no satisfactory defensive plan, he resigned.

When we sacrifice to open the enemy King position we would like to have the King completely open. Where this ultimate objective is not possible, a "semi-open" condition may be perfectly satisfactory as a goal, as long as the sacrifice is not too expensive. Such a condition exists in Diagram 82, E. Torre–R. Byrne, Leningrad Interzonal 1973, after Black's 28th move. Black has sacrificed the Exchange for a pawn and thus is about ½–pawn down. But look what he has at this minor cost: an open KB file, an active centrally placed Queen, a Bishop attacking White's key QP, and White's King being uncomfortably and loosely placed in the center. White just can't organize any kind of a satisfactory defense:

29 R/1–N2

DIAGRAM 82

BLACK

WHITE

Torre–Byrne
Leningrad 1973
after Black's 28th

Worse is 29 R/3–N2?! R–B6! 30 R–Q2 BxP! 31 RxB QxKPch and Black wins.

29 . . . Q–R8ch 30 K–K2 R–B8! 31 Q–Q2 R–QN8 32 Q–N5

The immediate attempt at fleeing, 32 K–B3, fails to 32 . . . Q–B3ch 33 K–K3 (33 K–N4 R–KB8 34 Q–N5 Q–B1, and the King open on the edge will soon be lost) 33 . . . Q–Q5ch 34 K–B4 P–K4ch 35 K–N4 Q–Q2ch 36 K–R4 R–KB8, and again the King will be cornered and killed.

32 . . . R–K8ch 33 K–B3 Q–Q8ch 34 K–B4 R–B8ch 35 K–K5 Q–R8ch

Though in the diagram above the King seemed at least somewhat sheltered, note how quickly he has been driven into the open for certain death. If now 36 K–Q6, 36 . . . Q–Q5ch 37 K–B6 R–B2 etc.

36 KxP B–B1ch 37 K–Q6 R–B3ch 38 K–B7 B–K3! 39 P–Q4 QxQP 40 R–Q2 R–B2ch 41 K–N8 QxP White resigns

There is no reasonable way of preventing . . . Q–QN2mate. Note how successful, in practical terms, Black has been: not only has White's King been chased across the open board to its imminent death, but Black here even has a slight *material* advantage!

SECTION 2. The King Is Safe

For the King to be safe when out in the open, one of the following basic conditions must exist:

(1.) The King's side has such a commanding positional superiority that the opponent has no prospects of organizing a coordinated assault, or

(2.) The King's side has a sufficient material advantage so that the preponderance of defenders can beat back the attackers.

There are various shadings of these conditions, of course, and these will be explored as part of this section. The situations where the King is safe because its forces are able first to achieve decisive victory someplace else were discussed in Chapter 13 ("To be or not to be afraid").

The kind of position which is obviously overpowering is illustrated in the following position, J.R. Capablanca–A. Schroeder, New York 1916, after Black's 23rd move. White: K—e1 Q—g5 R—c1, h1 P—a4, b3, e3, f2, g2, h2 Black: K—d6 Q—a5 R—a8, e8 B—c5 P—a7, b4, e6, f7. White has sacrificed a piece for two pawns to drive Black's King into the open, yet needs his KR to hope to finish the job. The safe, obvious move, therefore, is 24 0–0, and it is O.K. The course of play however, may well require White to enter an endgame, and in such a case White's King at KN1 would be far away from any potential action. Therefore

Capablanca chooses a King move whereby he can kill both birds: mobilizing the KR and placing his King advantageously for the endgame.

24 K–K2!

The King is perfectly safe here since neither Black's Queen nor Rooks have a prayer of getting at it (24 . . . Q–R3ch 25 R–B4 leads to nothing) and Black's KB is obviously impotent as an attacker.

24 . . . QR–B1 25 R–B4 K–B3 26 KR–QB1 K–N3 27 P–R4!

With all of Black's pieces in a bind White sets the KRP in motion for its winning run. Black is lost; the main line, according to Capablanca, goes as follows: 27 . . . R–B2 28 P–R5 R/1–QB1 29 P–R6 B–Q3 30 QxQch KxQ 31 RxR RxR (after 31 . . . BxR?! 32 R–B6! all of Black's pieces are paralyzed) 32 RxR BxR 33 P–B4 B–Q1 34 P–N4 B–B3 35 P–N5 B–R1 36 P–K4 K–N3 37 P–B5 PxP 38 PxP K–B4 39 P–N6 PxP 40 PxP, followed by 41 P–N7. It is true that in this variation the pawns win by themselves with no need for assistance from the King. Yet from the practical side it is good to be in a position for the King to be able to help, if required. *No one* could exactly foresee this variation when contemplating the diagram position.

The above analysis shows that Black is theoretically lost; in the game the end comes very quickly.

27 . . . P–B4?! 28 Q–N7! R–K2 29 Q–K5 R–B3?! 30 RxB!
Black resigns

After 30 . . . RxR 31 Q–Q6ch is decisive.

Unquestionably White's King is more open in the position below, B. Spassky–A. Miles, Bugojno 1978, after Black's 25th move. White: K—f1 Q—e6 R—c6 N—b3 P—a2, c2, c3, g3, h2 Black: K—h8 Q—e8 R—d8 B—f6 P—a7, e7, g6, h7. Yet White's Q and R exert such a bind over Black's position that the King can remain safely on KB1 while White activates his Knight:

26 N–B5! BxP 27 N–K4

The Knight is now ideally placed for both offense and defense.

27 . . . B–Q5   28 P–B3 B–N3   29 K–K2!

With White's pieces controlling the board and with access to White's Q2 and KB2 squares denied to Black, White centralizes his King both for potential endgame play and to prevent any checks along the KB file.

29 . . . Q–Q2   30 QxQ RxQ   31 P–B4 R–Q5?!   32 N–N5 P–KR3?

White's passed QBP gives him a decisive advantage in any case, but the text loses heavy material. The only move to prolong resistance was the retreat 32 . . . R–Q2.

33 R–B8ch Black resigns

Now we come to the cases where King safety is based on having considerable material advantage. An effective defensive strategy in many such situations is to give back some of the material in order to break the back of the attack by removing a sufficient number of attackers from the board. Consider the play from Diagram 83, D. Bronstein–J. Nogueiras, Jurmala (Riga) 1978, after Black's 20th move. The position is starting to look both equal and barren and heading for a draw. Such a prospect is of no interest to Bronstein, and he prefers to sacrifice a Rook for "nothing":

21 RxP?! KxR   22 B–N3 R–K4!

The Rook is actively placed here, while the discovered check can do no serious damage.

23 N–B4ch K–K1   24 Q–N4 N–K2   25 R–Q1 QxRch!!

In exchanging his Queen for 2 Rooks, Black gets full material equivalence. Additionally, White is left with insufficient force to continue the attack, while Black's Rooks quickly establish strong pressure against White's position.

26 QxQ R–Q1   27 Q–KB1 R–Q7!   28 P–KR4 R–KB4!   29 P–N3 R–K4!   30 P–N4 R–KB7   31 Q–KN1 R–Q7!, with at least full equality for Black.

DIAGRAM 83

BLACK

WHITE

Bronstein–Nogueiras
Jurmala (Riga) 1978
after Black's 20th

He can satisfy himself with a draw after 32 Q–KB1 R–KB7 33 Q–KN1 R–Q7! or perhaps look for more with a different 32nd move. In the game, Black, out of carelessness, blundered with 31 . . . RxP?, and after 32 Q–QB1 R–KB7 33 N–Q3 lost an Exchange and subsequently the game on Move 50.

An unsafe King in the center becomes safe when the material advantage useful for warding off short–term threats can be combined with attacking chances against the enemy King. A marvelous demonstration of this occurs in the play arising from the following position, L. Polugaevsky–E. Torre, Manila Interzonal 1976, after Black's 26th move. White: K—c1 Q—b4 R—g1 B—e3 N—a3, h4 P—d5, f2, h3 Black: K—h8 Q—a2 R—f8 B—e4 N—f6 P—d6, e5, h7. Black has sacrificed a full piece to rip open White's King position. White's pieces are rather scattered for effective defensive work, but they exist, are one greater in number than Black's attackers, and for the time being can protect the King. The decisive element in the position becomes the less than secure position of Black's King:

27 QxP! R–B1ch 28 K–Q1 Q–R8ch 29 K–K2 Q–N7ch

Black must continue the attack, as clearly hopeless is 29 . . . QxR? 30 QxNch etc.

30 B–Q2 NxP

It turns out that this can be parried fairly easily. White's task would be considerably tougher after 30 . . . B–Q6ch!? 31 K–B3! (Losing is 31 KxB? Q–Q5ch 32 K–K2 N–K5) 31 . . . N–K5 32 Q–K7!! (it's the attack that will make the difference) 32 . . . NxBch 33 K–N2 N–K5 34 N–B2!! R–KN1ch 35 K–R2 RxR 36 Q–B8ch!! R–N1 37 N–N6ch! PxN 38 Q–R6mate. Beautiful!!

31 R–N4! N–B5ch   32 K–K3!

White's King is safe because Black has no time to coordinate his forces when he himself is threatened with mate.

32 . . . N–Q4ch   33 KxB Q–Q5ch   34 K–B3 R–B6ch

White sidesteps 34 . . . P–K5ch with 35 K–N3. After the text combination, Black is left with only a Queen against an overpowering White army.

35 BxR Q–Q6ch   36 K–N2 N–B5ch   37 RxN QxQ   38 N–B3

Sufficient to win, but White could have held on to all of his pieces with 38 N–B4! Q–Q4ch 39 N–B3.

38 . . . QxN   39 BxPch K–N1   40 R–N4ch K–B2   41 R–N7ch K–K3   42 RxP Black resigns

A recurring happening in master play is the trading of one advantage for another so as to make winning easier. Sometimes such an approach is required to win, period. The kind of thinking involved is beautifully evident in the course of play arising from Diagram 84, A. Gipslis–J. Plachetka, Tiflis/Suhumi 1977, after Black's 23rd move. Black has sacrificed his QR to bring about the position shown. White's King is in the open and must cope with three Black attackers. Can White win? In a comprehensive analysis of the position, another side of Black's position appears: Black's Kingside development is incomplete. This factor becomes significant in White's ultimate success:

24 K–B3!

DIAGRAM 84

BLACK

WHITE

Gipslis–Plachetka
Tiflis/Suhumi 1977
after Black's 23rd

Only a draw results after 24 K–N3 N–B5ch as the King must head back with 25 K–B2; the active 25 K–R4?? runs into the devastating 25 . . . N–N3ch!!.

24 . . . N–K8dblch   25 K–N4!! QxRch

Black does win back the Rook, but the time spent doing so allows White to get his attack going. As Gipslis points out, the alternatives are no better:

(1.) 25 . . . NxP   26 B–B3!;
(2.) 25 . . . B–K7ch   26 K–R4;
(3.) 25 . . . P–R4ch   26 K–R4;
(4.) 25 . . . P–B3 26 QxNP, followed by 27 NxPch.

26 K–R3 Q–N6ch   27 B–B3 N–Q6   28 QxP!

White has Q, B and N in the attack, with the KR ready to join. If now 28 . . . N–B5ch,   29 K–R4! wins.

28 . . . R–B1   29 R–R1! Q–B7

This leads to a middlegame loss. The alternative was a most unsatisfactory endgame after 29 . . . Q–N3   30 P–KN3! N–B7ch   31 NxN QxN   32 QxKPch K–Q2   33 Q–Q4ch! QxQ   34 BxQ B–Q6   35 RxPch K–Q3   36 K–N4! (Gipslis).

30 BxP! Q–K7

Or 30 . . . N–B7ch 31 NxN QxN (31 . . . QxBPch 32 Q–N4) 32 RxB QxBPch 33 K–R4 Q–K5ch 34 P–KN4 Q–K8ch 35 B–N3 Q–K2ch 36 Q–N5, and White remains a safe Bishop up.

31 N–B6ch K–K2 32 B–Q6ch KxB 33 QxRch K–B2 34 QxPch K–N3 35 N–Q7ch K–N4 36 Q–N3ch

White has a winning material advantage to go with his attack. The win is assured.

36 . . . N–N5 37 Q–R4ch K–B5 38 R–QB1ch K–Q4 39 Q–Q1ch! QxQ 40 RxQch Black resigns

Section 3. The Situation Is Unclear

What we're concerned with here are the cases where one side has sacrificed material to open up the enemy King position or to chase the King into the open—but the outcome remains in doubt. A winning attack can not be demonstrated, but neither can the attack be dismissed out of hand. Of course we are concerned with the practical requirement of evaluating a position. Given an unlimited amount of time (easily upwards of, say, 200 hours), the actual condition of a middlegame position can be clarified, but who has that kind of time?

So what I'll do is discuss what type of positions should be inherently considered as unclear. If a position is thought to be unclear, there is no need to waste scarce time in "over-evaluating" it. In deciding whether or not to accept it, personal tastes and intuition become important. Here psychological factors start playing a major role. An attacking player may be perfectly happy to sacrifice a piece to bring about an "unclear" attacking position; he will be doubly happy if he knows that his opponent dislikes defending. The converse is also true: positional players will tend to "sacrifice" material when the "certainty of soundness" is high.

A revealing look at the way playing style affects such decisions is provided by Diagram 85, J. Kupper–M. Tal, Zurich 1959, after Black's 20th move. Equally illuminating is how different analysts evaluate the same "unclear" position. I'll let them speak for themselves. They are: (1) Tal, himself (attacker *par excellance*),

DIAGRAM 85

BLACK

WHITE

Kupper–Tal
Zurich 1959
after Black's 20th

(2) GM Shamkovich (daring and creative attacker) (3) GM Pachman (iron–logic strategist).

The diagram shows that Black has sacrificed a piece for a pawn to get White's King out in the open. White's defenders are well clustered around their King and nothing approaching a forced win for Black is in sight. I call this position "perfectly unclear." Tal had no lack of confidence, however, when he made his sacrifice to bring about this type of position. His words: "In sacrificing the Knight I did not calculate variations. It would be strange if after this sacrifice White were able to find a defense against Black's overwhelming attack." Black's immediate threat is obvious: 21 . . . BxN 22 KxB (22 NxB? R–B6ch wins the Queen) 22 . . . RxB. Of course 21 RxB? allows 21 . . . QxR. Therefore White decides to protect the KR:

21 Q–B2

The defensively logical 21 KR–QB1 cries out for consideration. Shamkovich doesn't even consider it; Tal dismisses it with the comment "An interesting continuation was 21 KR–QB1, after which Black would have the choice of 21 . . . BxN 22 RxB B–N3 or even the sharper 21 . . . P–K4 with very complicated play."

Pachman points out that in the first line White can defend himself for the time being with 23 R/1–QN1 QxP 24 R/7xB. During the game Tal had planned to continue with 21 . . . B–R1 22 B–N3 R–B4, after which White could play either 23 P–N5 or 23 Q–K3 (Pachman) when "the further progress of the game is hard to investigate even in analysis."

21 . . . B–R1

Tal: "The further sacrifices 21 . . . RxB or 21 . . . BxN, however tempting, do not work. After the text move all of Black's threats retain their full power."

22 KR–QB1!

Again the only sensible plan. In the game White blundered with 22 R–N3? (Shamkovich doesn't even give this a question mark) and the game ended drastically: 22 . . . P–K4! 23 P–N5 PxN 24 NxP (24 PxB RxB! 25 KxR QxPch 26 R–N2 R–B1ch) 24 . . . BxN White resigns.

Tal does query 22 R–N3? and says: "In my opinion a better chance was 22 P–N5 B–Q1 23 KR–QB1," and then confidently adds "but even then after . . . P–Q4 or . . . P–K4 the fall of White's King would be unavoidable."

The text must be played: White brings the "on-looking" KR over for critical defensive work. The further course could be

22 . . . P–K4!? 23 N–QN3! Q–N4ch 24 K–Q2 P–Q4!

Shamkovich breaks off his analysis here, convinced, just like Tal, that White must lose, with the terse comment "Black's attack is very strong." But let's continue playing:

25 K–K1 QPxP with an unclear, perhaps equal position.

Pachman concludes here with "The White King no longer faces any direct threats, but Black does have two pawns for the piece and a very active position. Both sides again have chances, just as before the start of all the complications." Instructive also is what Dr. M. Euwe (another logical strategist) says about this position: "With a good defense by White, in most cases an endgame will result where Black will have to be satisfied with having two to three pawns for the piece. Most likely a draw."

So, what's the conclusion on Diagram 85? You choose your style and draw your own conclusion! For the practical player, the important conclusion is that "it's unclear."

A special kind of "unclear positions" are those in which to retain the initiative, one must start sacrificing and continue sacrificing material; else the position would peter out in a draw. The attitude to keep in mind here is that, although, of necessity, the coming course will lead to unclear positions, the attack—if there is justice in chess—should be good enough for at least a draw.

An excellent example of the practical application of such an attitude is demonstrated by this position, A. Karpov–V. Korchnoi, 1971 Training Match, Game 3, after White's 22nd move. White: K—c1 Q—e7 R—f1 B—b5 N—d2 P—a2, b2, c2, g2, h4 Black: K—g6 Q—f2 R—a8, h8 B—f5 P—a7, b7, d5, f6, h5. White has had a clear initiative since Black committed an inaccuracy on Move 7 of a French Defense. Yet to keep up the pressure White has had to sacrifice an Exchange. Black's King is rather open, and Black must use great care in safeguarding it:

22 . . . Q–Q5!

The centralized Queen covers the widest area, and this is an absolute must for defending here. Losing are both 22 . . . QxRP? 23 RxB! KxR 24 B–Q3ch K–B5 25 Q–N4ch K–N6 (25 . . . K–N4 26 N–B3ch) 26 N–B1ch and 22 . . . QxNP? 23 RxB! KxR 24 B–Q3ch K–B5 25 QxBPch.

23 RxB!

A further sacrifice is required to get the King fully into the open. White's army of attackers is now severely depleted, however.

23 . . . KxR   24 B–Q3ch K–B5   25 Q–Q6ch Q–K4   26 Q–N4ch K–N6!

Instead in the game Black lost after 26 . . . P–Q5?! 27 N–K4! K–B4? 28 QxNP K–N5 29 B–K2ch KxP 30 P–N3ch K–R6 31 N–B2ch K–R7 32 Q–R1ch KxP 33 N–K4ch K–B5 34 Q–B3mate. Korchnoi calls this one of Karpov's best games.

The text is Korchnoi's recommendation, with the strategic point that White's Knight is kept away from the active K4 square.

27 N–B1ch KxP   28 Q–Q2ch K–R6   29 B–B5ch!?

Also unclear is 29 Q–B2 KR–N1   30 B–B5ch R–N5 (Korchnoi).
After the text, 29 . . . QxB? allows 30 Q–R2ch K–N5   31
Q–N3mate.

29 . . . KxP "Unclear," according to Korchnoi.

So it is! White should have enough to keep bothering Black's
King for a perpetual check; yet the coordination of White's pieces
isn't sufficient for a decisive attack.

In the previous example, the "unclearness" involved a King
chase. A more usual situation during an attack is where the King
position is opened up, yet the King remains in the same general
area. A typically unclear situation under such conditions is shown
in Diagram 86, D. Andreev–J. Estrin, USSR Correspondence
Championship 1977–78, after Black's 21st move. White has made
two separate combinations to arrive at this position. He's a Rook
down and obviously must continue attacking, come hell or high
water:

22 B–K5ch! NxB!

DIAGRAM 86

BLACK

WHITE

Andreev–Estrin
USSR Correspondence
Championship 1977–78
after Black's 21st move

One of the cardinal principles of successful defense is to eliminate as many attackers as possible. Therefore the text, whereby Black exchanges off his Knight for White's strong attacking Bishop, is the only move which makes sense. In the game Black unaccountably played 22 . . . K–K2?, and was forced to resign after 23 BxP!! K–Q1 24 P–Q5! R–K1 (24 . . . PxP 25 PxP N–N1 26 N–K6ch BxN 27 PxB Q–K2 28 R–Q1ch K–B1 29 BxR!! QxQ 30 P–K7 and wins) 25 PxN BxP 26 R–Q1ch K–B1 27 B–K5 Q–K2 28 N–B7!.

23 PxNch K–K2!

The King must stay near home territory. Losing are both 28 . . . KxP?? 24 QxNPch and 23 . . . KxN?? 24 P–B4ch K–N5 26 Q–N6ch K–R5 27 Q–N5mate.

24 QxNPch K–K1 25 R–Q1! R–Q1!

Using *all* his pieces for defense. Faulty is 25 . . . Q–K2? because of 26 Q–N6ch K–Q1 27 NxPch K–B1 28 NxR QxN 29 P–K6 B–B3 30 Q–R7.

26 Q–N6ch K–K2 "Unclear"

While it is true that White can force perpetual check (27 Q–N7ch etc), an attempt at winning would lead to unclear consequences.

The ultimate in unclear positions arise where both sides have attacking chances. In the position below, Gruenfeld–Stein, 1978 Israel Championship, after White's 19th move, White: K—g1 Q—d5 R—a1, f1 N—b5 P—a2, c4, e4, f2, g3, h2 Black: K—d7 Q—g5 R—a5, g8 B—c8, f8 P—d6, e5, f5, f7, h7, White has sacrificed a piece for a pawn to open up the position and have Black's King exposed in the center. White does have attacking chances, yet the only objective evaluation of the position is that it is unclear. It must also be pointed out that Black has attacking chances against the enemy King—along the KN, and, perhaps, (after a . . . P–KR4, P–R5) the KR files. White's immediate threat is 20 QxBPch, and Black prevents that and brings back his Queen for defense by playing:

19 . . . Q–B3! 20 KR–Q1 Q–K3 21 Q–B5 RxN!

The threatened 22 Q–B7ch forces this countersacrifice.

22 QxRch K-K2   23 P-B5!

Open lines is what White's Rooks need. In the game Black accommodated his opponent with 23 . . . QPxP? and lost after 24 PxP QxBP   25 Q-N6! B-Q2   26 QR-N1! Q-K3   27 Q-R7 R-N5   28 QxPch K-B3   29 QxB R-Q5   30 RxR PxR   31 R-N6!.

23 . . . K-B3!!

The King is relatively safe here, and the diagonal of Black's KB is now open. White has nothing better than to capture the QP.

24 PxQP B-Q2! "Unclear"

White's passed QP is blockaded, and materially Black has the Bishop pair to counter White's R and 2P. The advanced QP could well turn out to be weak in the endgame. With Black's King relatively safe, he can now turn to action along the KN file. All in all, the situation is unclear—and it must be appreciated that it is so.

CHAPTER 18
The King on a Forced Flight

To get at the enemy King so as to send him packing is a major goal of middlegame play. During the opening phase, a King on a forced flight is on a journey with most likely an unpleasant end. The King's chances of surviving a middlegame flight into enemy territory are even smaller, because generally the enemy pieces are already sufficiently developed and thus ready for action. Under such circumstances, even heavy material sacrifices are well worth making, just to get the enemy King in one's own territory. A typical example is the following, from Püchele–P. Feustel, East Germany 1977, White to move. White: K—g1 Q—e3 R—f1, f4 N—d4 P—d3, e6, h3 Black: K—g7 Q—a2 R—b2, h8 B—g2 P—a6, b5,e7, f6, g6, h6. Black's King has a shelter of four pawns all right, but little other support. Therefore, sweeping the pawns aside should leave the King indefensible:

1 RxP!! PxR

The win is more prosaic after 1 . . . BxR 2 R–B7ch K–N1 3 Q–K5.

2 N–B5ch! PxN 3 Q–R7ch K–N3 4 Q–B7ch K–N4 5 Q–N7ch K–R5 6 QxBPch K–N6 7 Q–K5ch KxP 8 QxPch K–N6 9 Q–B4ch K–R6 10 Q–R2ch K–N5 11 R–B4ch K–N4 12 Q–N3ch K–R4 13 R–R4mate

It was hardly surprising that the undefended Black King couldn't cope with the battery of White's Q and R.

The prospects of getting at the exposed King when he is on the enemy side of the board are so bright that very often full Queen sacrifices are affordable. Where the King's defenders are at least temporarily out of action, then it may even be sufficient to get at the King on its own side of the board. Consider Diagram 87, T. Petrosian–L. Pachman, Bled 1961, after Black's 17th move. Black's Queen is stuck on the Queenside, his Kingside is weakened and without sufficient defenders—is it any surprise that White already has a decisive combination?

18 R–K4?!

DIAGRAM 87

BLACK

WHITE

Petrosian–Pachman
Bled 1961
after Black's 17th

Ever cautious, Petrosian brings up the Rook before getting ready for the decisive blow. Immediate glory was possible with 18 QxBch!! KxQ 19 B–K5ch K–N4 20 B–N7!, and Black's King can't get back to safety. (See the game continuation for a possible finish.)

Black's position is inherently indefensible, anyway, so that from the standpoint of chess beauty, is just as well that he allows the same combination on the next move.

18 . . . R–Q1?! 19 QxBch!! KxQ 20 B–K5ch K–N4 21 B–N7!! Black resigns

There is absolutely nothing to be done about the coming 22 P–R4ch K–R4 23 B–B3mate. If 21 . . . P–K4 22 P–R4ch K–B4 23 B–R3mate.

Most of the time, though, a Queen sacrifice is followed by a traditional King chase. This is what happens in the play arising from Diagram 88, Y. Averbakh–A. Kotov, Zurich Candidates Tournament 1953, after White's 30th move. White's Kingside is somewhat open, yet he does have a number of defenders nearby, and, after the coming 31 N–N1, the KRP will be secure. Black therefore must strike while the chance is there:

30 . . . QxPch!!

DIAGRAM 88

BLACK

WHITE

Averbakh–Kotov
Zurich 1953
after White's 30th

An electrifying shot, giving a Queen for a pawn to be able to chase White's King into Black's half of the board.

31 KxQ R–R3ch 32 K–N4 N–B3ch 33 K–B5

Now Black, somewhat short of time, continued with 33 . . . N–Q2?!, giving White some chances for defense with 34 R–N5!.

The further course of the game was: 34 . . . R–B1ch　35 K–N4
N–B3ch　36 K–B5 N–N1ch　37 K–N4 N–B3ch　38 K–B5 NxQPch
39 K–N4 N–B3ch　40 K–B5 N–N1ch　41 K–N4 N–B3ch　42 K–B5
N–N1ch　43 K–N4 BxR　44 KxB (Even after the better 44 B–K3
B–K2　45 BxKBP PxB　46 NxP R–R5ch　47 K–N3 R/5xN White is
quite lost.) 44 . . . R–B2!　45 B–R4 R–N3ch　46 K–R5 R/2–N2　47
B–N5 RxBch　48 K–R4 N–B3　49 N–N3 RxN　50 QxQP R/6–N3 51
Q–N8ch R–N1　White resigns.

Instead, Black can immediately set White unsoluble problems
with Stahlberg's:

33 . . . N–N5!!

. . . which, by preventing 34 R–N5, leaves White defenseless.

34 KxN

The "thematic" move. To prevent mate White must play 34
QxBP PxQ　35 P–K5—hardly of great practical note!

34 . . . R–N1ch　35 K–B5 R–B3mate

Successful practical play consists of always getting the maximum
reasonable result out of any position. If the position is inferior,
then a draw becomes a very worthwhile object. Therefore, forcing
the King into the open to achieve a perpetual check draw is a
logical tool of the chessmaster. This is well demonstrated in the
play arising from the following position, A. Miles–J. Timman, Las
Palmas 1977, after Black's 22nd move. White: K—e2 Q—c7 R—
g1, g2 B—b2 P—a3, b3, d3, e3, e5, f2 Black: K—g8 Q—h3 R—a8,
c6 N—h5 P—a5, b7, f7, g7, h7. Both sides seem to have attacking
chances, yet those of Black are inherently greater. Miles gives the
following convincing analysis: 23 QxNP? R–B7ch　24 K–K1 (24
K–Q1!? QR–QB1!　25 P–K6 QxKP/3　26 RxPch NxR　27 RxNch
K–B1　28 RxRP Q–N5ch, and Black wins) 24 . . . R–KB1! 25 B–Q4
P–N3!, with Black's King being safe and threats such as 26 . . .
N–B5! and 26 . . . KR–B1 in the air. Therefore White immediately
goes for a drawing combination:

23 RxPch!! NxR　24 RxNch KxR

Not 24 . . . K–R1?? because after 25 P–K6! White even *wins*.

25 P–K6ch! K–R3!　26 Q–B4ch K–R4!　27 QxPch K–N5!

Black's King will be chased around, but not captured. Therefore: an honorable draw.

28 Q–N7ch K–B4   29 Q–K5ch K–N3   30 Q–N7ch K–B4   31 Q–B6ch K–N5   32 Q–B4ch Draw

The situation is unclear if the chased King can manage to stay on his side of the board and the enemy pieces are not well mobilized to attack the King immediately. A truly incomprehensible situation results in the play arising from Diagram 89, A. Lein–J. Watson, New York International II 1977, after White's 27th move. White has just played 27 P–KB4, uncovering on Black's Knight. Since retreat would obviously be unsatisfactory, Black correctly decides to press on by sacrificing the Knight to get White's King out on a "mini-flight:"

27 . . . NxNP!   28 KxN Q–N8!   29 N–K3! PxPch   30 NxP B–R5ch   31 K–N4 Q–R7   32 N–R5!

DIAGRAM 89

BLACK

WHITE

Lein–Watson
N.Y. 1977
after White's 27th

The play over the previous moves has been excellent on both sides. Black has mobilized everything immediately available for the attack, whereas White has brought over both Knights to guard important squares. This is the critical position of the game. White is an eyelash away from consolidating. What can Black do to keep his attack going?

32 . . . R–B4?

This obvious try is easily parried. A subsequent analysis by Watson showed the correct idea to be 32 . . . B–Q1!!. The possibilities then are immensely complicated. Three of them:

(1.) 33 N–B5? R–B6! 34 BxR RxB 35 N/B–N3 N–K4ch 36 K–B4 RxN! 37 NxR B–N4ch!, and Black wins.

(2.) 33 N–Q5? BxN! 34 RxB (34 PxB P–B4ch! wins) 34 . . . RxP 35 R–Q2 RxB!, and Black wins.

(3.) 33 K–B3! (Home where it is bound to be safer!) 33 . . . N–R5ch! 34 K–N4! (Unfortunately 34 K–B2? NxB 35 NxN B–R5ch 36 K–K3 R–K2! leads to a very strong attack for Black) 34 . . . N–N3! 35 K–B3!, and neither side may have anything better than to acquiesce to a draw.

33 N–B5!

White's pieces spring to life (the major threat is 34 R–R1), and Black has nothing to show for his material disadvantage. White wins easily enough:

33 . . . P–Q4   34 BxP P–R3   35 PxP Q–B2   36 NxB Q–Q2ch 37 N–B5 R/1–B3   38 N–B6ch RxN   39 BxR P–R4ch   40 K–N5 Black resigns

For the King to feel secure during a flight, the flight must take place within its own territory on something like a strictly horizontal route. Such a situation arises in the following position, E. Ubilava–N. Radev, Tiflis/Suhumi 1977, after Black's 21st move. White: K—g1 Q—d7 R—a1 N—b3 P—a2, c2, c3, g3, h2 Black: K—g8 Q—e3 R—f8 P—a6, b5, e6, f7, g7, h7. In the previous play, both sides were agreeable to a series of combinations which led to White winning a piece. What of the diagrammed position? White can, of course, play the safe 22 K–N2, but then after 22 . . . Q–K7ch Black continues his checks (23 K–R3 Q–R4ch etc). In order to win, White's King must try to flee to the Queenside. Of necessity this means sacrificing the rest of his Kingside pawns:

22 K–B1! Q–B6ch   23 K–K1 Q–R8ch   24 K–Q2 QxPch   25 K–B1 QxP   26 K–N2

White's King has safely reached the Queenside. Materially Black is quite well off and in an endgame his four passed pawns would no doubt be decisive. However, the position is very much a middlegame and White is able to make decisive use of his extra, nimble Knight.

26 . . . P–KR4   27 R–KB1! P–R5   28 N–Q4 Q–N5

There was no time for 28 . . . P–R6? because of 29 NxP!.

29 N–B6! Q–K7   30 R–B4 P–N4   31 R–B6 Q–K5   32 Q–Q2!

The weaknesses in Black's Kingside offer White's pieces the necessary targets.

32 . . . Q–N5   33 N–K5 Q–N6   34 Q–Q4! P–R6 Black overstepped the time limit.

There is no defense after 35 R–R6!, e.g. 35 . . . K–N2   36 NxPch! P–K4   37 Q–K4! etc.

CHAPTER 19
The Aggressive King

So far in Part II the major emphasis has been on an inherently defensive King, though in some cases the King had to become active in order to save his own life. In this and the next chapter we'll see a King who is aggressively a part of the major action. This chapter will consider successes; the negative side will be looked at in Chapter 20.

SECTION 1. Forming Part of an Attack

In the endgame the King becomes a very important attacking piece. Yet there also are times in the middlegame when it can play a vital role as an attacker. The most important examples are those where the King is an integral part of an attack against the enemy King. Consider first the play possible from Diagram 90, J. Klovans–L. Gutmans, Riga 1977, after Black's 27th move. White is up a piece; Black seems to have certain attacking chances based on the position of the White King. The location of the White King is the crux of the position: is it a strength or a liability on KN4? White has a marvelous chance to demonstrate the strength of his King by playing:

28 NxR!

Instead, White continued routinely with 28 BxN? and lost after 28 . . . RxB   29 QR–Q1 P–KR4ch   30 PxPe.p. R/1xN   31 RxR RxR   32 RxR QxR   33 PxP KxP   34 P–B6ch K–R2   35 P–KR4 P–N4   36 P–R5 Q–B5   37 QxQ PxQ   38 K–B4 K–R3   39 K–K4 KxP   40 K–Q4 K–N3   41 KxP KxP White resigns.

DIAGRAM 90

BLACK

WHITE

Klovans–Gutmans
Riga 1977
after Black's 27th

28 ... P–KR4ch   29 K–R4! NxQ   30 RxRch   K–R2   31 P–N6ch PxP   32 PxPch NxPch   33 KxP White wins

White's King activity effects the devastating threat of 34 BxN mate. Black is defenseless; 33 ... Q–R4 ch   34 R–Q5 gives Black the unpalatable choice between being mated immediately (34 ... QxN   35 BxNch K–N1   36 R–Q8) or after a slight delay (34 ... Q–N3   35 R–KN5 etc).

In a way we can say that in the example above the hunted King became the hunter. There is something of this shadow also over the next three King hunts. The first arises from the position after Black's 31st move in V. Korchnoi–A. Karpov, 1978 World Championship Match, Game 17. White: K—g1 R—b7, f1 P— a4, g2, h2 Black: K—e5 R—a6 N—a3, f6 P—g7, h7. White is for choice because the doubled Rooks can menace Black's King and Black is in real danger of losing all of his Kingside. Yet Black's King also has the potential for being a genuine attacker—watch how this turns the tables a bit later on.

32 R–K7ch

Sending the King further from the Kingside so that he is not able to help out there.

32 . . . K–Q5   33 RxP?!

Still too early. More promising were 33 R–Q1ch! K–B6   34 R–QB7ch K–N6   35 RxP (Larsen) or 33 R–B4ch! K–Q4   34 RxP K–K4   35 P–N3 (Pachman). In either case, White's winning chances are excellent.

33 . . . N–B5   34 R–B4ch N–K5   35 R–Q7ch?!

A time pressure type of check, which only serves to turn Black's King into a more potent attacker. The immediate 35 RxP! was correct, though after 35 . . . RxP   36 P–R4 N–K6! (Habbel) the active position of Black's pieces is just enough to hold the draw.

35 . . . K–K6   36 R–B3ch K–K7   37 RxP N/B–Q7!   38 R–QR3 R–QB3!

With his last two moves Black emphasizes his interest in active play. Necessary to draw were either 39 P–N3! or 39 P–N4!. Instead, Korchnoi sees the simple threat but not the more sophisticated one.

39 R–R1?? N–B6ch!! White resigns

After the forced 40 PxN R–KN3ch   41 K–R1, Black mates with 41 . . . N–B7. In the success of Black's combination, his King played an integral part.

If the successful trek of Black's King seemed surprising in the above example, it was nothing compared to what happens in the play arising from the following position. M. Filip–K. Darga, 1961 European Team Championship, White to move. White: K—g1 Q—d6 R—d1 P—a2, e3, f2, g3, h2 Black: K—g8 Q—b7 B—c8 P—a5, e6, f6, h7. Black's position is truly resignable: he has no compensation for the missing Exchange and pawn, has no counterplay and has an exposed King. But watch a miracle unfold:

1 Q–Q8ch

O.K., but simpler is 1 R–QB1!.

1 . . . K–N2 2 P–KR4?!

Here too the logical move is 2 R–QB1!: 2 . . . B–Q2 3 R–B7 Q–N8ch 4 K–N2 Q–K5ch 5 P–B3, and Black must resign.

2 . . . Q–B6! 3 R–QB1 B–N2

Now Black has a mate threat; even so White's attack should come first.

4 R–B7ch K–N3 5 Q–N8ch K–B4

White now has the following forced win: 6 P–N4ch! K–K4 7 R–B5ch K–Q3 8 Q–KB8ch! K–Q2 9 Q–B7ch K–Q1 10 Q–B7ch K–K1 11 Q–N8ch K–B2 12 R–B7ch, followed by 13 QxB. Instead, a combination of carelessness, greed and blindness, makes White play:

6 QxRPch?? K–N5 White resigns

Whether White plays 7 Q–N6ch or 7 RxB, 7 . . . K–R6! sets up mate on KN7, with the attempt at fleeing (after 7 RxB K–R6) by 8 K–B1 allowing 8 . . . Q–Q8mate. In the meanwhile Black threatens the immediate 7 . . . Q–N7mate.

A sharp up–and–down struggle in Jelen–B. Larsen, Ljubljana/Portoroz 1977 led to the position of Diagram 91, after Black's 32nd move. Black's King is in the open and White can win by 33 RxB! RxR 34 R–K1 with the major threat being 35 P–R4ch K–B3 36 Q–KR8mate, and with the "minor" threat of 35 NxPch. The only defense, 34 . . . R–K7, loses to 35 RxR! QxR 36 P–R4ch K–B3 38 QxPch K–K4 39 Q–K7ch, followed by 40 QxQ. Instead White is a bit overeager:

33 NxPch? K–N5!

The Black King now becomes a dangerous attacking weapon.

34 RxB! RxR 35 P–B3ch K–R6 36 Q–B8ch!

The move White was counting on. If now 36 . . . RxQ??, 37 N–N5mate! Yet Black also has a surprise in store . . .

36 . . . Q–N5! 37 N–N5ch! RxN 38 PxQ R–KN7ch 39 K–R1 R–QB4!?

DIAGRAM 91

BLACK

WHITE

Jelen–Larsen
Ljubljana/Portoroz 1977
after Black's 32nd

Black could have grabbed an immediate draw with 39 . . . RxRPch 40 K–N1 R–KN7ch etc. But as this always remains in hand, he tests White with the text move.

40 Q–Q8??

In time pressure, White obliges. To keep the draw White's Queen had to remain on the Black King's diagonal, i.e. 40 Q–K6! or 40 Q–Q7!. For instance 40 Q–Q7 RxRPch (Black has no time for 40 . . . PxP?? because of 41 Q–R7ch R–KR4 42 Q–QN7!) 41 K–N1 R–KN7ch etc.

40 . . . RxRPch 41 K–N1 P–KN4!! White resigns

He's defenseless! For instance, 42 Q–K8 R/B–QB7 43 QxPch KxP or 42 PxP R/B–QB7 43 Q–Q5 (43 Q–Q7ch P–N5) 43 . . . R/B–N7ch 44 QxRch RxQch 45 K–R1 P–N6 46 P–R6 P–N7 47 P–R7 R–R7ch 48 K–N1 KxP. In fact, White did play 42 R–N1 but then resigned in view of 42 . . . R/B–QB7 43 Q–Q5 R/B–N7ch 44 QxRch RxQch 45 K–R1 PxP 46 RxP RxP 47 RxQNP R–R6, etc. with an easily won R and P endgame.

Periodically the King is even useful in "attacking" the major pieces. Of course, where the Queen is concerned this cannot be done directly. Yet the King can be very effective as part of the attack. Such an attack allows White to save a draw from Diagram 92, V. Korchnoi–G. Kuzmin, Leningrad Interzonal 1973, after Black's 27th move. White's in serious trouble: he's a pawn down already and still has all kinds of remaining pawn weaknesses. Korchnoi spies an opportunity for a perpetual attack on Black's Queen:

28 R–N5! QxBP

DIAGRAM 92

BLACK

WHITE

Korchnoi–Kuzmin
Leningrad 1973
after Black's 27th

The "normal" move, though as GM I. Zaitsev has suggested, the electrifying 28 . . . RxB!! could well have given excellent winning chances.

29 B–B1 Q–R5   30 K–N2!

A key point of White's plan: the King takes away White's KR3 square from Black's Queen. Thus the Queen will be "semi-trapped."

30 . . . P–R6

The alternative is to sacrifice an Exchange with 30 . . . R–N7!?.

31 N–B3 Q–R3

After this the game continued 32 R–N3?! Q–R4 33 R–N5 Q–R3 34 R–N3?! Q–R4 draw!, but Black could have played on with 34 . . . QxB!! 35 RxQ R–N7 36 K–B1 RxQ 37 KxR N–R7!. The accurate move was:

32 R–N4! Draw

Now 32 . . . QxB doesn't lead to anything because after 33 RxQ R–N7 34 K–B1 RxQ 35 KxR N–R7 36 R–QR1 N–B6ch 37 K–Q2 R–N1 White has 38 RxQP.

The King can, of course, attack Rooks with impunity. A particularly effective example — though bordering on an endgame— occurs in the play arising from the position below, A. Alekhine–F. D. Yates, London 1922, after Black's 34th move. White: K—f4 R—c7, f7 N—e5 P—a3, b2, d4, e3, f3, g3, h5 Black: K—h7 R—a8, g8 B—a6 P—a4, b3, d5, e6, f5, g7, h6. White has an unquestionable advantage with Rooks doubled on the 7th rank and the superior minor piece. Yet at the moment Black is defending everything and he retains some chances for counterplay along the QB file. Alekhine demonstrates a forced win by virtue of having the aggressive King:

35 N–Q7 K–R1

Required because of the threatened 36 N–B6ch. But White continues with his Knight maneuver, anyway.

36 N–B6! R/N–KB1

Forcing the exchange of a pair of Rooks, no?

37 RxP!

Nothing doing!

37 . . . RxN 38 K–K5 Black resigns

This King move is the point of White's play. The Rook is attacked, and it can neither retreat to KB1 nor be protected by the other Rook, as in either case White has a mate in two: 39 R–KR7ch K–N1 40 R/B–KN7. Thus there is no defense to 39 KxR, after which Black still remains in great danger of being mated.

Section 2. Entering the Enemy Camp

Often there is no sharp dividing line between the King entering the enemy camp on general principles and the King having a specific part of the attack, as in the previous section. Consider Diagram 93, V. Korchnoi–M. Tal, 1962 USSR Championship, after Black's 43rd move. Clearly White's Q and B have Black's King in a box, but there doesn't seem enough firepower nearby to bring Black down. Therefore Korchnoi fashions a King trek to KN5. The King will be safe there and will be in an active attacking position to take advantage of whatever specific possibilities will then develop:

44 K–N3! R–N1

DIAGRAM 93

BLACK

WHITE
Korchnoi–Tal
1962 USSR
Championship
after Black's 43rd

Obviously 44 . . . P–R5?? is not feasible because of the overloaded condition of Black's Queen, with White simply playing 45 RxP!.

45 K–R4 Q–KB2   46 K–N5! PxP   43 PxP B–Q2

After 47 . . . QxQch? 48 KxQ White's active King is immediately decisive.

48 R–QB4 P–R5   49 R–B7 P–R6

With the following Exchange sacrifice White gets his connected passed pawns going for a certain win. Black has no defense, anyway, e.g. if 49 . . . QxQch   50 KxQ P–R6, then 51 P–K6! PxP 52 PxB R–KB1ch   53 K–N5! P–N8 = Q   54 R–B8! (Korchnoi).

50 RxB! QxR   51 P–K6 Q–R2   52 Q–K5! PxP   53 P–K7 K–B2 54 P–Q7! Black resigns

After 54 . . . QxP White mates with 55 Q–B6ch K–K1   56 Q–B8. Here too White's King has a meaningful role to play.

The following three examples show the motif of the King entering the enemy camp in purer form. Three different situations are possible: (1) King activity is primarily defensive in nature, (2) King activity is primarily offensive in nature, and (3) King activity has both defensive and offensive characteristics. The latter is illustrated by the play from the following position, E. Mednis–F. Gheorghiu, Cleveland 1975, after Black's 29th move. White: K—b3 Q—g3 R—e4 P—b2, b5, c3, f4, h3 Black: K—h7 R—b1, d2 B—f6 P—a6, e6, f7, g7, h6. In the previous action, Black had been furiously attacking my King, whereas I—confident of the ultimate safety of it—had mobilized my Queenside pawn majority. I saw no reason not to carry out my plan consistently.

30 PxP! R/7xPch

White's King is also O.K. after 30 . . . R/8xPch   31 K–R4!.

31 K–B4 R–QR8

Black was quite confident of his chances here; therefore White's next move came as a shock.

32 Q–Q3!!

The Queen returns to action and threatens a horrible discovered check (32 . . . RxP?? 33 RxPch). Being short of time Black is unable to formulate a correct approach to the position. Imperative was to aim for a draw with 32 . . . P–N3! 33 Q–Q7 RxP! (33 . . . K–N2? 34 RxP!) 34 QxPch B–N2 35 RxP RxR 36 QxR R–QB7 and the meager amount of material remaining does not give White any real winning chances.

32 . . . R–R5 ch?

Chasing the King to safety on the Queenside. Black now is lost.

33 K–B5 R–R4ch   34 K–B6 P–N3   35 R–N4!

Making sure that White can hold on to the valuable QRP.

35 . . . R/7–QR7   36 R–N6 R/7–R6   37 K–N7! RxBP

There is no defense. If 37 . . . R–Q4   38 QxR! PxQ   39 RxB.

38 Q–Q7 B–N2

Or 38 . . . K–N2   39 RxP! etc.

39 QxBP R–KB4   40 QxKP R–KB3   41 QxR

Not required, of course, but an endgame a Rook ahead is quite tempting.

41 . . . BxQ   42 RxB Black resigns

The other two examples will be two titanic R. Fischer–T. Petrosian struggles from the 1959 Candidates Tournament. First for a King march primarily for defensive purposes. Diagram 94 shows Fischer–Petrosian, Rd 16, after White's 38th move. White has a definite advantage: he has an extra passed KNP (great for a potential endgame!) and his double Queens are well placed for an attack against Black's rather exposed King. Black now plays:

38 . . . K–B4!

To which Fischer adds the following (as always, perceptive) comment: "Curiously the King will be safer in White's territory where it obtains shelter from the cluster of pawns."

39 Q–KB8?

Fischer querries this and recommends instead 39 Q–R2!: 39 . . . Q–B3   40 P–N5; 39 . . . Q–R8   40 Q–N7; 39 . . . Q/2–K2   40 Q–QR8.

39 . . . Q/2–K2   40 Q–R8

Here Fischer thought that he was winning; but Black's King turns out to be "slippery as an eel."

40 . . . K–N5!   41 Q–KR2 K–N6!   42 Q–QR1?!

DIAGRAM 94

BLACK

WHITE

Fischer–Petrosian
1959 Candidates,
Round 16
after White's 38th

An obvious sealed move, which, however, leads to naught. More dangerous for Black was 42 P–B5! QxP 43 Q–KN8ch K–R6 44 Q–QB2 Q–N5 45 Q–QR8ch Q–QR5 46 Q/2xQch NxQ 47 QxP, though after 47 . . . N–B6 "it's likely Black can draw" (Fischer).

42 . . . Q–R6 43 QxQch KxQ 44 Q–R6 Q–KB2! 45 K–N2 K–N6!

With the threat of 46 . . . N–Q8!. The chances here are equal—Black's piece activity compensates for the missing pawn.

46 Q–Q2 Q–KR2! 47 K–N3

After 47 P–N5, Black has 47 . . . Q–R5.

47 . . . QxP! 48 Q–KB2?

The only correct move is 48 P–N5! with equal chances.

48 . . . Q–R8! Draw

Offered by Fischer, who admits that Black is already better, e.g. 49 P–N5 P–K5! or 49 B–N2 Q–R3.

The following position, Fischer–Petrosian, 1959 Candidates, Rd 2, after White's 46th move, White: K—g2 Q—h6 R—d1 B—f3 P—e5, f2, g3 Black: K—a7 Q—d7 R—d4 N—c5 P—a5, b6, d2, f7, is easy to evaluate: Black is better. The reasons are equally easy: he is a pawn up, the advanced QP ties White down so that White is essentially without counterplay, Black has two connected passed pawns on the Queenside. What is not easy is to transform these advantages into a win. The basic problem is that Black's passed pawns are where his King is and that advancing the pawns will necessarily open up his King position. The way that Petrosian uses his King in assisting the pawns to advance, while simultaneously not allowing White any attacking chances, deserves the highest praise:

46 . . . P–N4!

Black's pieces (and QP) are at their optimal present positions so that it is time to start mobilizing Black's major trump—the connected passed pawns.

47 Q–K3 K–N3!   48 Q–R6ch N–K3   49 Q–K3 K–R3

The simplest way to prevent the threatened 50 RxP. In the next part Black slowly yet surely continues to push his Q-side pawns.

50 B–K2 P–R5   51 Q–QB3 K–N3   52 Q–K3 N–B4   53 B–B3 P–N5   54 Q–R6ch N–K3   55 Q–R8 Q–Q1   56 Q–R7 Q–Q2   57 Q–R8 P–N6!

Black's King position has become loosened, thus giving White's Queen some attacking prospects. With some sharp calculation and guts Black decides to send his King into White's Queenside. He reasons that not only will his King be safe there (because White's Rook must watch the QP) but that it will be of significant help to its Queenside pawns.

58 Q–QN8ch K–R4   59 Q–QR8ch K–N4   60 Q–QN8ch K–B5!   61 Q–N8 K–B6!   62 B–R5 N–Q1   63 B–B3 P–R6   64 Q–B8 K–N7!

Guarding Black's QR6 square and getting ready to take command of QR8.

65 Q–R8 N–K3   66 Q–R8 P–R7   67 Q–R5 Q–R5!   68 RxPch K–R6! White resigns

Black's QRP will turn into a new Queen—thanks to major assistance from its King.

Section 3. Generally Unafraid

There are plenty of times when the King has an active role to play during the middlegame. It is important to get away from the "King tucked away in the corner is the safest" syndrome. During the middlegame King safety is a major consideration in the evaluation of any position. Nevertheless, this doesn't mean that the King can't take part in the action. It simply means that *prior to* making the decision to have the King participate, it must be determined that the aggressive King will also be a safe King.

The decision is fairly easy to make from the following position, B. Larsen–L. Polugaevsky, Lone Pine (Calif) 1978, after White's 34th move. White: K—g1 Q—c3 R—c8 P—a2, b2, f2, g3, h4 Black: K—g7 Q—e7 R—d7 P—a7, b6, f5, g6, h7. The apparently safer 34 . . . K–B2 leads to great problems after 35 R–KR8!; therefore required is the "generally unafraid"

34 . . . K–R3! 35 Q–B1ch K–N2!

But further aggressiveness is foolhardy: 35 . . . K–R4? 36 R–K8! Q–B3 37 R–KB8! Q–K2 38 R–B7!, and the mate threat on KN5 wins at least a Rook for White.

36 P–R5! Q–K7!

White's coordinated attack with his Q, R and KRP is very dangerous, and to blunt it Black must create threats of his own.

37 P–R6ch K–B2 38 K–N2 Q–K5ch 39 K–R2 Q–Q5 40 Q–B2 P–B5 41 P–KN4 K–B3!

Heading for KN4, where it will not only be safe but also could form a part of an attack against White's King. Therefore White decides to allow an equal R and P endgame.

42 R–B4! Q–Q7! 43 QxQ RxQ 44 RxPch K–N4 45 K–N3 KxP!

Careless would be 45 . . . RxNP 46 R–B7 RxRP??, because Black gets mated after 47 P–B4ch KxP 48 P–N5ch K–R4 49

RxKRP. Therefore Black's King itself works to prevent this possibility.

46 R–B7 P–KN4! 47 RxQRP RxNP 48 P–R4 Draw

The exchange of Queenside pawns will lead to dead equality.

Strictly a defensive King, yet one which is very much unafraid, is shown in Diagram 95, V. Korchnoi–A. Karpov, 1978 World Championship Match, Game 5, after Black's 43rd move. The open character of the position must favor White's Bishop pair, and there is a pawn loose for the taking. White therefore grabs his chance, even though his King will have to start feeling ill at ease:

44 QxP! Q–Q7ch 45 K–N3 N/2–B3 46 R–N1 R–K1 47 B–K4!!

DIAGRAM 95

BLACK

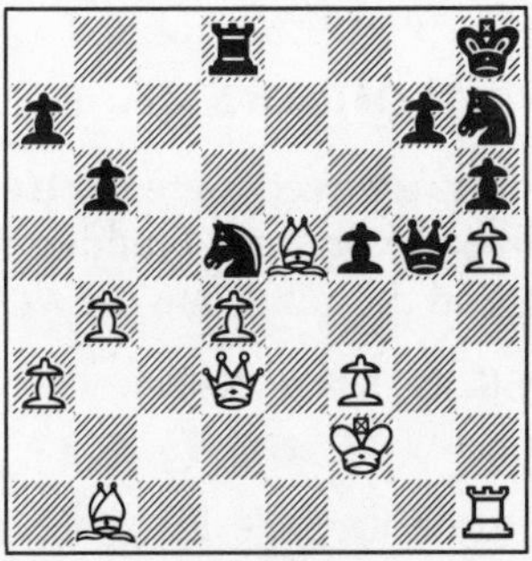

WHITE

Korchnoi–Karpov
1978 World Championship
Match Game #5
after Black's 43rd

Effectively centralizing both Bishops and neutralizing Black's cheapos, e.g. 47 K–R3? RxB!.

47 . . . N–K2 48 Q–R3 R–QB1

After the other try at activating the Rook, 48 . . . R–KB1, White achieves a winning endgame: 49 R–N2 NxBch 50 K–R2! N–N4 51 RxQ NxQ 52 KxN RxPch 53 K–N4 (Tal).

49 K–R4!!

Allowing White to mobilize Q and R along the KN file and thus preempt Black's counterattack.

49 . . . R–B8   50 Q–N3

Good, but even stronger is 50 Q–N2!, forcing off the Queens. White's impressive King aggressiveness is best illustrated if Black, after 50 Q–N3 (or 50 Q–N2!), plays 50 . . . Q–N4ch   51 QxQ PxQch   52 RxP R–KR8ch   53 K–N3 R–KN8ch. True that 54 K–B4! N/3–Q4ch   55 BxN NxBch   56 K–B5 N–K2ch   57 K–K6! RxR   58 KxN RxP   59 P–B4 leaves Black temporarily the Exchange up, but White's active King will force Black's Rook to sacrifice itself for the QP.

50 . . . RxR   51 QxR K–N1   52 Q–N3 K–B2?!

Here and on the next move, Black's King should satisfy itself with the "modest" KB1 square.

53 B–N6ch K–K3?!   54 Q–R3ch K–Q4   55 B–B7ch

Of course, this leads to a forced mate. Instead—with seconds left for his next two moves—Korchnoi blundered with 55 B–K4ch?? NxB   56 PxNch KxP, and the game was drawn on Move 124 (!).

55 . . . K–B3   56 Q–K6ch K–N4   57 Q–B4ch K–R5   58 Q–R6mate

In the next three examples, the King (always Black's!) is truly unafraid, doing anything and everything that comes into view. First, let us look at the following position, B. Ivanović–E. Bukić, 1978 Yugoslav Championship, after White's 27th move. White: K—c1 Q—e7 R—f1 N—c4 P—a2, b2, c2, g2, h2 Black: K—g6 Q—a7 R—a8, h8 B—c8 N—d1 P—b7, e5, f5. White has sacrificed a Rook and Bishop to get this position. Black's King is open and has a dearth of defenders nearby. For quite some time to come it must do a series of "dances:"

27 . . . P–N4!   28 NxPch K–R4   29 Q–B6 R–KN1!   30 R–B3 N–B7!   31 P–KN3! Q–Q5!   32 P–N4ch PxP

Throughout, Black has been finding the only existing defenses and so here too, since 32 . . . RxP? allows 33 Q–R8ch K–N4   34

Q–N7ch K–R4 35 Q–KR7ch K–N4 36 Q–N6ch K–R5 37 Q–KR6mate.

33 Q–B7ch K–R3 34 Q–B6ch K–R4 35 Q–B7ch K–R3 36 R–B6ch K–N4 37 N–B3ch! PxN 38 QxRch KxR! 39 Q–R8ch K–B4 40 QxQ N–K5!

If Black could immediately coordinate his pieces he would even have the advantage, as he has more wood. Unfortunately that is not possible, and he correctly parts with his Rook (40 . . . B–N2? 41 Q–Q7ch wins for White) so that his active King can make a power out of the KBP.

41 Q–Q5ch K–B5 42 QxR P–B7 43 Q–N8ch K–B6 44 QxP K–N7!

44 . . . B–R6? loses to 45 Q–Q3ch.

45 Q–K2 B–B4! 46 P–B4 K–N8!

What a King!

47 Q–K3 K–N7 48 Q–K2 draw

Neither side can do better than repeat moves.

In the following two cases Black's King receives a full point for his fearless work. The statics and dynamics of the position below, K. Honfi–T. Horvath, Subotica 1978, after White's 21st move, are quite different from each other. White: K—e1 Q—a5 R—a1, f1 N—d5 P—a2, b2, f2, h2 Black: K—d8 Q—c2 R—h8 B—c8, h6 P—d4, d6, f5, f7, h7. Having the advantage of an Exchange for a pawn White is somewhat ahead in material, and this characteristic is significantly magnified by Black's having two sets of isolated doubled pawns. Yet dynamically Black has a large advantage: his Q, 2 Bs and advanced QP are ready to menace White's King and the KR is ready to join in via K1. This latter reason explains why Black doesn't want to play 21 . . . K–K1 now, but instead

21 . . . K–Q2! 22 Q–R7ch

After the "fancy" 22 Q–R4ch QxQ 23 N–N6ch K–B3 24 NxQ, Horvath demonstrates the following winning line for Black: 24 . . .

B–R3   25 P–B3 R–K1ch   26 K–B2 B–K6ch   27 K–N2 R–KN1ch
28 K–R1 BxR   29 RxB P–Q6.

22 . . . K–K3   23 QxP

After 23 N–B7ch Black's King continues "attacking:" 23 . . .
K–K4! 24 P–B4ch BxP 25 RxB KxR 26 QxPch Q–K5ch   27 QxQch
PxQ, with a won endgame for Black.

**23 . . . B–R3!   24 Q–B6ch KxN   25 R–Q1ch B–Q6!   26
QxBP/5ch K–B3**

Black's King now is "safely home," while the attack rolls on. The
main line is 27 RxB R–K1ch   28 R–K3 Q–B8ch!   29 K–K2 RxRch
30 PxR QxKPch   31 K–Q1 Q–Q7mate.

**27 Q–B3ch B–K5!   28 Q–B6 B–Q4!!   29 QxB R–K1ch   30 Q–K3
R–K3 White resigns**

Black is satisfied with nothing but mate, e.g. 31 R–KN1 B–B6!.

An inscrutable position is shown in Diagram 96, B. Ivanović—
E. Sveshnikov, Yugoslavia–USSR 1976, after White's 19th move.
White is a pawn ahead and has connected passed pawns, while
Black's King seems rather open in the center. Yet things are not
that simple, since Black has a strong center and White's KR is out
of the game. Black understands this position quite well and plays:

19 . . . R–R2!

Piece activity, not King "safety," is what is required! Inferior is
the "safe" 19 . . . B–N2? 20 Q–Q7ch K–B1 21 QxQPch K–N1 22
P–QR4! BxP   23 R–Q1, and White is on his way to winning.

20 Q–K8ch?!

Better is 20 P–QR4; best is 20 P–QR3! with the plan of
mobilizing the Queenside pawns via 21 P–QN4.

20 . . . K–B3   21 P–KN4?!

Weakens the King position too much. Better is 21 P–KN3 or 21
P–KR4.

21 . . . R–K2   22 Q–N8 K–K4!

DIAGRAM 96

BLACK

WHITE

Ivanović–Sveshnikov
Yugoslavia–USSR 1976
after White's 19th

Threatening 23 . . . B–N2, winning the Queen. White's best now is 23 B–B4, though after 23 . . . P–B5! 24 Q–N3 Q–Q7! (Schwarz) Black has a definite plus.

23 P–B4ch?! KxP 24 K–K2

There also is no hope in 24 QxPch R–K4!.

24 . . . K–K4! 25 KR–KB1 PxP!

Maximum care was required here. Thus 25 . . . P–B5? loses to 26 RxP!! KxR 27 QxPch R–K4 28 Q–KB6ch KxP 29 R–KN1ch, and the Black King in the open by itself goes under: 29 . . . K–R6 30 R–N3ch KxP 31 Q–R4mate.

26 P–N4

Finds an elementary refutation, but there is also no longer term hope in 26 B–B4 Q–Q7ch! 27 KxQ B–R3ch 28 K–B3 RxQ 29 P–N4 P–B4 etc.

26 . . . B–N2!

Not 26 . . . QxNP? because of 27 R–B5ch! KxR 28 B–Q7ch and 29 QxQ.

27 PxQ RxQ   28 QR–N1 P–B4   29 P–R6 P–B5!   30 B–B6 P–B6ch
31 K–B2 RxR   32 RxR K–B5!   33 R–N4 B–B6   34 R–B4 B–R4   35
K–B1 B–N3   36 B–N7 P–R4   37 R–B6 P–K6   38 R–B4ch K–N4
White resigns

CHAPTER 20
Erroneous King Activity

Now let us see under what conditions the King should stay put, i.e., under what circumstances King activity is erroneous. The first typical error is *over-activity in its defensive area.* Consider first Diagram 97, Z. Veröci–R. Kas, 1977 Hungarian Women's Championship, after White's 20th move. White has a moderate advantage in view of the slight weakening of Black's Kingside and the superiority of White's extra Knight to Black's Bishop. Black should now play 20 . . . Q–Q3, followed perhaps by 21 . . . QR–B1. Instead:

20 . . . P–KR4?!

DIAGRAM 97

BLACK

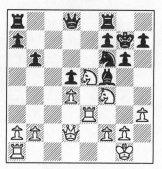

WHITE

Veröci–Kas
Hungary Women's
Championship 1977
after White's 20th

241

This is nothing but an unmotivated weakening of the Kingside.

21 Q–K2 Q–Q3   22 R–KN3 K–R2?!

The preferable way to protect the KRP was 22 . . . R–R1.

23 R–N5 K–R3?

Exposing itself, while "forcing" White to make a winning sacrifice. Necessary was 23 . . . B–Q2.

24 RxB! PxR   25 Q–K3 K–R2   26 Q–Q3! N–K5   27 Q–B3

The Queen "triangulation" has gained a valuable tempo for the attack and Black is defenseless. If now 27 . . . Q–R3, White wins after 28 NxRP N–Q3   29 N–Q7 KR–Q1   30 N/R–B6ch K–R1   31 QxQP N–K5   32 Q–K5.

27 . . . N–B3   28 NxRP NxN   29 QxNch Q–R3   30 QxBP/5ch K–N1   31 R–K1!

White now has a material advantage to go with his decisive attack.

31 . . . QR–K1   32 R–K3 Q–R2   33 R–KN3ch K–R1   34 Q–B6ch Black resigns

The second type of error is *leaving the actual safety of the castled position for illusory safety somewhere else*. In general the safest location for the King is its castled position. Look at the position below, J. R. Capablanca–R. Black, New York 1915, after White's 38th move. White: K—g1 Q—a2 B—d5 N—d2, e2 P—e4, f3, g4, h3 Black: K—g8 R—d8 B—b8, g6 N—c5, e6 P—d6, e5, f7, g7, h6. Black's King looks absolutely secure on his KN1. For the Queen Black has R, B and P—almost sufficient compensation. Black's position, though passive, is very solid, and it is difficult to see where White can make decisive progress. Capablanca himself doubted that White could win. But Black, not satisfied in leaving well alone, starts his King on a suicidal mission:

38 . . . K–B1?   39 N–QB4 K–K2??

39 . . . K–N1 or 39 . . . B–B2 were in order.

40 N–R5 K–B3???

Capablanca comments here: "Worse and worse. The King is now in a mating net."

41 N–B6 R–QB1 42 P–R4! B–B2 43 P–B4!

Decisive. By threatening both 44 P–N5ch and 44 P–B5 White wins a piece and the game. If 43 . . . NxBP 44 NxN PxN 45 Q–QN2mate—made possible only by the Black King's ridiculous position on his KB3.

43 . . . BxP 44 P–N5ch PxP 45 RPxPch NxNP

45 . . . K–N3 or 45 . . . K–B4 allow 46 N–K7ch.

46 PxNch KxP 47 BxB NxB 48 QxP B–N3ch 49 K–N2 RxN 50 QxPch K–R4 51 Q–R7ch K–N4 52 QxN, and Black finally resigned on Move 63.

The third characteristic error is *"preventing" a draw by sending the King to prospective death.* Diagram 98, Readers of Pioneerskaya Pravda–M. Tal, 1977, after Black's 18th move, shows a "romantic" position of the type common over 100 years ago. Black has sacrificed three (!) minor pieces to expose White's King, while his own is also "characteristically" unsafe. At first "The Readers" show good nerve and judgment:

19 K–R4!

A simple perpetual check results after 19 K–R2 Q–B7ch etc. After the text, 19 . . . QxRch? is refuted by 20 B–R3ch (20 . . . KxN 21 Q–K6mate).

19 . . . Q–B7 ch! 20 K–R5?

But this further aggressiveness is foolhardy, as the King is now in enemy territory and will be unsafe. Necessary is 20 K–R3 Q–B6ch etc, with a draw.

20 . . . RxN! 21 BxRdblch KxB 22 R–R2

White is playing without his Queenside forces and the other pieces can't protect the overexposed King. If 22 Q–Q5ch, simply 22 . . . K–B1, with the dual threats of 23 . . . N–B5ch and 23 . . . N–N6ch.

DIAGRAM 98

BLACK

WHITE

"Readers"–Tal
USSR 1977
after Black's 18th

22 ... Q–B6ch   23 K–R4 P–N4ch!!   24 QxP R–KN1   25 Q–KR5ch QxQch   26 KxQ

Black seems to have almost no attacking power left—but in fact he has three attackers. The grandmaster now erred with 26 ... N–N6ch?, and after 27 K–R6 N–B4ch 28 KxP R–N2ch a draw was agreed on. Yet Black can win by:

26 ... N–B5ch!   27 K–R6

Or 27 K–R4 P–KR4!, and there is nothing to be done about the coming 28 ... R–N5mate.

27 ... R–N3ch   28 KxP R–N2ch   29 K–R6 K–N1!! Black wins

Next comes 30 ... R–N3mate. The respective Kings made for the game result. Black's King made possible the winning mating net, whereas White's foolhardy 20 K–R5? exposed his King to the coming trouble.

The fourth error is *unnecessarily sending the King on an attacking mission.* Remember that the King never feels comfortable when exposed in the middlegame, and that this is particularly true when the opponent's pieces have a fair amount of scope. White:

K—g1 Q—f5 R—f7 P—a2, c2, c3, g4, h2 Black: K—g8 R—a8, e8 B—f8 P—a7, c6, g7, h6. In this position M. Tal–V. Simagin, 1956 USSR Chaxpionship, after Black's 31st move, Black is close to the end of his rope. He's down a significant amount of material and has no play to talk about. If White now plays some sensible move like 32 R–Q7, it is even possible that Black may resign. Yet Tal gets an "inspiration" to send his King into enemy territory and this immediately presents Black with chances:

32 K–B2? B–B4ch! 33 K–N3 R–K6ch 34 K–R4 B–K2ch!

In the game Black failed to utilize the given chance and lost after 34 . . . QR–K1? 35 RxNPch! KxR 36 QxB R/1–K3 37 QxRPch K–N3 38 Q–R8 K–B3 39 P–R4 K–K4 40 P–R5 K–Q4 41 Q–Q8ch K–K5 42 P–R6 K–B6 43 P–R7 R–K7 44 Q–Q3ch R/3–K6 45 QxR/3ch.

35 K–R5 R–Q1!

With the obvious threat of 36 . . . R–Q4, and after 36 P–B4, strong is 36 . . . R–Q3. White's coming combination is also insufficient to win, because of the precarious King location.

36 RxPch KxR 37 Q–N6ch K–B1 38 QxRPch K–B2 39 QxR R–R1ch 40 Q–R6 RxQch 41 KxR Equal

Tal rates this endgame as equal and there is no reason to doubt him.

The fifth type of error is thinking that if *an exposed King is safe at present, then it will also remain safe in the future.* This is a very dangerous falacy, well illustrated by the course of play from the position below, G. Sax–O. Castro, Budapest 1977, after Black's 23rd. White: K—h4 Q—d3 R—a1, f1 B—d2 P—a2, b2, c3, d4, e5, g4, g5 Black: K—g8 Q—e6 R—a8, f8 N—c4 P—a7, b6, c7, d5, g7, h7. White has won a valuable pawn, with the last move in the combination consisting of White's King capturing Black's Knight on KR4. At the moment—and for some time to come—White's King is safe on KR4. Play continued:

24 P–N3! NxB 25 QxN R–B2 26 RxR QxR 27 R–K1 R–KB1!? 28 P–K6 Q–K2 29 P–B4?!

Here was the right moment to head back via 29 K–N3!. White's winning chances then are bright, e.g. 29 . . . Q–Q3ch 30 K–N2!

R–B5   31 P–K7! RxPch   32 K–B1 R–B5ch   33 K–N1 R–N5ch   34 Q–N2!!.

29 . . . PxP   30 PxP P–KR3   31 R–K5?

Now Black gets serious counterplay. After 31 K–N3! White would still be better.

31 . . . R–B6!

White's King from now on is unpleasantly caught on the edge of the board.

32 R–KB5 R–R6!   33 P–Q5 P–QR4   34 Q–QN2 R–K6   35 Q–B1 R–Q6   36 Q–B1 R–QB6   37 R–K5?

Loses. Probably even chances would be retained with 37 Q–B4.

37 . . . PxPch   38 RxP P–N3!

The threat of 39 . . . Q–R2ch is devastating. The only try by White is the endgame after 39 Q–B7ch QxQ   40 PxQch KxP   41 P–Q6!, which, however is probably lost.

39 Q–K1?! R–Q6   40 Q–K4 Q–R2ch   41 R–R5 P–KN4ch! White resigns

And so White even loses a Queen instead of a Rook—all because of the recently unsafe King location on KR4.

CHAPTER 21
Voluntary King Repositioning

Back in Chapter 11 we learned that very often the King must get out of the way prior to the start of action. There, though, a small step was all that was required. Periodically the need arises for the King completely to leave the area where it is located—otherwise the required piece activity or line opening just can't be accomplished. I call such cases of the King getting out of the way "voluntary King repositioning." Practical play affords many opportunities for such repositioning.

An excellent example occurs from Diagram 99, A. H. Williams–A. Karpov, 1974 Nice Olympiad, after White's 15th move. Black has somewhat more central space and the superior pawn formation. These give him several dynamic possibilities, such as attacking White's QB4 pawn, or executing a central avalanche with . . . P–KB4 and . . . P–KB5, or gaining control of the KR file. Yet as long as Black's King is in the center he is in no position to undertake anything active. Therefore Karpov sends his King to the furthest reaches of the Queenside, where it will achieve two goals: be safe itself and guard the Queenside territory.

15 . . . K–Q1!! 16 P–R4 P–R4!

White's encumbering 17 P–R5 must be stopped. White should now play 17 N–B1!, with the idea of reaching QN5 via QN3–Q2–QN1–QR3. As played, White accomplishes nothing and wastes lots of time.

17 R–QR2?! K–B2! 18 R–R6?! R–R3!

DIAGRAM 99

BLACK

WHITE

Williams–Karpov
Nice 1974
after White's 15th

A great spot for the Rook, protecting the QR and Q pawns, the QN3 square, and allowing the King to sneak in behind it for total safety.

19 Q–N5 K–N1! 20 R–N2 K–R2!

Karpov is not about to allow Black any counterplay as, for instance, after 20 . . . R–QN3?! 21 QxR NxQ 22 QRxN. White should now imitate Black and try to send his King to relative safety on QR1. The King will turn out to be unsafe in the center as soon as Black gets his KBP going.

21 Q–N3?! N–N5 22 R–R1 P–B4! 23 K–Q1 R–QN3! 24 Q–R2 RxR 25 QxR P–N3! 26 B–N3 B–R3 27 N–B1?!

White's position is miserable, but the release of control over KB4 accelerates the end. Required was 27 K–K1, and if 27 . . . N/2–K4, 28 BxN.

27 . . . N–B1! 28 Q–K2 N–N3! 29 K–Q2 N–B3! 30 Q–Q1 P–B5 White resigns

After 31 B–KR2 R–KR1! White has no satisfactory way to prevent Black from doubling on the KR-file via . . . R–KR3 and

. . . Q–KR2, after which Black must gain material. If White's Knight returns to K2 (32 N–K2 for instance), 32 . . . N–N5! is decisive. Note how tranquil and safe Black's King is on QR2!

A successful King repositioning under fairly open conditions occurs from Diagram 100, L. Vadasz–D. Bronstein, Tallin 1977, after Black's 41st move. The position is a rather fantastic one.

DIAGRAM 100

BLACK

WHITE

Vadasz–Bronstein
Tallin 1977
after Black's 41st

Materially White is up the Exchange for a pawn, yet the advanced passed QNP is a threat to be reckoned with. On the other hand, White's advanced passed KBP can be a real thorn in the side of Black's King. Who's better? Who can tell! Seriously, the chances are probably in dynamic balance—but oh, how easy it is to lose such positions for either side!

42 Q–N5 K–B1!

Envisioning a possible P–R5, Black places his King a bit to the side of the potential break.

43 K–R2 K–K1! 44 Q–K5ch K–B1

With White's Queen powerfully placed on K5, 44 . . . K–Q2?! risks danger after 45 B–N3.

45 Q-N5 K-K1   46 P-R5?

White wants more than a draw, but the resultant line opening will lead to chances for Black to get at White's King. In the meanwhile Black very consistently sends his King to safety on the Queenside.

46 . . . K-Q2!   47 N-Q1 K-B1!   48 B-N3 PxP!   49 PxP B-K1!   50 Q-B5ch K-N2   51 Q-B4

This is a waste of time, yet there is nothing good to recommend. White's position on the Kingside has become a sieve, and its penetration by Black's Q and QB can't be prevented, e.g. 51 P-R6 Q-R4ch!, and Black wins.

51 . . . K-R3!   52 K-N1 R-N3!   53 R-B2 P-K6!   54 QxP QxRP   55 Q-K5 Q-N3   56 R/1xP NxR White resigns

In the above example, both Black and his King had to endure some nerve wracking moments in connection with the King flight originating from KN1. The voluntary King repositioning from Diagram 101, T. Petrosian–W. Unzicker, USSR–West Germany 1960, after Black's 28th move, is a much smoother affair. Petrosian has his typical bind on the position as well as the more flexible (and useful) minor piece. Yet at the moment Black is just able to guard all further significant infiltration squares on the Queenside. This suggests that White should want to open another theatre of war—on the Kingside. But White's King would probably be in the way as well as be potentially vulnerable. Thus as his first step Petrosian sends his King unhurriedly to safety on the Queenside:

29 K-B1! K-B1   30 P-R4 P-R4

Prevents P-KR5, but at the cost of allowing a line opening P-KN4 later on. In either case, only with a miraculous defense can Black hope to salvage a draw. In practice such positions are invariably lost.

31 R/1-B2 K-N2   32 K-K1 K-N1   33 K-Q1 K-R2   34 K-B1 K-N1   35 K-N1! K-R2?!

Since White will be breaking via P-KN4, Black's King is poorly

DIAGRAM 101

BLACK

WHITE

Petrosian–Unzicker
USSR–West Germany 1960
after Black's 28th

placed on the KR file. Better defensive prospects are offered by shuttling it between KN2 and KB1.

36 Q–K2 Q–N2   37 R–B1 K–N2   38 Q–N5 Q–R1

The endgame after 38 . . . QxQ?! offers even less chance than the middlegame.

39 P–B4 K–R2?!   40 Q–K2 Q–N2   41 P–N4! PxP   42 QxP

The first file opened.

42 . . . Q–K2   43 P–R5 Q–B3   44 K–R2! K–N2   45 PxP QxNP 46 Q–R4

White has now opened two lines against Black's King on the Kingside, while still having an absolute grip on the QB file. White's King is completely safe. Such positions are always won— especially in the hands of someone who is both accurate and careful.

46 . . . B–K2   47 Q–B2 K–B1   48 N–Q2 R–N2   49 N–N3 R–R2 50 Q–R2! B–B3   51 R–B8! R/2–Q2   52 N–B5! P–N6ch   53 KxP R–Q3   54 P–B5! R–N3ch   55 K–R2 Black resigns

If 55 . . . QxP,   56 N–Q7ch wins a Rook.

The voluntary repositioning of both Kings under basically closed conditions will be seen from Diagram 102, A. Alekhine–O. Chajes, Carlsbad 1923, after Black's 23rd move. It is clear that Black's position is very passive and that White must be significantly better.

DIAGRAM 102

BLACK

WHITE

Alekhine–Chajes
Carlsbad 1923
after Black's 33rd

Yet the closed nature of the position means that White's road to victory must indeed be long and hard. According to Alekhine, White's winning plan consists of the following three steps:

1. White brings his King to the center, so that after the exchange of all major pieces along the KR file, White's King can penetrate via QR5.

To counter this plan, Black's King will also have to head towards the center and perhaps the Queenside.

2. By threats against Black's King (which now is on the Queenside or in the center) and Black's pawns, White forces the Black pieces to leave the Kingside.

3. At the proper moment White doubles Rooks on the KR file, forces the exchange of Queens and Bishops, and penetrates with his Rooks into Black's Kingside.

Of course, the execution takes time, but Alekhine never loses the thread of the position. Since it is White who has the position of strength, his King maneuver will be successful, whereas Black's King repositioning will be for naught:

34 N–Q3!

Care is always required. After the immediate 34 K–K2?, Black gains the advantage with 34 . . . P–K4!.

34 . . . B–K1   35 K–K2! K–B1   36 K–Q2 R–N2   37 B–B3 K–K2 38 KR–K1 N–B1   39 N–N4 K–Q1   40 K–Q3! R/KN–K2   41 Q–Q2! R–R2   42 R–KR1 R/K–QB2   33 R–R2

With Black's pieces starting to clutter the Queenside, Alekhine swings his Rooks over to the KR file.

43 . . . B–N3   44 Q–K3 K–B1   45 QR–KR1 K–N2   46 K–Q2 R–K2   47 N–Q3 N–Q2   48 B–R5!

Alekhine shows excellent judgment here. Though Black's Bishop is totally impotent as a potential attacker, it is the glue that holds together Black's Kingside. By exchanging it off, White is sure to penetrate along the KR file.

48 . . . R–R1   49 BxB PxB   50 R–R7 R/R–K1   51 N–K5!

The Knight establishes itself at this powerful location, since 51 . NxN?! 52 BPxN Q–B1 allows 53 Q–N5!, winning the KNP.

51 . . . N–B1   52 R–R8!

The Rooks keep Black in a bind, and, to accentuate this, White now prepares to exchange Queens.

52 . . . R–N2   53 N–B3! R–QN1   54 N–N5 R–K2   55 Q–K5! QxQ   56 BPxQ K–R1   57 R–N8 P–N5   58 R/1–R8! R/K–K1   59 PxP K–R2   60 K–B3 K–R3   61 N–B7!

White goes for the jugular. A prosaic win was 61 NxP.

61 . . . R–R1   62 N–Q6 R/K–N1   63 R–R1! N–Q2   64 R–R1!! Black resigns

It is not too difficult to see that Diagram 103, J. Fernandez–G. Kuzmin, Budapest 1978, after Black's 30th move, must be

DIAGRAM 103

BLACK

WHITE

J. Fernandez–Kuzmin
Budapest 1978
after Black's 30th

favorable for White. He has two nice Bishops and attacking chances against Black's Kingside, whereas Black's minor pieces are passive and the potential play along the King-file easily stoppable. However, White does need a plan of procedure. What should it be? The reader shouldn't find it hard to see that a logical approach is:

1. First 31 B–Q4!, to stop any play along the K-file,
2. Then King repositioning to the Queenside,
3. Finally, an appropriately timed Kingside break, with the obvious break method being via P–KN4.

Yet White is oblivious to all these possibilities. Note how quickly he goes from a superior to a lost position:

31 B–K5?! R–B1   32 R–R5?

It was not too late to play 32 B–Q4!.

32 . . . RxB!   33 PxR P–N3   34 R–R3 R–K1   35 R–B3 QxKP   36 QxQ RxQ

Black has one pawn for the Exchange in a sound position. The chances are even.

37 R–N2 P–N4   38 R–KN3??

By immobilizing his own Rook for the rest of the game, White finds himself, for practical purposes, a whole piece down. The normal 38 K–B2 was correct.

38 . . . P–N5! 39 P–R3 P–R4 40 PxP RPxP 41 B–B2 K–N2 42 K–B2 N–B2 43 R–N1 N–K1 44 R–KR1 N–B3 White resigns

Black can exchange his Knight for White's Bishop and can always threaten to exchange his Rook for White's "normal" Rook. In either case Black would be playing with an extra Bishop because White's KN3 Rook is absolutely nothing but a spectator.

CHAPTER 22
Correct/Incorrect King Moves

To complete this section on the middlegame, I will discuss several typical errors involving King moves. These are recurring, and affect all of us, including the greatest. Nevertheless, by disciplined approach, their occurrence in actual play can be minimized.

The most important error, and the one which is the easiest to prevent, *is carelessness in considering enemy moves.* This can also be stated as "not bothering to consider moves by the opponent which are technically very obvious." A perfect example is afforded by the following position, J. R. Capablanca–A. Alekhine, 1927 World Championship Match, Game 27, after Black's 36th move. White: K—g1 Q—e4 R—e6, g6 P—a4, b2, f4, g2, g3 Black: K—h7 Q—c5 R—f7, g8 P—a6, b7, c6, h6. Black's game is in its last moments: he's a pawn down and about to be mated. His only hope lies in some Queen checks. Of course, White can't play 37 K–R2?? because 37 . . . Q–KR4ch wins the Rook; however winning is:

37 K–B1 Q–B8ch

Now White can get out of checks and win with the accurate 38 K–K2!: 38 . . . QxNPch 39 K–B3 Q–N6ch 40 K–B2! Q–N7ch 41 K–N1 Q–B8ch 42 K–R2. Black's "attack" is over and White's will be quickly decisive.

But why play the "risky" 38 K–K2 when there is a safer, clearer King move?—this was White's reasoning when he played
. . .

38 K–B2??

Now after 38 . . . QxNPch?? 39 K–N1 White's King escapes to immediate safety. Yet now came the unanticipated . . .

38 . . . Q–Q7ch! Draw

It is exactly this check which 38 K–K2! prevented. Note that the check on Q7 occurs much closer to White's King than the one after taking off the QNP. Yet White ignored it because it didn't involve capture of material by Black. Now White can't get out of perpetual check: 39 K–N1 Q–Q8ch 40 K–B2 (40 K–R2?? Q–R4ch) 40 . . . Q–Q7ch etc.

This kind of error is preventable by simply considering all possible enemy moves in the vicinity of one's own King.

The second type of error is *a kneejerk avoidance of a dangerous looking King move in favor of a safe move, without actually looking at the specifics of the position.* Such errors occur mostly in time pressure situations; avoiding them is managed by "always looking before you leap." A typical case is the following position S. Gligorić–L. Portisch, 1974 Nice Olympiad, after Black's 53rd move. White: K—h2 Q—d5 B—b6 P—a6, d6, g2 Black: K—g6 Q—h7 R—e4 P—g5, g4. Black is up the Exchange for a pawn, yet on a strategic basis White's two far advanced passed pawns are full compensation. In the meanwhile, though, White's King is in check and must move to one of two possible squares. But where?

54 K–N1??

Surely not here, because after Black's most obvious response White's King is in a mating net. If White had bothered to consider Black's reply, he never would have played the text move. White's error lay in considering just *his own* moves on a general strategic basis—without any specific consideration of Black's possible replies.

For better or worse 54 K–N3! had to be played, and, in fact, analysis shows that it would have been for the better. Then 54 . . . P–B5ch? accomplishes nothing but the loss of a pawn after 55 KxP, while 54 . . . Q–R1 is parried by 55 B–R5! R–K4 56 Q–Q4 P–B5ch 57 QxP! RxB 58 Q–K4ch, and White will have perpetual check. Even though this conclusion was not obvious at the time of his 54th move, the alternative, as played, is instantly hopeless.

54 . . . P–N6

It is not surprising that White must now be lost. If 55 Q–Q1, 55 . . . R–KB5, followed by 56 . . . Q–R7mate. Fleeing is also no answer:

55 K–B1 Q–R8ch White resigns

It's mate after 56 B–N1 QxBch! 57 KxQ R–K8.

The third type of error is *eschewing the correct King move, because it "only leads to a draw."* Success in chess requires a never–ending quest for the truth. Any deviation from this approach brings much more sorrow than happiness. It is always necessary to retain as much objectivity as possible in evaluating a position. The best and only effective way of preventing this kind of error is to require yourself to be objective and insist on playing the *best* move. Otherwise, "playing to win" is usually synonymous with "playing for a loss." This is what happens in the play arising from Diagram 104, H. Bird–P. Morphy, London 1858, after White's 20th move. Morphy has sacrificed a Rook for this position yet a draw is all that he has in hand:

20 . . . Q–R8ch 21 K–B2 Q–R5ch!?

DIAGRAM 104

BLACK

WHITE

Bird–Morphy
London 1858
after White's 20th

Of course, Black can force an immediate perpetual check with 21 . . . Q–R7ch 23 K–B1 Q–R8ch etc. But he sees no harm in the text move, which tempts Bird to aim for more than a draw.

22 K–N2??

Walking "right into it." There is little objective basis in forcing Black to play the following obvious combination. Perhaps White overlooked Black's 25th move; even so his move smacks of foolish optimism. The only correct move is the simple 22 K–B1!, after which Black has nothing better than to grab the draw after 22 . . . Q–R8ch. The further sacrifice 22 . . . BxP? 23 PxB RxP is unsound because White has then an extra defensive tempo and can play simply 24 Q–B2 Q–R6ch 25 K–Q2 R–N7 26 R–QB1, and, with White's King safe, the material advantage will be decisive. It is even possible that White can hold on to more material by playing 24 Q–N5!?.

22 . . . BxNP! 23 PxB RxPch 24 QxR QxQch 25 K–B2

The only way to play "for a win." Other moves give no better *drawing* chances, e.g. 25 K–R2 P–B4! 26 R–QN1 (26 PxP P–Q5!) 26 . . . Q–R4ch 27 K–N3 B–Q2! and Black wins (Euwe).

25 . . . P–K6!! 26 BxP B–B4ch 27 R–Q3

Equally bad is 27 B–Q3 Q–B5ch.

27 . . . Q–B5ch 28 K–Q2 Q–R7ch 29 K–Q1 Q–N8ch! White resigns

He loses a Rook for nothing.

A fourth type of erroneous King move crops up in situations where after a hard fight a position is reached which, according to previous calculations, must be considered as won. There is a tendency to start relaxing and to give preference to the "safest" King move, rather than continuing to strain one's head to ascertain the best move. An instructive—though to me painful—case is shown from Diagram 105, E. Bogdanov–E. Mednis, World Student's Championship, Helsinki 1961, after White's 28th move. I had prepared and executed a creative combination involving the sacrifice of two pieces. White's only defensive method has been to

DIAGRAM 105

BLACK

WHITE

Bogdanov–Mednis
World Student's 1961
after White's 28th

aim for a perpetual check with his Queen, and to escape this my King has fled from the Queenside to KB3. In my earlier calculations I had envisioned this position and formed the opinion that "after a simple King move it would be all over." Thus, when the position actually arose, despite having lots of time left on the clock, I quickly glanced at 28 . . . K–N4, saw that it wins, but then decided "not to take any more chances" and just play the simple and safe:

28 . . . K–N3?

Correct and winning is 28 . . . K–N4!, as 29 QxPch is obviously inconsequential, all of Black's mating threats remain, and the game continuation is not possible.

29 R–Q2

Obviously the only way to prevent mate.

29 . . . RxR   30 Q–N4!

Suddenly things are not at all clear. Thus 30 . . . R–Q8 is foiled by 31 QxKP with *check*, and the attempt to protect the advanced KP with 30 . . . P–B4 looks unplayable because of the simple 31 BxP R–Q8   32 BxPch. Flustered by the unexpected 30 Q–N4!, I didn't bother to look any further—when in fact the accurate King move 32 . . . K–B2! would still have led to an ultimate win. Instead I settled on trapping the KB, but White had an unexpected move in this line also.

30 . . . P–QR4? 31 QxKPch QxQ 32 PxQ P–R5 33 P–B4!

The surprise. Black's next is forced and White's recapture gains a key tempo by the attack on the Rook.

33 . . . PxB 34 NxP R–Q1 35 PxP White is better

The White passed pawns are certain to produce a new Queen. Only with the greatest of effort and accuracy was I able to achieve a draw in a Q and P endgame (two pawns down) on Move 89! All of this was a direct result of taking it too easy on Move 28, and not concentrating sufficiently on Move 30.

There is one last type of error which in the practical game is almost unpreventable. This lies in not finding the correct move in an extremely complicated position, where the benchmarks for a correct decision are not apparent. In such cases only a considerable amount of actual specific calculation can be expected to give the correct answer. Under tournament play conditions unerring consistency in such analysis is not possible. For correspondence play or analysis of an adjourned position, the advice is easy to give and difficult to execute: "Analyze any and all reasonable moves." The course of play from the position below, F. Gheorghiu–L. Polugaevsky, Petropolis Interzonal 1973, after Black's 40th move, shows this very well. White: K—h3 Q—h5 R—g5, h4 P—a4, c3, f3, g6 Black: K—h8 Q—c4 R—d2, g7 P—a5, e5, f4, h7. After mutual errors in time pressure, the indicated position was reached, with the game to be adjourned and White sealing his next move:

41 RxKP Q–B8ch 42 K–N4

This position was easy to anticipate and it was not difficult to determine that Black loses after 42 . . . RxP ch? and draws with 42 . . . R–KN7 ch. However, the Soviet analysts had discovered a very surprising and unpleasant continuation:

42 . . . R–Q1!!

This move was not expected by White and therefore he was totally unprepared for it. Subsequent extensive analysis showed that the only correct reply is the paradoxical looking 43 K–N5!! After 43 . . . R–KB1 White plays 44 QxPch RxQ 45 RxRch K–N1 46 K–R6!, and after 43 . . . Q–KN8ch 44 R–N4 Q–QB8, 45 Q–R2! holds. In fact, Polugaevsky had intended 43 . . . Q–B7, but then after 44 KxP!! R–KB1ch 45 R–KB5 R–B1 46 R–K5 R–B1ch 47 R–KB5 Q–Q7ch 48 K–N3 Q–Q3ch 49 K–N2 RxPch 50 R–N4 RxRch 51 PxR, only a draw could have been expected.

43 KxP?

Wrong—because of the following diagonal check. The only way to have known is to have analyzed in depth the position after Black's 42nd.

43 . . . Q–B8ch! 44 K–N3

After 44 K–B5 Black wins with 44 . . . R–KB1ch! 45 K–K4 QxP 46 Q–N4 Q–B3ch 47 K–K3 RxNP 48 Q–K4 Q–B8ch, while after 44 K–K4 QxP White's King is again without hope.

44 . . . RxPch 45 R–KN4 Q–N8ch 46 K–R3 RxR 47 QxR Q–R8ch 48 K–N3 R–KN1 49 R–KN5 Q–N8ch 50 K–B4 Q–B8ch 51 K–B5 R–B1ch 52 K–K4 QxP 53 R–K5?

Loses immediately, yet the King in the center looks like a sitting duck, anyway.

53 . . . Q–K8ch 54 K–Q5 R–Q1ch 55 K–K6 R–K1ch White resigns

Part III

THE ENDGAME

It is in the endgame that the King is King. Of necessity sheltered through the opening and middlegame, in the endgame the King becomes a valuable, important, fighting piece. Mikhail Tal has intriguingly suggested that the value of an active King in the endgame is "three points," i.e. equivalent to a Bishop or Knight.

Just as the dividing line between the opening and middlegame is not sharp, so too the transition from the middlegame to the endgame is often blurred. For an endgame to have arisen, to my mind the following two things must exist: (1) Some exchanges of material must have taken place, and (2) The important characteristics of midlegame play, such as the importance of superior piece coordination and/or attacking prospects against the enemy King, *must be absent*. Note that the mere absence of Queens, however, is never enough to indicate the start of an endgame. Conversely, Queen and pawn endgames are an important part of the genre. If a large number of pieces have been exchanged and the Kings look safe—then you can feel confident that you're in an endgame.

The basic objective of the endgame is to queen a pawn. Thus, much of the action revolves around creation of passed pawn(s) and the attempt to transform the passed pawn into a new Queen. The King is of major importance, both as an attacker and defender, in these operations.

CHAPTER 23
The Helpless King

Because, by definition, the occurence of an endgame requires that a considerable amount of material has left the board, the remaining forces—pieces *and* pawns—increase in importance. Therefore, it follows logically that the King takes on a significantly increased role. The side with a King unable to participate fully is under a very serious handicap.

SECTION 1. King Cut Off from Specific Field of Action

Middlegame positions usually suggest relatively broad possible scenes of action; in the endgame the fruitful area of play is much more localized. If the King can not get to this area, the ultimate result of the game may be decided: i.e. a potentially drawn position lost, or a favorable position only drawn. The most important scene of action is the attempt at queening a pawn. If the defender's King is cut off from this area, the loss is almost inevitable.

A classic example is Diagram 106, J. Bednarski–E. Geller, Siegen Olympiad 1970, after Black's 24th move. White is a pawn up, but Black's active Rook appears to be sufficient compensation. Yet note that Black's King is cut off from returning to the Kingside. This enables White to achieve a forced win starting with

25 P–B4! PxP   26 P–K5 R–QN8

DIAGRAM 106

BLACK

WHITE

Bednarski–Geller
Siegen 1970
after Black's 24th

Since Black's King can't help out, the Rook must rush back. Unplayable for White now is 27 P–K6??, as 27 . . . R–N3 both stops and wins the KP. White's King now enters the fray however, and, with Black's King effectively absent, the unequal fight for promotion of the KP must end in White's favor.

27 K–B3! R–KB8ch 28 K–N4 P–N4 29 P–K6 R–K8 30 K–B5 R–K6 31 K–B6 P–B6 32 PxP RxBPch 33 K–N7 R–K6 34 K–B7 R–B6ch 35 K–K8 P–B3 36 R–Q8ch K–B2 37 R–Q7ch K–B1 38 RxP RxP 39 P–K7 RxP 40 K–B8 R–K7 41 P–K8 = Qch Black resigns

The need for the defending King to control the queening square is clear, and should serve as a guiding beacon in positions where a choice of moves is possible. Consider next the following position L. Polugaevsky–V. Korchnoi, 1977 Candidates Match, Game 6, after White's 43rd move. White: K—f4 R—b8 P—b5 Black: K—d5 R—b3 P—d6, f5. Black is a pawn up, and it is easy to envision White's QNP and Black's KBP being lost. This will leave Black's QP as the only pawn remaining, and the question will be whether White (with the necessary assistance of the King) can stop it. Black's next is straightforward:

43 . . . K–B4

White should now play the obvious 44 KxP, and after 44 . . . RxP, 45 R–QR8!, to keep the Rook active. He can then hold the position after either 45 . . . K–Q5ch 46 K–B4 R–N8 (46 . . . R–K4 47 R–R4ch! K–Q6 48 R–R3ch K–B5 49 R–R6!) 47 R–R4ch K–Q6 48 R–R3ch K–B5 49 K–K3 or after 45 . . . R–N5 46 R–R5ch! K–N3 47 R–R8! R–Q5 48 K–K6.

44 R–B8ch??

Short of time, White commits a horrible, thoughtless blunder.

44 . . . KxP 45 KxP R–K6!

The move White had overlooked when he indulged in his "automatic" check. White's King now is and remains cut off from the Black pawn's queening march, with the position becoming a routine theoretical win.

46 K–B4 R–K8 47 R–Q8 K–B4 48 R–B8ch K–Q5 49 K–B3 P–Q4 50 K–B2 R–K4! 51 R–QR8 K–B6 52 R–R3ch K–N5 53 R–R1 P–Q5 54 R–QB1 P–Q6 55 R–B8 P–Q7 56 R–N8ch K–B6 57 R–B8ch K–Q6 58 R–Q8ch K–B7 59 R–B8ch K–Q8 White resigns.

Black has obtained the "Lucena position"—known as a win since the end of the 15th century! The proof: (1) 60 R–B7 R–B4ch 61 K–N2 K–K7 62 R–K7ch K–Q6 63 R–Q7ch K–K6 64 R–K7ch K–Q5 65 R–Q7ch R–Q4, and (2) 60 R–Q8 R–K7ch 61 K–B1 (61 K–B3 K–K8) 61 . . . R–K8ch 62 K–B2 K–B7.

In K and P endings, the need for the King to control the enemy pawn's queening square is, of course, absolute. Disaster, however, can strike in various forms. First consider the position below, A. Lein–P. Biyiasas, New York International 1977, after Black's 37th move. White: K—g2 R—f2 P—a2, f5, g4, h5 Black: K—f6 R—c4 P—a6, b4, g5. Though White is a pawn up, the activity of Black's Rook and the weakness of White's KNP means that there is no win:

38 K–N3 R–B6ch

White has nothing better than to acquiesce to 39 K–N2 R–B5

40 K–N3 etc., with a draw, as the passive 39 K–R2 R–B5   40 R–KN2 gives no winning chances and Black can choose either 40 . . . P–R4 or 40 . . . K–N2. Yet White "decides" to commit suicide:

39 R–B3??

With the point that after 39 . . . RxRch??   40 KxR White's King is close enough to the Queenside to stop Black's pawns, thereby giving White a won endgame. With his unexpected (by White) reply, Black wins a key tempo and completely turns the tables.

39 . . . P–R4!

After 40 RxR PxR the BP queens, and if White tries to get out of the pin with 40 K–B2, he is one move too late after 40 . . . RxRch 41 KxR P–R5   42 K–K2 P–N6   43 PxP P–R6!.

40 P–R6 P–R5 White resigns

After 41 P–R7 RxRch   42 KxR K–N2 Black's King is close enough to the scene of action, but White's King isn't.

In the previous example White's King was simply arithmetically too far away from the Queenside. Often the King seems to be close enough, yet use of appropriate interference prevents it from reaching his goal. This is what happens to the play arising from Diagram 107, A. Pomar–Cuadras, Olot 1974, after Black's 62nd move. Playing White, the Spanish GM has obtained only a materially even endgame against his unheralded opponent. The endgame offers nothing but equality, and the best way to maintain the status quo is with 63 K–Q4 K–K3   64 K–B4 K–Q3   65 K–Q4 K–K3   66 K–B4. But Pomar, unmindful of potential danger, thinks only of winning:

63 K–Q6??

. . . and allows Black a characteristic winning breakthrough with

63 . . . P–B5!!   64 K–Q5

The danger has been perceived, but the King won't be able to get back in time. Alternately, 64 NPxP P–R5 will give Black a winning passed RP, and, after 64 KPxP P–R5!   65 PxP P–N6! 66 PxP P–K6 the KP can't be caught.

DIAGRAM 107

BLACK

WHITE

Pomar–Cuadras
Olot 1974
after Black's 62nd

64 . . . P–R5! 65 KxP P–B6!!

The key interference move, preventing White's King from getting to KB3, as after 65 . . . P–R6?? 66 PxRP PxRP 67 K–B3.

66 PxBP P–R6 White resigns

There are, of course, many, many other types of action. Particularly important for practical play is the type shown in the position below, P. Ostermeyer–J. Dueball, Manheim 1975, after Black's 53rd move. White: K—g3 R—b5 P—f2, g4 Black: K—g6 R—c3 P—b4. Such endgames are generally won for the stronger side, *provided that his King can assist in the advance of his pawns.* This principle should serve as the basis for White's decisions. Because it doesn't, White doesn't win:

54 K–N2?!

A serious, though not fatal misstep. Correct is 54 P–B3, with the usual objective of using the King to assist the pawns to advance. Black has two defenses, neither sufficient: (1) 54 . . . P–N6 55 K–B4! R–B5ch 56 K–K3 R–B6ch 57 K–K4 K–B3 (57 . . . R–B5ch? 58 K–Q3 R–B5 59 K–K3) 58 P–B4 R–B5ch 59 K–K3 R–B6ch 60 K–Q4 R–N6 61 R–N6ch K–K2 62 P–N5, followed by K–K4, K–KB5, etc. Slowly and surely White keeps moving forward. And (2) 54 . . . R–B5 55 R–N6ch K–N2 (55 . . . K–N4? 56 P–B4ch! RxP 57 R–N5ch wins the Rook) 56 P–B4!, followed by P–N5, P–B5, etc. With the King on the third rank the pawns can advance by themselves since a . . . R–QB4 is easily met by K–N4.

54 . . . P–N6   55 P–B4??

But after this there is no win since White's King remains cut off. It was still not too late for bridge building with P–B3, K–N3, etc. White has lost some time, but Black can't do anything of substance with it.

55 . . . K–B3!

Surely not 55 . . . R–B7ch?? 56 K–B3, and the King gets out.

56 R–N6ch K–B2   57 P–N5 K–N2   58 P–B5

Acquiescing to an immediate draw. With White's King relegated to the second rank there is no way to make progress.

58 . . . R–B4!

Now there is no way to protect the overly advanced pawns.

59 R–N7ch K–N1   60 R–N8ch draw

A possible continuation is 60 . . . K–N2 61 P–B6ch K–B2 62 R–N7ch K–B1 63 P–N6 R–N4ch and 64 . . . RxP.

Section 2. King Generally Imprisoned

There are two problems with a King who is so contained that it must be considered to be imprisoned. First, it is of no offensive help and, except for the few squares immediately around it, also of no defensive value. Secondly—and particularly in positions containing one or more major pieces—the King can be readily vulnerable to a mating attack.

An absolutely hopeless position, for practical purposes, is shown in Diagram 108, L. Shamkovich–A. Soltis, 1978 U.S. Championship, after White's 33rd move. Not only is Black a

DIAGRAM 108

BLACK

WHITE

Shamkovich–Soltis
US Champ 1978
after White's 33rd

pawn down, but his King and Bishop are contained on the first rank. White's immediate threat is 34 P–Q6, so Black plays

33 . . . R–N2

Or 33 . . . R–Q6   34 R–Q8, followed by 35 K–K2; or 33 . . . K–N2   34 K–K2 R–N7ch   35 K–Q3 R–N6ch   36 K–Q2 R–N7ch 37 K–B3, followed by 38 B–Q4ch.

34 B–Q4 P–R3   35 P–R4 R–N6ch   36 K–K2 R–N2   37 R–B8!

Black would be in complete *zugzwang* after 37 . . . P–R4   38 P–N3. Therefore he allows an immediate end.

37 . . . R–N5   38 P–Q6! Black resigns

Of course a position doesn't have to be as hopeless as the above still to be hopeless. This is true of Diagram 109, L. Polugaevsky–V. Korchnoi, 1977 Candidates Match, Game 2, after Black's 34th move. Though material is even, Black's Rook has penetrated into White's position and Black's Kingside pawns will form a fence around White's King. White is simply lost; the course was as follows:

DIAGRAM 109

BLACK

WHITE

Polugaevsky–Korchnoi
1977 Match, Game 2
after Black's 34th

35 B–B3 R–QB8 36 B–Q2 R–B7 37 P–QR4 P–B5 38 P–R3 P–B6ch 39 K–B1 P–KR4 40 PxP PxP White resigns

Here the game was adjourned and White took 45 minutes to seal his move, 41 K–K1. He resigned without continuing, since 41 . . . B–B4! keeps White in a hopeless hammerlock. No better would have been 41 R–Q4, as the following analysis by Robert Byrne shows: 41 . . . R–N7 42 B–K1 RxNP 43 RxP R–N8 (Shades of Shamkovich–Soltis, reversed!) 44 R–K4 B–N5 45 R–K6 K–B2 46 R–K3 K–N3 47 R–K6ch K–B4 48 R–K3 RxBch 49 RxR BxR 50 KxB K–K5, and Black wins the K and P endgame.

There are times when the greatest of sophistication is required to recognize the ultimate danger of having a contained King. The following position, E. Mednis–L. D. Evans, New York International II 1977, after Black's 40th move, appears to hold no dangers for Black. White: K—g2 R—c7 B—f4 P—e4, f2, g3, h4 Black: K—g8 R—a8 N—c8 P—e6, f7, g7, h5. With his next move however, White sets a sophisticated trap:

41 R–B5!

Attacking the RP, which therefore should be defended, yes?

41 . . . P–N3?

No! Correct is 41 . . . P–B3!, as White can not afford to play 42 RxP?! because of 42 . . . P–K4 43 B–K3 N–Q3, and White's Rook is semi-trapped. Therefore best would have been 42 P–K5!, but with only a slight advantage for White.

42 R–B6!

Black now is lost: his King and Knight are contained, and this also chains his Rook to the first rank. Moreover, the "holey" nature of Black's pawn formation enables White's King to penetrate into Black's Kingside.

42 . . . N–K2 43 R–B7! N–B1 44 B–K5! N–N3 45 B–Q4 R–N1 46 K–B3! N–B1 47 B–K5 N–N3

Loses immediately, but after 47 . . . R–R1 48 K–B4 White's King starts marching in.

48 R–B6! R–N2 49 B–Q4 Black resigns

After 49 . . . N–Q2 50 R–B8ch N–B1 (50 . . . K–R2 51 R–KR8mate!) 51 B–B5 White wins the pinned Knight.

The imprisoned King is such a liability that the only correct advice to give in how to defend such positions is: AVOID THEM! A graphic illustration of the never–ending problems resulting from such a King position is demonstrated in the play arising from Diagram 110, E. Mednis–I. Csom, Budapest 1978, after Black's 33rd move. Though a pawn down, Black is already better here, because of his active Rook and the ultimate vulnerability of all of White's Kingside. Being short of time, however, I didn't appreciate the additional risk of getting my King imprisoned:

34 P–B4?

For better or worse, 34 P–N3! had to be played. White's King would then have obtained a fair amount of mobility.

34 . . . K–B3! 35 B–K3 R–B6 36 PxPch KxP 37 B–N6 P–N6!

It is this move to which I had neglected to give the necessary

DIAGRAM 110

BLACK

WHITE

Mednis–Csom
Budapest 1978
after Black's 33rd

respect. White's King now remains contained for the rest of the game.

38 PxP PxP   39 B–B7 R–R6   40 R–Q1ch K–K5   41 B–Q6

The adjourned position. Analysis showed that as long as Black is careful to keep the bind, White's chances of survival are nil.

**41 . . . B–Q1   42 B–B5 B–B2!   43 R–K1ch K–Q4   44 B–Q6
B–R4!   45 R–Q1ch   K–K5   46 B–B5 B–Q7!   47 B–B2 KxP   48
B–K1 B–B5   49 B–B3ch K–B4   50 R–KB1 RxP   51 B–K1 R–R6
White resigns**

White's King is still contained while he is already down material.

The practical considerations that exist in an actual game are excellently shown by the course of play from Diagram 111, J. Benjamin–P. Biyiasas, New York International II 1977, after Black's 41st move. The time control is over, Black is two clear pawns down, and his King is rather exposed. White's win should not be far away. Instead note what happens and why it happens:

42 Q–Q4??

DIAGRAM 111

BLACK

WHITE

Benjamin–Biyiasas
N.Y. 1977
after Black's 41st

According to conventional thinking, a good plan: White exchanges the Queens and remains two pawns up in the endgame. Yet a deeper consideration shows it to be wrong because White's King will remain imprisoned and unsafe during the play to come, whereas, with the Queens off, Black's King is safe. It is most doubtful if the endgame is a win for White; of course it shouldn't be lost.

Correct for White would have been a "middlegame" move, such as 42 R–K1.

42 . . . QxQ!   43 RxQ R–K2

Already Black is operating with mating threats!

44 R–Q1 R–K5   45 R–KB1 K–N2   46 P–Q6 P–R4   47 N–Q5 R–K7   48 N–N6 P–R5   49 NxBP?!

Both 49 P–Q7! and 49 NxRP! are better.

49 . . . B–K3   50 R–Q1 K–B1!   51 N–R3?!

51 P–R3! is better.

51 . . . K–K1   52 P–B4 RxKNP   53 P–B5 K–Q2   54 N–N5 B–N5 55 R–QB1?

55 R–K1 should still be good enough for equality.

55 . . . R–QB7! 56 R–KN1 RxBP 57 N–B3 B–K3 58 NxP R–QR4 59 N–B3 KxP 60 R–Q1ch K–K2

With his King still imprisoned, White now is lost. After winning White's KRP Black will have a decisive KRP of his own.

61 R–K1 K–B2 62 R–KB1ch B–B4 63 R–B4 K–B3 64 N–R4 K–N4 65 R–B4 KxP 66 PxP K–N4 67 R–B1 P–R4 68 R–N1ch K–B5 69 R–B1ch K–N6 70 R–N1ch K–B7 71 R–R1 B–K5 72 R–R4 B–B6 73 K–N1 K–N6 74 R–QB4 P–R5 75 N–B3 R–K4 76 R–B8 P–R6 77 R–N8ch B–N5 78 R–KR8 P–R7 79 K–B2 R–KR4 80 N–K4ch K–B5 81 RxR BxR 82 N–B2 K–B6 White resigns

CHAPTER 24
The Active King Wins

SECTION 1. King + Pawn Endgames

As the only piece left—by definition—the King's power in K and P endgames is awesome. Apart from general King activity, the technical King movements called "opposition" and "triangulation" are also of major significance. Since these will be considered in detail later on in the book, any appearance in this section will be only noted tangentially. King activity is always of paramount importance, and when I talk of the "active King" what I mean is that *the King can get to where it wants to go*.

A basic, important, position is of the type shown below, White on move. White: K—f3 P—b4 Black: K—a8 P—b6. Ideally, White wants to capture Black's pawn while Black wants to capture White's. Clearly Black's King is too far away to do that. As a secondary goal, Black wants to be able to protect his pawn. This also will be shown to be impossible. Thirdly, Black would want to lose the pawn only under such circumstances that he can still hold the position for a draw. Yet if White plays correctly, this too can be avoided. White to play wins as follows:

1 P—N5!!

Overeager is the immediate 1 K—K4?, as Black draws after 1 . . . P—N4!! 2 K—Q5 K—N2 3 K—B5 K—R3 4 K—B6 K—R2 5 KxP K—N2!, and a position known as a theoretical draw has been reached. White can always capture Black's pawn; the key to the win of the game is to do it the right way.

1 ... K-N2 2 K-K4 K-B2 3 K-K5! K-Q2 4 K-Q5! K-B2
5 K-K6 K-B1 6 K-Q6! K-N2 7 K-Q7! K-N1 8 K-B6 K-R2 9
K-B7 K-R1 10 KxP

And so, at long last, White's active King has captured the
pawn. Since White's King is on the *sixth rank in front of its
pawn, the position is won irrespective of who is on move.*

10 ... K-N1 11 K-R6 K-R1 12 P-N6 K-N1 13 P-N7
K-B2 14 K-R7 White wins

The active King is potentially even more dangerous when
there are pawns on both sides of the board. This situation, with
the pawn formations unbalanced, is shown in this position, S.
Kalinichev–Y. Gutop, 1978 Moscow Championship, after
White's 49th move. White: K—c2 P—a2, b3, f2, g3, h4 Black:
K—d4 P—a6, e5, f5, g6, h6. It is obviously Black's King which
is active, and he won as follows:

49 ... P-N4! 50 PxP PxP 51 K-Q2 P-K5 52 P-R3 P-B5

Black can readily create a passed pawn from his majority,
whereas the overpowering location of Black's King prevents
White from achieving the same.

53 PxP PxP 54 P-N4 K-B5! 55 K-B2 K-N4! 56 K-B3 K-R5 57
K-Q4 P-K6! 58 PxP P-B6 White resigns

After 59 K-Q3 KxP 60 P-K4 KxP Black's King can stop White's
KP but White's can't get to Black's QRP.

A more sophisticated demonstration of the value of the active
King is shown in the play arising from Diagram 112, A.
Jusupov–Ionov, USSR 1977, after Black's 45th move. White has
two advantages here: the obvious one of having the active King
and the less obvious one of having the potential Queenside pawn
breakthrough (because of Black's doubled QNPs), similar to that of
Diagram 107. The basic winning method is for White's King to
force Black's far enough away from the Queenside to allow the
break to be executed. The course of the game:

46 P-N4 K-B3 47 P-N5

DIAGRAM 112

BLACK

WHITE

A. Jusupov–Ionov
USSR 1977
after Black's 45th

White's QNP is now in place. Black has nothing better than continued passivity, since 47 . . . P–N4ch 48 K–N4 K–N3 loses to 49 P–R3! K–B3 50 K–R5 K–B4 51 P–QR4! K–B3 52 K–R6 K–B4 53 K–N7, and White's King will be the first one to do damage.

47 . . . K–N3 48 K–N4 K–B3 49 P–KR4 K–N3 50 P–R5ch K–R3?!

Makes White's task routine. More logical was 50 . . . K–B3! 51 K–B4! K–K2 (also losing is 51 . . . P–N3 52 P–R6! P–N4ch 53 K–K3!, and Black can't go after the KRP because of White's pawn breakthrough) 52 K–N5 K–B2 53 K–B5 K–K2 54 K–N6 K–B1 55 P–R4!, and after the forced 55 . . . K–N1, White wins with 56 P–B5!: 56 . . . QPxP 57 P–R5! PxP 58 P–N6! PxP 59 P–Q6 K–B1 60 P–Q7 K–K2 61 KxP P–R5 62 P–R6 P–R6 63 P–R7 P–R7 64 P–Q8 = Qch KxQ 65 P–R8 = Qch.

51 P–R4 P–N3 52 P–B5! PxRPch

Or 52 . . . QNPxP 53 P–R5 P–B5 54 P–R6 PxP 55 PxP P–B6 56 P–R7 P–B7 57 P–R8 = Q PxPch 58 K–B5! (the active King) 58 . . . P–B8 = Q 59 Q–R8mate.

53 K–B3!

But here it is important for the King to be able to stop the pawns, as 53 K–B5? allows 53 . . . P–R5!, and if White stops the KRP with 54 K–N4, the mate threat apparent in the above note has evaporated. In the game Black resigned after the text. Jusupov gives the following likely continuation:

53 . . . NPxP   54 P–R5 P–B5   55 P–R6 PxP   56 PxP P–B6   57 K–K3 White wins

Black's QBP gets stopped; White's QRP promotes.

The active King doesn't necessarily have to be gaining material to be doing its part in winning. Gaining territory or preventing threats is often equally desirable. The following position, a 1932 study by N. Grigoriev, at first glance offers scant winning hopes for White. White: K—g6 P—a2 Black: K—f3 P—c7. Yet sophisticated and *active* King movements lead to the following forced win:

1 K–B5! K–K6   2 K–K5 P–B3

To prevent White's K–Q5. After 2 . . . K–Q6   3 K–Q5 K–B6   4 K–B5! White's win is routine.

3 P–R4 K–Q6   4 P–R5 P–B4   5 P–R6 P–B5   6 P–R7 P–B6   7 P–R8 = Q P–B7   8 Q–Q5ch!

Black is just an eyelash away from a stalemate draw. To win, White must put his Queen on the correct square and then move his King down to create a mating net.

8 . . . K–K7

After 8 . . . K–K6 White wins with 9 Q–N2! followed by 10 Q–N5(ch).

9 Q–R2! K–Q8   10 K–Q4! P–B8 = Q   11 K–Q3! White wins.

Mate is unpreventable, e.g. 11 . . . Q–B5   12 Q–B2ch K–K8   13 Q–K2.

The above is a study, yes. But now let us see how the themes of preventing Black's pawn from queening and utilizing the King as part of the mating attack are transferable to real life. An excellent practical case is shown in the position below, Dr. Mändler–

Prochaska, East Germany 1976, White to move. White: K—c6 P—a3, b4, g2, h3 Black: K—f2 P—a7, h4. White is two pawns ahead, yet Black's King is at the throat of White's Kingside. Routine play is insufficient for the full point, e.g. 1 P–N5 KxP 2 K–N7 KxP 3 KxP K–N5 4 P–N6 P–R6 and, after both sides Queen, White's QRP on the third rank is not enough to win. The win requires a different type of King activity:

1 K–Q5!! KxP 2 K–K4 KxP 3 K–B3

White's plan is clear: he wants to keep Black's K and KRP contained long enough to enable him to make a Queen from his Queenside pawn majority. Black's only practical hope is to try to create a stalemate on the Kingside.

3 . . . K–R7 4 K–B2!!

Only so! After 4 P–N5 K–N8!! 5 K–N4 K–N7! 6 KxP K–B6 Black's King gets back in time to the Queenside; after 4 P–R4 P–R6 5 K–B2 P–R4!! 6 PxP K–R8 7 P–R6 P–R7 Black has created stalemate.

4 . . . P–R6 5 P–N5! K–R8 6 K–B1! P–R7 7 P–N6!! P–R4!?

The only try, since 7 . . . PxP 8 P–R4 P–N4 9 P–R5 allows White to promote with checkmate.

8 P–N7 P–R5 9 K–K2!

Unfortunately White must release the stalemate. However, White's King remains close enough to Black's so that the coming Q and P endgame is won.

9 . . . K–N8 10 P–N8 = Q P–R8 = Q 11 Q–N6ch K–R7 12 Q–Q6ch K–N8

Or 12 . . . K–R6 13 Q–R6ch K–N7 14 Q–N5ch K–R6 15 Q–R5ch K–N7 16 Q–N4ch K–R7 17 K–B2!, and White's King is close enough to mate Black's.

13 Q–Q4ch K–R7 14 Q–R4ch K–N7 15 Q–N4ch K–R7 16 K–B2! Black resigns

Imminent mate is unavoidable.

Section 2. Minor Piece Endgames

Since, as mentioned in the introductory section, the value of the active King in the endgame is approximately 3 points, the strength of the active King in a minor piece endgame is equivalent to a whole minor piece. This means that in minor piece endgames the active King is a tremendous power and most of the time is the winning factor. A crossection of minor piece endgames will demonstrate this principle as well as give guidance in the proper utilization of the King.

Instructive play in a same–color Bishop endgame arises from Diagram 113, Tarasov–T. Petrosian, 1957 USSR Championship, after White's 40th move. Superficially, White's position may look O.K. He has the Queenside majority and his pawns there are on the "right" color. Yet it will become apparent very soon that Black has in fact a decisive advantage because he can rapidly mobilize his King:

40 . . . K–N2!

DIAGRAM 113

BLACK

WHITE

Tarasov–Petrosian
1957 USSR
Championship
after White's 40th

Black plans simply to run his King along the KR1–QR8 diagonal to QN7. White suffers from having his King stuck on the edge of the board at KR2. Therefore, to try to slow down Black's King, White must use his KBP—but this leads to a chronic weakening of White's Kingside.

41 P–B4 K–B3   42 P–N3 K–B4!   43 B–N1ch B–K5   44 B–R2 B–Q6   45 K–N2 K–K5   46 PxP

Allows Black two connected passed pawns in the center, to go with his active King. But equally unattractive is 46 K–B2 PxPch 47 KxP K–Q5.

46 . . . KxP   47 K–B2 K–K4!   48 B–N3

Black's King and passed pawns now can become active. But 48 K–K3 loses a pawn after 48 . . . B–B4.

48 . . . K–Q5   49 B–Q1 P–K4   50 P–R5 PxP   51 BxP P–B4   52 P–KR4 P–B5   53 B–Q1 P–K5!   54 P–R5 K–K4!

Passed pawns must be pushed!—and both sides strive to follow this principle. Black's connected passed pawns remain a powerful force, but first Black's King neutralizes White's pawn.

55 P–R6 K–B3   56 B–N3 P–K6ch   57 K–B3 B–K5ch!   58 K–K2 K–N3

Eliminating the KRP.

59 B–K6 KxP   60 B–Q7 K–N4   61 P–R4 K–B3!

Moving over to neutralize White's Queenside prospects.

62 P–N5 PxP   63 PxP K–K4   64 B–N4 K–Q4 White resigns

After the forced 65 P–B6 PxP   66 PxP KxP Black is up the two passed pawns. Over-all, what a colossal job by Black's King!

The King's importance is even greater in an opposite–color Bishop endgame. Since each Bishop "does its own thing," it is the King's role which most often is the decisive factor. It is very much so in the play arising from Diagram 114, E. Mednis–W. Lombardy, 1978 U.S. Championship, after Black's 46th move. White is up a sound pawn, but the blockading tendencies of the

DIAGRAM 114

BLACK

WHITE

Mednis–Lombardy
1978 US Championship
after Black's 46th

opposite–color Bishops makes the potential win far in the future. White's general strategy is as follows: his King will head to the Queenside; Black's King will have to do likewise or White's QRP will promote. White's Bishop then will capture Black's KB2 pawn. With Black's Kingside thus weakened, White's King will return to it and penetrate decisively. This is exactly what happens—though it takes patience.

47 K–K4 B–B7   48 B–B8 K–Q1   49 B–B5

White has accomplished his first objective: the Bishop is on the proper diagonal for getting to KR7, Black's potential counterplay via . . . P–B4 is stopped, and White's King is free to head to the Queenside. Black has no time for an immediate King foray there: 49 . . . K–B2   50 B–R7 K–N3   51 B–N8 K–R4   52 BxP KxP   53 K–B5 B–R5   54 K–K6 etc., with White King's penetration decisive.

49 . . . B–K8   50 B–R7 K–Q2   51 K–Q3 K–Q1   52 K–B4 K–B2 53 K–N5 B–N6   54 P–R5 B–K8   55 B–Q3

Prior to executing the indicated plan, White kills a bit of time in order to reach the time control on Move 56. This is a common tournament technique when the opponent—such as Black here— has no way of improving his position.

**55 . . . B–R5   56 B–K4 B–K8   57 K–R6 B–R5   58 B–R7 B–N4
59 B–N8 B–Q7**

After considerable thought Black again sticks to his passive
approach. Of course, the only reason I hesitated about playing
B–N8 was to decide on how to respond if Black plays . . . P–B4,
i.e. here 59 . . . P–B4. I felt fairly certain that 60 PxP P–B3   61
B–B7 should win, as White eventually gets in P–KB4 and Black
also has to reckon with a potential P–QB5 break. Nevertheless, I
had decided that even surer is 60 BxP, with the following
possibilities: (1) 60 . . . P–B5   61 B–N6 B–R5   62 B–B5 B–B7   63
K–N5 B–N6 64 P–R6 B–B7   65 P–B4 B–N6 (65 . . . B–B4   66 P–R4
etc.) 66 P–R7! K–N2   67 P–R8 = Qch KxQ   68 K–B6; (2) 60 . . .
P–K5   61 PxKP PxKP (61 . . . P–B5   62 B–K8, followed by 63
B–N5) 62 B–N6 P–K6   63 B–Q3 and in due course White will
fashion a passed pawn on the Kingside to win; (3) 60 . . . PxP   61
BPxP!, and again White will obtain a winning Kingside passed
pawn.

60 BxP B–B6   61 B–N6 B–K8   62 B–B5 B–B6   63 K–N5

With objective 2—winning the KB2 pawn—achieved, White's
King heads back to go for objective 3: penetration of Black's
Kingside.

**63 . . . B–K8   64 P–R6 B–B7   65 K–B4 K–N3   66 B–B8 K–B2
67 B–N7 K–Q1   68 K–Q3 K–K2   69 K–K4 B–N3   70 B–B8 B–B4
71 B–K6 K–B1   72 K–B5 K–N2   73 P–B3 B–B7**

Black seems to be just holding by a hair, as 74 B–B8 can be met
by 74 . . . K–B2. But a simple tactical deflection maneuver immediately shows up the deficiencies in Black's camp.

74 B–N8! B–B4   75 K–K6

Black must now capture, as otherwise White plays 76 B–B7 and
has penetrated for nothing.

75 . . . KxB   76 KxP

Thus White has achieved his third objective: his King has
penetrated into Black's position. The cost (White's Bishop) is easily
affordable, as his Bishop had no offensive power and neither
Black's King nor Bishop has any offensive possibilities. On a purely

material balance, White has three pawns for the piece, which is
fully sufficient.

76 . . . K–R2

Leads to an immediate disaster, yet 76 . . . K–B1 is only
marginally better: 77 P–QB4 K–N1 (After 77 . . . K–K1 78 K–N7!
White makes a winning passed KNP) 78 P–R4! B–B7 79 K–K6
B–B4 80 K–Q7, followed by K–B7, K–N7, P–R7 etc.

77 K–B7!

Black now is helpless against the coming Kingside pawn advance. The conclusion was:

**77 . . . B–B7 78 P–R4 B–B4 79 P–N5 PxP 80 PxP B–N3 81
P–N6ch K–R3 82 P–N7 K–N4 83 P–N8 = Qch K–B5 84 Q–N4ch
K–K6 85 Q–N1ch KxP 86 QxB P–K5 87 P–R7 P–K6 88
P–R8 = Q P–K7 89 Q–K8 P–K8 = Q 90 QxQ Black resigns**

Even at the master level it must be emphasized over and over
again how critical one's position can become if the opponent has
the active King. An excellent illustration in a Knight endgame is
provided by Diagram 115, Segal–B. Ivkov, Sao Paulo 1978, after
Black's 22nd move. White—a Brazilian master—had just rushed to
exchange off all the Rooks in the expectation that this will bring
him closer to a draw. His Knight is well placed and pawn formation faultless. But the more experienced Yugoslav Grandmaster
had correctly reasoned that the imminent activity of his King will
suffice to win. Black's King is already centralized; White's is not.
Note how quickly Black's King attains a dominating position:

23 K–B1 K–Q3! 24 K–K2 K–Q4 25 N–B3

White's Knight looks for a more stable location. After 25 K–Q2
Ivkov gives the following winning procedure: 25 . . . N–K5ch 26
K–K2 K–B5 27 P–B3 N–B4 28 K–Q2 P–K4, followed by 29 . . .
K–N6.

25 . . . P–K4 26 N–Q2 P–K5 27 P–KN4

To prevent 27 . . . P–B4, yet this pawn advance weakens the
Kingside.

**27 . . . N–R5 28 P–N3 N–B6ch 29 K–B1 P–N4 30 K–N2
P–R5!**

DIAGRAM 115

BLACK

WHITE

Segal–B. Ivkov
Sao Paulo 1978
after Black's 22nd

Both fixes White's QRP and opens up Black's QB5 square for potential infiltration by the King or Knight.

31 P–N4 K–K4! 32 K–N3 P–B4

Black first strengthens his Kingside pawn formation. The Queenside play won't run away.

33 PxP KxP 34 P–B3 K–K4! 35 K–B2 P–B4 36 K–N3 N–Q8 37 PxP NxP 38 PxP NxPch 39 K–B3 K–Q5!

Black's King is now ready to devour White's Queenside, while the exchange of Kingside pawns has greatly decreased Black's vulnerability there. White is totally lost.

40 K–B4 N–Q3 White resigns

In Bishop vs. Knight endgames the role of the active King can be considered a "normal" one, thus being very often the decisive factor in such endings. Success for the side with the Bishop is demonstrated from the following position, V. Korchnoi–L. Portisch, Sousse Interzonal 1967, after White's 63rd move. White: K—f4 B—b5 P—a2, b3, d5, e4, g5 Black: K—f7 N—e5 P—a5, b4, c5, d6. White is up a passed KNP, yet his Bishop is unable to attack any pawns, while Black's Knight has an unassailable position on K4. White's King is actively placed, however, and Black can't prevent it from penetrating. Therefore White wins:

63 . . . K–N2

White's KNP will advance if Black places his King on K2. White also wins after 63 . . . P–B5 64 PxP N–Q6ch 65 K–B5 N–B4 66 P–K5 PxP 67 KxP P–R5 68 BxP! NxB 69 P–Q6 (Korchnoi).

64 K–B5 K–B2

If 64 . . . N–B6, White's active King wins as follows: 65 K–K6! N–Q5ch 66 KxP NxBch 67 KxP N–B6 68 P–K5 N–K5ch 69 K–N6 NxP 70 KxP N–B6 71 P–K6 etc.

65 B–K2 P–R5 66 PxP P–B5 67 B–R5ch! K–N2 68 B–Q1 P–B6 69 K–K6 N–B5 70 P–R5! Black resigns

After 70 . . . NxP 71 KxP White's active King provides decisive support for the march of the passed center pawns.

The active King helps the side with the Knight to win in Diagram 116, A. Rubinstein–A. Alekhine, London 1922, after Black's 50th move. Black's KP and Knight keep White's King away from the Queenside and Black wins by walking his King over:

51 K–N1 K–B1! 52 K–N2 K–K2 53 B–N8 K–Q3 54 B–B7 K–B4 55 BxP

Passive resistance would have been obviously hopeless.

55 . . . NxP 56 K–B3

A slightly better try was 56 P–N4, after which Alekhine gives the following winning line: 56 . . . N–Q5 57 P– N5!? PxP 58 PxP NxP 59 B–B7 K–Q5 60 K–B1 K–Q6 61 K–K1 N–R5 62 B–Q5 P–N6!.

56 . . . K–Q5 57 B–B7 K–Q6!

The active King makes possible this quick combinational solution.

58 BxN K–Q7! 59 B–B4 P–N6 60 BxP P–K7 White resigns

DIAGRAM 116

BLACK

WHITE

Rubinstein–Alekhine
London 1922
after Black's 50th

What about the relationship of the King (and pawns) in the fight versus a single minor piece? As is well known, one minor piece is usually regarded as equivalent to 3 pawns. It must be always kept in mind that as the total force level decreases, the balance turns more and more in the favor of the pawns. In the ultimate case of K and minor piece vs. K and 3 pawns, it is obvious that the side with the pawns has zero losing chances and excellent winning prospects. When the side with the pawns also has the active King, its winning chances are fantastic. Since the active King is equivalent in value to a minor piece, it can be postulated that in such situations the "pawns" side has in effect the material advantage of three pawns. The conclusion of play from Diagram 114 demonstrated how easily the active King + three pawns win against a Bishop.

Very often the active King needs much less pawn power to be certain of victory. Excellent food for thought is provided by, J. Pinter–E. Mednis, Budapest 1976, after White's 57th move. White: K—g4 B—c1 P—a3, b2, c3, g5 Black: K—c6 R—g6 P—a7, b6, c4. White has a passed pawn for the Exchange and his King is able to support the pawn's advance. The ultimate evaluation of the position seems unclear, though in fact Black has an electrifying forced win:

57 . . . K–N4!!

Alas, I never considered playing this move. To set the stage for what follows: the game was to be adjourned at that moment with Black to seal his move. After some thinking, it seemed clear to me that it was important both for general principles and in this specific case to activate my passive Rook, and I sealed 57 . . . R–K3?, whereupon White just managed to draw: 58 K–B5 R–K8 59 B–B4 K–Q2 60 K–B6 R–KB8 61 K–K5 K–K2 62 P–N6 K–B1 63 B–R6ch K–N1 64 K–Q5 R–QN8 65 KxP RxP 66 P–R4 P–R3 67 K–Q5 P–N4 68 PxP RxPch 69 K–B6 R–N6 70 P–B4 R–N6 71 B–Q2 RxPch 72 K–N7 R–Q3 draw.

During his home analysis, my opponent had quickly noted the power of 57 . . . K–N4!!, which idea is diametrically opposite to mine when I played 57 . . . R–K3?. Black not only keeps his Rook passive but must sacrifice it soon for White's KNP. On the other hand, he activates his King and it sweeps into White's Queenside along the weak light squares and eats up White's pawns. A whole night of analysis by Pinter produced no saving plan for White— there is none. So Black's correct plan was to sacrifice his Rook and activate his King. Yet it never occurred to me to leave my Rook passive. What advice can I give myself for the future? Perhaps, to always repeat in my mind: "the active King," "active King," "active King". . .

58 K–B5 R–N1   59 P–N6 K–R5   60 K–B6 K–N6   61 K–B7 R–KR1   62 P–N7 R–R2   63 K–N6 RxPch   64 KxR K–B7   65 B–B4 KxP   66 P–R4 KxP   67 B–N8 P–R3   68 B–B7 P–N4   69 PxP PxP   70 K–B6 K–Q6   71 B–Q6 P–B6   72 K–K5 P–B7   73 B–R3 P–N5   74 B–N2 K–B5   75 K–K4 K–N6   76 B–B1 K–R7   77 K–Q3 K–N8   78 B–N5 P–N6   79 K–B3 P–N7 Black wins

Of course, the above is just one illustrative variation. Yet no matter what White tries, Black's active King is decisive.

SECTION 3. Rook Endgames

The most important single factor in R and P endgames is Rook activity. This is so because the Rook, though excellent as an attacker, is a clumsy defender. By itself, the active King in R and P endgames is less of a power than in minor piece endgames. When teamed with an active Rook, however, it becomes very significant. The awesome power of such a combination is excellently demonstrated in the play arising from Diagram 117, E. Torre–P. Biyiasas, Cleveland 1975, after White's 54th move. Both sides have active Rooks and have passed pawns. The cardinal difference, therefore, is the location of the Kings. Whereas White's is passively placed and even in danger of being mated, Black's can be used as an active attacking piece. Therefore, 54 . . . KxP?! would be incongruous. Instead decisive is:

54 . . . K–B6!!

DIAGRAM 117

BLACK

WHITE

Torre–Biyiasas
Cleveland 1975
after White's 54th

Confining White's King to the first rank and enabling Black's connected passed pawns to roll forward. White's response is as good as any.

55 P–R6 RxP

The mate threat wins a tempo.

56 K–N1 P–B5!

Black is now able to utilize both the Q– and QR– files for his Rook's attacking purposes. If now 57 R–Q7, 57 . . . P–N6 58 P–R7 P–N7, followed by 59 . . . R–R8mate.

57 R–KB7 RxP!

With the mate threat 58 . . . R–Q8ch   59 K–R2 P–N6ch   60 K–R3 R–QR8. Too eager is 57 . . . P–N6?   58 RxP P–N7?? because of 59 R–B3ch.

58 K–B1 P–N6   59 R–QN7 R–Q7! White resigns

After 60 P–R7 RxP   61 P–R8 = Q comes 61 . . . R–B8mate, and 61 K–Q1 R–KR7 allows Black to stop the KRP, whereupon his passed pawns will be decisive. An ending where the difference lay in the activity of the respective Kings.

Often the relative pawn count is of considerably less significance than the activity of K and R. This was already noted in Diagram 117. An even more dramatic demonstration occurs in the play arising from this position, S. Gligorić–E. Geller, Zurich Candidates Tournament 1953, after White's 60th move. White: K—g2 R—e2 P—a2, c4, d5, g3 Black: K—f6 R—c1 P—d4, d6. White is up two pawns and has two passed pawns, yet Black's single passed pawn wins by force because his King can be rapidly mobilized to help out:

60 . . . P–Q6   61 R–B2ch

Now Black's King is liberated; if the Rook remains on the K-file, however, the pawn promotes by itself.

61 . . . K–K4   62 K–B3 K–Q5!   63 P–N4 K–B6   64 K–K4 R–K8ch   65 K–B5 P–Q7   66 RxP KxR   67 P–N5 K–Q6!

Black's Rook stands well enough and it is again time for King work. Since passive defense is hopeless, White tries an interesting pawn breakthrough, coming in the end only a tempo short.

68 P–B5 PxP   69 P–Q6 R–K1   70 P–Q7 R–QR1 White resigns

The likely end would have been: 71 K–K6 P–B5   72 K–K7 P–B6 73 P–Q8 = Qch RxQ   74 KxR P–B7   75 P-N6 P–B8 = Q   76 P–N7 Q–N4ch.

The next three examples are more "normal," in the sense that there exists material equality. In each case, the decisive factor is the active King. A strategically clear situation exists in Diagram

118, T. Petrosian–S. Furman, 1958 USSR Championship, after Black's 38th move. White obviously has the active Rook, yet Black can protect all of his weak spots against attack from that source. Therefore, White's Rook needs help from its King. Petrosian achieves this effectively with

39 P–K4!!

DIAGRAM 118

BLACK

WHITE

Petrosian–Furman
1958 USSR
Championship
after Black's 38th

Voluntarily allowing Black to exchange off his isolated QP Petrosian has correctly seen that this is hugely compensated for by what White gets in return: a dominant, centrally active King and a passed QP.

39 . . . PxPch   40 KxP K–K2   41 R–QR8 K–K3   42 P–Q5ch!

Utilizing all of White's strengths

42 . . . K–Q3   43 R–K8! R–QB2   44 R–K6ch K–Q2   45 R–B6! Black resigns

The active King from the R and P endgame gets transferred into the winning active King in the K and P endgame after 45 . . . RxR 46 PxRch KxP   47 K–B5. Also hopeless is the passive 45 . . . R–N2, with White having the delightful choice between 46 RxBP and 46 K–B5.

White also has a significant strategic advantage in the following position, A. Alekhine–M. Euwe, 1935 World Championship Match, Game 27, after Black's 31st move. White: K—f2 R—a8 P—a2, b4, f3, g2, h2 Black: K—h7 R—c3 P—b6, e6, f7, g6, g7. White, of course, can readily fashion a passed pawn on the Queenside, whereas it will not be so easy for Black to achieve the same on the Kingside. More importantly, White's King can get to the Queenside and assist his pawn(s) in queening. The game continued:

32 P–QR4?

Alekhine queries this because Black's Rook now gets access to his QN6 and QR6 and White's King is a move behind in various races to the Queenside. Consistent and decisive was the immediate 32 K–K2!. If Black defends passively, White wins as in the game, and after 32 . . . R–B7ch 33 K–Q3 RxNP 34 K–B4! White's King assists his Queenside pawns for a certain win (Alekhine).

32 . . . R–N6?

This loss of time seals Black's fate, something which according to Alekhine wouldn't have been as clear after the correct 32 . . . P–K4!. Of course, 32 . . . R–B7ch? would have been no better than in the previous note.

33 P–N5 P–N4   34 K–K2! P–K4   35 K–Q2 P–B3   36 K–B2 R–N5 37 K–B3 R–Q5   38 R–R6

Black has prevented White from achieving connected passed pawns, but one passed pawn, supported by the King, will also be victorious.

38 . . . K–N3   39 RxP RxP   40 R–R6 R–Q5   41 P–N6 Black resigns

After 41 . . . R–Q8   42 R–R2! R–Q1   43 K–B4 White's King assists in the promotion of the QNP, while Black's King remains toothless.

In a quick look at Diagram 119, J. R. Capablanca–S. Tartakower, New York 1924, after Black's 34th move, it may not be obvious that White is better. For instance, if anything, it is Black who has the more active Rook. Yet Capa in fact aimed for this position, convinced that his King activity must lead to a win. White's King heads for KB6 from where it will threaten Black's with a mate and also be in a position to assist in the advance of the Kingside pawn(s).

35 K–N3! RxPch 36 K–R4 R–B6

DIAGRAM 119

BLACK

WHITE

Capablanca–Tartakower
New York 1924
after Black's 34th

Black decides to at least eliminate the possibility of White having connected passed pawns. Other continuations are also unsatisfactory: (1) 36 . . . R–B8 37 K–R5! K–N1 38 R–Q7; (2) 36 . . . P–R4 37 P–N6 P–N4 38 PxP P–R5 39 K–N5 P–R6 40 K–B6. In both cases, White's active King is the winning factor.

37 P–N6 RxPch 38 K–N5 R–K5

A forced mate occurs after 38 . . . RxP?! 39 K–B6 K–N1 40 R–Q7.

39 K–B6 K–N1 40 R–N7ch K–R1 41 RxP R–K1 42 KxP!

The sacrificed material has been regained, with White still having the active King and now also the active Rook. White's win is assured, e.g. 42 . . . P–R3 43 R–R7 P–N4 44 P–R5!, and White will capture Black's RP and then promote his own.

42 . . . R–K5 43 K–B6! R–B5ch 44 K–K5 R–N5 45 P–N7ch K–N1

Or 45 . . . RxP 46 RxR KxR 47 KxP, and White's active King decides the K and P endgame.

46 RxP R–N8 47 KxP R–QB8 48 K–Q6 R–B7 49 P–Q5 R–B8 50 R–QB7 R–QR8 51 K–B6 RxP 52 P–Q6 Black resigns

Section 4. Queen Endgames

The Queen is such a powerful piece that of necessity the King's role is less than that in other endgames. Nevertheless, the active King is still of considerable value and power. It is completely wrong to feel that since the Queen is so powerful, the King may as well remain placidly at home.

A good practical illustration of the need always to consider the potential usefulness of the active King is shown in the play arising from the position below, K. Treybal–A. Alekhine, Pistyan 1922, after Black's 39th move. White: K—g2 Q—b8 P—b2, g5, h4 Black: K—f7 Q—c1 R—f8 P—g7, h7. Alekhine had started a combination on Move 33, with the key position resulting after White's next move:

40 P–N6ch!

In the game White inexplicably played 40 Q–N3ch? and resigned after 40 . . . K–N3, as the checks will soon be over (41 Q–K6ch K–R4 42 Q–K2ch KxP etc.). The text is the main line that Alekhine had considered when preparing to play his 33rd move.

40 . . . KxP!!

Playing for the active King in a Q and P endgame is in fact the *only* way to win. Obviously inadequate is 40 . . . K–N1? because of 41 PxPch etc. However, the obvious, materialistic 40 . . . PxP? also only draws because White can force perpetual check. Alekhine provides the following line: 41 Q–N3ch K–B3 42 Q–B3ch K–K2 43 Q–R3ch K–K1 44 Q–R4ch! K–Q1 45 Q–R8ch K–K2 46 Q–R3ch K–B2 47 Q–N3ch etc.

41 QxR QxPch 42 K–B3 Q–B6ch 43 K–N2 Q–Q7ch 44 K–N3 Q–K6ch 45 K–N2 Q–K5ch 45 K–N3 Q–K4ch 47 K–N2 K–R4!

The active King! Since there is no satisfactory way to protect the RP, White must initiate its exchange.

48 Q–B3ch KxP 49 Q–R3ch K–N4 50 QxP Q–K7ch 51 K–N3 Q–N5ch 52 K–R2 Q–R5ch Black wins

After the exchange of Queens, the active position of Black's King leads to an easily won K and P endgame.

A more traditional starting position for King activity is the following, Y. Averbakh–A. Suetin, 1954 USSR Championship, after Black's 41st move. White: K—h2 Q—f7 P—f2, g3, h3 Black: K—h7 Q—e2 P—e5, g7. White is a pawn ahead, but no direct method exists for realizing this advantage. Moreover, Black's remaining pawns seem to be quite secure in their present locations. Clearly White can not hope to achieve anything by utilization of only the Queen and pawns. The winning ingredient is White's King, as follows:

42 P–N4!

Freeing the KN3/KR4 route as an outlet for the King.

42 . . . Q–Q7 43 K–N3 Q–B6ch 44 K–R4 Q–Q5 45 Q–B5ch P–N3

Weakening the King position. Equally unpalatable however, is the retreat 45 . . . K–N1, as White's King rolls forward by 46 K–R5.

46 Q–B7ch K–R3 47 Q–B6 K–R2

The threat was 48 Q–R8mate. Now White's King starts his decisive march.

48 K–N5! Q–Q7ch 49 P–B4 PxP 50 Q–B7ch K–R1 51 K–R6! Black resigns

Mate can't be prevented; if 51 . . . P–B6ch, then 52 P–N5 is the end.

The active King proves itself quite as valuable through three phases of the Q and P endgame ensuing from Diagram 120, V. Kuznetsov–E. Tiolin, USSR 1978, after Black's 46th move. Though material is even, Black seems to be for choice, because his Queenside pawn majority will readily generate a passed pawn. On the other hand, for White to achieve the same on the Kingside seems a much slower process. Yet White demonstrates that because of the advantageously active location of his King, the chances are fully balanced:

47 P–KN4!

DIAGRAM 120

BLACK

WHITE

Kuznetsov–Tiolin
USSR 1978
after Black's 46th

The first phase is a single Queen endgame. White starts pushing his Kingside pawns.

47 . . . P–N5   48 K–N6! Q–K5!

Otherwise 49 P–B6.

49 K–N5! Q–Q4!   50 K–N6! P–R6?

Black seriously overvalues his prospects. Correct was 50 . . . Q–K5!, with a likely draw.

51 PxP PxP   52 P–B6 Q–K3

Clearly unsatisfactory is 52 . . . P–R7? 53 QxPch K–B3 54 P–B7 P–R8 = Q   55 P–B8 = Q Q–N8ch 56 P–B5.

53 P–N5 P–R7   54 P–B5 Q–K4   55 Q–N8 P–R8 = Q?!

Better drawing chances were to be had with 55 . . . PxP 56 QxP PxP.

56 P–B7 P–Q4

A frustrating position for Black. Even though he has queened ahead of White, the two Queens can't get at White's active and sheltered King. Yet as soon as White gets a second Queen, Black's King will be in mortal danger. The double Q endgame is the second phase.

57 P–B8 = Q Q–R3ch   58 P–B6 Q–Q6ch

After 58 . . . PxP, White wins with 59 Q/N–N7ch K–B3 60 Q/BxPch QxQch 61 QxQch K–N4 62 QxQch KxQ 63 K–B5!.

59 K–B7 Q–K3ch   60 K–N7 QxQch   61 QxQ PxP   62 PxP

Here starts the third phase. The further advanced passed pawn, aided by the King, leads to a forced win.

62 . . . Q–Q5   63 Q–B7ch K–B3   64 Q–K6ch K–N4   65 K–B8 Q–K5   66 Q–K7 Q–KR5   67 K–K8 Q–R7   68 K–Q7 Q–R3   69 Q–K6 P–Q5   70 P–B7 Q–N2   71 K–K8 Q–R1ch   72 P–B8 = Q Black resigns

An instructive Q and N endgame is shown in the play arising from the following position M. Matulovic–U. Andersson, Belgrade 1977, after Black's 54th move. White: K—h2 Q—e5 N—e3 P—a2, b2, f4, g3 Black: K—g8 Q—b6 N—f6 P—a6, f7, h5. True, White is up a Queenside pawn, yet it is quite difficult to fashion a passed pawn there, and, in general, Black is not only able to protect everything, but even has counterchances. For example, Black's immediate threat is 55 . . . QxN!. White, noting the vulnerability of many of Black's Kingside squares, comes up with the winning plan: activization of his own King:

55 K–R3! Q–B3   56 K–R4! Q–R8ch   57 K–N5 N–R2ch   58 K–R6 Q–B3ch

There is nothing else, but now White will be up two pawns.

59 KxP N–B3ch   60 K–N5 N–R2ch   61 K–R4, and White won on Move 73.

Black's immediate checks are at an end, e.g. 61 . . . Q–R3ch   62 K–N4 N–B3ch   63 K–B3 Q–R8ch   64 K–K2 Q–R7ch   65 K–Q3 or 61 . . . Q–R8ch   62 K–N4. Therefore the two pawn advantage leads to an easy win. Yet note that it was the active King that made this situation possible!

Section 5. Mixed Endgames

A cross section of other endgames are given in this section, all with the same basic important point: the active King wins. Consider first Diagram 121, E. Mednis–J. Fedorowicz, New York International 1977, after Black's 40th move. The fact that White is an Exchange down is a minor matter; some moves earlier White had sacrificed it hoping (expecting) to arrive at such a position. The connected passed pawns mean that White has a theoretical win; the way to win is to make full use of the active King:

41 K–R4! K–B1

41 . . . K–B2 is also met by 42 K–N5! and Black's K and R are in *zugzwang*. Neither does Black have time for Rook activity with 41 . . . R–K2, as 42 P–R6 wins, e.g. 42 . . . R–K8   43 K–N5 R–QR8 44 K–N6, followed by 45 P–R7.

42 K–N5!

The first step is for White's King to achieve a dominating presence. White's King should be where it can be of greatest help in the pawns' advance. Less clear would be 42 P–N5 R–B2!   43 P–N6 R–B4, and Black is getting counterplay.

42 . . . K–N1

Or 42 . . . K–B2   43 P–R6, and Black is again in *zugzwang* and must allow the further advance of White's King.

DIAGRAM 121

BLACK

WHITE

Mednis–Fedorowicz
New York 1977
after Black's 40th

43 K–N6! R–K2   44 P–R6 R–B2

There is no hope. If 44 . . . R–R2   45 P–N5 and the Rook must move, whereupon 46 B–N7 wins.

45 B–N7!

The threat of 46 P–R7mate requires the reply which leads to an elementary K and P endgame win.

45 . . . RxBch   46 PxR P–Q4   47 K–B5 Black resigns

With lots of free board room, in endgames of R and B vs. R and N the side with the Bishop has the advantage because the Bishop can control more territory than the Knight. The position below, V. Smyslov–V. Bagirov, Lvov 1978, after Black's 63rd move, shows that even in cases with minimum material, a win can be fashioned from a combination of small advantages. White: K—e4 R—f6 B—c5 P—c3 Black: K—g2 R—d7 N—h4 P—a5. White has a number of these: the Bishop, the active King, the temporary inactivity of Black's King. Therefore, even though each side has only one pawn, White's practical chances for a win are excellent. At first Black defends perfectly, yet just one slip is sufficient to cause a loss:

64 P–B4 P–R5   65 R–QR6 R–Q1   66 B–Q6!

Keeping the bind is much more important than winning the QRP. What White particularly wants to prevent is for Black's Knight to sacrifice itself for the QBP, thereby securing a theoretical draw.

66 . . . R–K1ch 67 K–Q5 N–B4 68 P–B5 N–K6ch 69 K–B6 R–K5 70 K–Q7! N–Q4 71 P–B6 R–QB5 72 K–K6 N–B6 73 K–Q7

Insufficient is 73 R–N6 because of 73 . . . P–R6! 74 BxP N–N4! 75 B–N2 N–R2.

73 . . . N–Q4 74 B–R3! K–B6?

Bringing back the King is strategically logical, but tactically wrong because White's King can now force Black's Knight away from its defensive bastion. Only with 74 . . . R–Q5! 75 B–B5 N–N5!ch 76 BxR NxR 77 B–K5 P–R6 78 K–B8 N–N5 (Bagirov) could Black draw.

75 K–Q6! N–B3 76 R–R8! R–B6 77 R–KB8! RxB 78 RxNch K–K7 79 P–B7 R–Q6ch 80 K–B6

The active King decides the R and P endgame.

80 . . . R–B6ch 81 K–N7 K–Q7 82 R–QB6 Black resigns

An elegant and sophisticated demonstration of the active King in a R and B vs. R and B endgame is given by White from Diagram 122, A. Alekhine–R. Teichmann, Berlin 1921 Match, Game 4, after Black's 26th move. Alekhine has sacrificed a pawn to arrive at this position, in full realization that the active King, active Rook, superior Bishop and passed QNP will give winning chances only to him:

27 K–Q3! K–N1?

As soon becomes clear, Black will have great difficulties in protecting his QBP. Therefore, Alekhine suggests 27 . . . P–K5ch! 28 KxP B–Q3, with some drawing chances.

28 K–K4! R–N1

Or 28 . . . R–B8 29 K–Q5! K–B2 30 R–R7.

29 P–N4 K–B2?!

DIAGRAM 122

BLACK

WHITE

Alekhine–Teichmann
1921 Match, Game #4
after Black's 26th

The only practical chance was 29 . . . BxP!?.

30 P–N5 K–K3   31 P–B4 K–Q2   32 R–R7! B–Q3   33 K–Q5!

Threatening the unpreventable 34 P–N6. Obviously White is entitled to more than 33 P–B5?! BxP!.

33 . . . P–K5   34 P–N6! R–KB1

After 34 . . . BxP Alekhine gives the following win: 35 P–B5 K–B1   36 K–B6 PxP   37 RxP!.

35 P–B5 R–B4ch   36 K–B4 Black resigns

The QNP is unstoppable: 36 . . . BxP   37 P–N7 R–B1 (37 . . . P–B3   38 P–N8 = Qch) 38 R–R8.

The active King becomes even more powerful when opposite–color Bishops are on the board. One such demonstration occurs in the play arising from the following position, E. Mednis–G. Kuzmin, Budapest 1978, after White's 79th move. White: K—g1 R—f7 B—f3 P—g4, h3 Black: K—e5 R—e6 B—e1 P—b4, f5, g5. The presence of opposite–color Bishops and the meager number of pawns seem to offer White realistic drawing chances; these would become much better after the "normal" looking 79 . . . PxP? 80 BxP!. Nevertheless, Black takes advantage of the active King to win by

79 . . . P–B5! 80 R–B5ch K–Q5 81 RxNP K–K6! 82 K–N2 B–B6 83 R–N8

With the idea 83 . . . R–Q3? 84 R–K8ch, and a likely draw. Material is now even and White could draw—thanks to the opposite–color Bishops—if he could chase Black's King away from its domineering location on K6. Yet he can not, and this fact will spell his end. Of course, 83 R–N5 loses to 83 . . . R–Q3.

83 . . . P–N6 84 R–QB8

When playing this, I overlooked the killing response. Also insufficient is 84 R–N8 P–N7, however, e.g. 85 P–N5 B–Q5! 86 R–N3ch K–Q7 87 B–N4 R–K7ch! 88 BxR KxB followed by 89 . . . P–B6ch etc.—the active King wins again!

84 . . . B–R4! 85 B–Q1

White's Bishop can't both stop the QNP and prevent the devastating . . . P–B6. 85 R–QN8 now fails to 85 . . . B–N3!.

85 . . . P–N7 86 B–B2 P–B6ch 87 K–N3 K–K7 88 R–B8 B–B2ch White resigns

Something like the ultimate in King activity in a mixed endgame where the major piece is the Rook occurs in the play arising from Diagram 123, C. de Villiers–R. Schackis, 1977 South African Championship, after Black's 39th move. We see White's King active from the initial position, in a R and opposite–color Bishop, and finally in a B vs. R endgame. The initial position is obviously very favorable for White, since he has a large space advantage and active pieces, while the dark squares in Black's position are chronically weak. Even so, the semiblockaded nature of the position makes progress difficult. White's winning plan is based on King power:

40 K–K3! K–R2 41 K–B4! K–R1 42 B–R3 K–R2 43 N–R3 K–R1 44 K–N5! R–QB1 45 K–B6! R–R1 46 N–N5 R–K1 47 B–B5 R–B2 48 R/1–N2! R–Q2 49 N–R7 R–R1

DIAGRAM 123

BLACK

WHITE

de Villiers–Schackis
South Africa
Championship 1977
after Black's 39th

Deciding that sacrifice of the Exchange is the best defensive plan. The alternative, 49 . . . R–B2, loses to 50 N–B8! N–Q1 51 B–Q6!, e.g. 51 . . . R–B1 52 B–K7! N–B3 53 NxB RxB (53 . . . NxB 54 N–B5) 54 RxN! (Walker).

50 N–B8 RxN 51 BxR K–R2 52 B–B5 K–R1 53 B–Q6 K–R2 54 P–B4! K–R1 55 RxN!

White must create new vulnerable points in Black's position. The sacrifice of two Exchanges does that trick, after which the domineering White King is decisive.

55 . . . PxR 56 R–N8ch K–R2 57 R–K8! K–N2 58 RxB

White's just a bit overeager here. More accurate was first 58 P–R5!, and only after 58 . . . K–R2, 59 RxB!. After the text Black is able to organize a bit of a defense.

58 . . . PxR 59 KxKP K–B1 60 P–R5 R–QN2 61 B–N4 K–Q1 62 K–Q6! R–QB2 63 B–B5 R–B1 64 B–N6ch K–K1 65 B–B7! K–B2 66 K–Q7! R–K1 67 B–Q6 R–K3 68 KxP R–K1 69 K–N7 Black resigns

White will win Black's QRP and then queen his own. What an awesome example of King power!

The last two examples will show the active King helping its Queen achieve success. First consider the position below, Banas–J. Plachetka, 1978 Czechoslovakian Championship, after White's 41st move. White: K—g1 R—b5 B—d5 P—b4, c4, f2, g3, h4 Black: K—f6 Q—f3 P—e4, f5, h5. For the missing Queen White has R, B and 2 pawns, which is full equivalence. White's main problem is that his pieces are not well placed for defensive work. Since Black can't hope to win without the participation of his King in any case, his next move is logical enough:

41 . . . K–K4!   42 B–B7ch?

This just further deflects the Bishop away from the defense, while chasing Black's King where it wants to go. Correct was to improve the defensive position of the Rook with 42 R–R5!. Chances would have then remain balanced.

42 . . . K–Q5   43 R–Q5ch K–B6   44 R–K5 Q–Q8ch   45 K–N2 P–B5!   46 RxP?

Allows an immediate forced win. The only move was 46 PxP! with the following continuation: 46 . . . Q–N5ch 47 K–B1 QxBP 48 R–K7 Q–B3 49 RxP! (Equivalent is 49 R–R7 P–K6 50 R–R3ch KxP 51 RxP) 49 . . . QxB 50 R–K3ch! KxNP 51 K–N2 Q–B5 52 R–KR3 Q–N5ch 53 R–KN3 QxRP 54 R–K3 KxP 55 R–KR3, and, according to Averbakh, White has obtained a theoretically drawn position.

46 . . . P–B6ch   47 K–R2 Q–K7!!   48 R–K3ch

There is nothing else, but now Black's active King will help the KBP queen. Note that White's Bishop is too far away to help.

48 . . . K–Q7!   49 K–N1 QxR!   50 PxQ K–K8   51 B–Q5 P–B7ch 52 K–R2 P–B8 = Q White resigns

Quite interesting is the play arising from Diagram 124, J. Smejkal–L. Ljubojevic, Moscow 1977, after Black's 52nd move. Having two Rooks for the Queen, Black even has a slight material advantage. White's passed KBP is such a power however, that it

DIAGRAM 124

BLACK

WHITE

Smejkal–Ljubojevic
Moscow 1977
after Black's 52nd

will tie down both of Black's Rooks to passive defense. This will allow White's King to infiltrate into Black's position and gain victory. The instructive course was:

53 Q–K5! R–Q8   54 Q–N8ch K–R4   55 K–K4

A shade more accurate was the move order 55 Q–N7! R/Q–Q3 56 K–K4 R–QN3   57 Q–QB7 R/Q–QB3 58 Q–Q7! (Filip) and Black, being in *zugzwang*, must lose immediately.

55 . . . R–Q2   56 K–K5 R/B–QB2   57 P–B6 P–R4

Or 57 . . . R–QN2   58 Q–K8 K–N3   59 Q–R5 P–R4   60 Q–N6! K–R2   61 Q–N1 K–N3   62 Q–QR1, and White will win in a way similar to that in the game.

58 P–R4 R–B2   59 Q–K8 K–N3   60 K–K6! R–KR2   61 Q–N8ch K–R4

No better is 61 . . . K–B3   62 K–B5 R–QN2   63 Q–N8 and White's win again is near.

62 K–B5 R/R–Q2   63 K–N6! R–QN2

Pretty is the end after 63 . . . R–B3:   64 KxP RxP   65 Q–QB8!.

64 Q–K5 K–N3   65 KxP R/N–B2   66 K–N5 P–R4 · 67 Q–R1!

Preventing any possible . . . P–R5 and getting ready to take advantage of the weakening of the QN5 square.

67 . . . R–B3   68 Q–R4 R–QR2   69 P–R5! R–R1   70 P–R6 R–N1ch   71 K–B5 R–QR1

The attempt at counterplay by 71 . . . R–KB1 is parried with 72 Q–N5ch K–B2   73 QxRPch K–Q2   74 Q–R1.

72 P–R7 Black resigns

Something in Black's position will have to give imminently.

CHAPTER 25
The Active King Achieves a Draw

If you can't win, by far the next best thing is to draw. To achieve this, it is very often necessary to create counterplay in order to compensate for either a material disadvantage or a positional problem someplace else. Since the King is an inherent power in the endgame, it follows that an active King can often create enough counterchances to attain a draw.

An excellent starting example is the following, V. Ceshkovsky–V. Bagirov, Lvov 1978, after Black's 55th move. White: K—b5 P—b3, c4 Black: K—g3 N—d3 P—c5. White of course is a piece down and has been so for quite some time. Nevertheless, he had activated his King, "tricked" Black into allowing the exchange of a pair of Rooks, and now exploits his King position to force a draw as follows:

56 P–N4!! PxP   57 K–R4! K–B5   58 P–B5 K–K4   59 P–B6 K–Q3   60 K–N3 Draw

Black's King is able to neutralize the QBP all right, but White's King can't be prevented from scissoring Black's pawn or Knight: 60 . . . KxP   61 K–B4 K–N3   62 KxN K–N4   63 K–B2 K–R5   64 K–N2, with an elementary draw.

There is no question that White is better in the following position, L. Portisch–T. Petrosian, 1974 Candidates Match, Game 12, after Black's 51st move: White is up a passed QNP. White: K—e3 R—b8 P—b4, f2, g3, h4 Black: K—h6 R—b2 P—

f6, g5, h5. Nevertheless, Black should be able to hold the draw, because his Rook has the ideal active location so that he can both watch the QNP and menace the Kingside pawns, while also the threat of infiltration by his King should keep White's King "honest." Play continued:

52 P–N5 PxP! 53 PxP K–N3 54 P–N6 K–B4! 55 K–Q4

Obviously the only winning try—the King tries to help the QNP's advance.

55 . . . RxBP?!

The first inaccuracy. The Rook stood well enough; it was the King that needed activation, thus: 55 . . . K–N5! 56 R–N8ch KxP 57 K–B5 R–B7ch! 58 K–Q6 R–Q7ch! 59 K–B7 R–B7ch! 60 K–N8 RxP 61 P–N7 R–QN7 62 K–B7 P–B4 63 P–N8 = Q RxQ 64 RxR P–B5 65 K–Q6 P–B6 66 K–K5 P–B7 67 R–KB8 K–N6 68 K–K4 K–N7, and it is White who needs to force the draw with either 69 K–K3 or 69 R–KN8ch.

56 R–QR8! R–QN7 57 K–B5 R–B7ch 58 K–Q4 R–QN7 59 R–R5ch K–N5!!

Only so—the King must be kept active. As pointed out by Averbakh, this is the only way to draw. Of course, this is nowhere as simple to see as was the correct way back on Move 55.

Even so, the passive 59 . . . K–K3? seems inherently hopeless, and in the game Black lost quickly: 60 K–B5 R–QB7ch 61 K–N5 K–Q3 62 K–R6! K–B3 63 R–R1 R–B5 64 P–N7 R–QN5 65 R–QB1ch K–Q2 66 R–B8 Black resigns. Note how the active King was victorious over the passive one.

60 R–R4! K–R6!!

To enable Black to reach the stalemate draw at the end, White's KRP must be allowed to live.

61 K–B5 P–B4 62 R–QN4!? RxR! 63 KxR P–B5 64 P–N7 P–B6 65 P–N8 = Q P–B7 Draw

The KBP on the 7th with the King to protect it is a theoretical draw. The blockaded KRPs do not affect this consideration.

Some virtuoso King activity allows White to hold the following inferior Q and P endgame, P. Keres–M. Taimanov, Zurich Candidates Tournament 1953, after Black's 31st move. White: K—e1 Q—f3 P—a3, b2, b4, g2, h3 Black: K—h7 Q—g6 P—a6, b5, e5, g7, h6. In effect Black is up the passed KP, since his two Queenside pawns easily hold White's three pawns there. Note how White's King first holds up any invasion by Black's Queen and then itself goes on an attack to secure a perpetual check draw:

32 K–Q2!

Centralization!

32 . . . P–K5   33 Q–B2 Q–N4ch

After 33 . . . Q–KB3?!   34 QxQ! PxQ   35 K–K3! P–B4   36 P–N4 K–N3   37 K–B4 the active King already means a slight plus for White.

34 K–K2 Q–Q4   35 K–K3! Q–Q6ch

White threatened 36 Q–B2, and 35 . . . K–N3 is of no help because of 36 Q–B2 K–B4   37 Q–B8ch.

36 K–B4 P–N4ch   37 K–K5! Draw

There is no reasonable way to prevent perpetual check, e.g. 37 . . . P–K6   38 Q–B7ch etc.

For a practical demonstration of how to fight back in a hopeless–appearing position, watch the play from Diagram 125, B. Amos–E. Mednis, New York International 1976, after White's 49th move. Black is a pawn down and has less than no compensation for that. Moreover his KRP is very weak and at the very least he will have to allow White a tremendous passed KRP. However:

49 . . . K–N3!

Never say die! In fact, after 50 B–B7?! K–B4   51 BxP? K–Q5! Black obtains excellent chances for at least a draw. Therefore White must mobilize the KRP immediately and this allows Black to exchange off his KRP, rather than lose it outright.

50 P–KN4 PxPch   51 NxP B–K2!   52 P–R5 K–B4   53 P–R6 B–B1   54 P–R7 B–N2   55 N–R6?

DIAGRAM 125

BLACK

WHITE

Amos–Mednis
N.Y. International 1976
after White's 49th

Black is on the verge of significant counterplay so that White's "straight-forward" attempt to win a piece by queening his KRP will be unfruitful. It was imperative to keep out Black's King with 55 K–K3! B–N8 56 P–R3!. White then should safeguard his KP with 57 B–Q5, move his King to a safe square, and then proceed with N–R6 and N–B7 to win Black's KB. As always, care is required, but the ultimate win is there! After the over-eager text Black obtains sufficient defensive resources to eke out a surprising draw.

55 . . . K–N5! 56 N–B7 B–N8 57 NxQP

A very unpleasant change of plans for White. There is less than no time for the intended 57 P–R8 = Q? BxQ 58 NxB because after 58 . . . BxRP and 59 . . . BxP Black's QRP is worth more than White's out-of-the-game Knight. Better than 57 P–R8 = Q? is 57 P–R4?!, as after the capture of both pawns Black's King will be placed less favorably on QR5 than on QN6 (or QN5) as in the above note. Even so Black has at least equal chances.

57 . . . BxRP 58 N–N7 B–N8!

Obviously Black is not going to exchange Queenside pawns with 58 . . . BxP??. If we compare the position after the text move with that just a few moves earlier, it is clear that Black has made giant strides towards the draw. He has traded his "useless" QP for White's valuable QRP, White's QNP is now weak and Black's King has an excellent active location hovering over it. In subsequent analysis, Amos and I were not able to find any win for White. White's next moves are quite logical: he protects his QP with the Bishop and then moves his King over to guard the QNP.

59 B–Q5 B–B7   60 K–K3 B–Q8!

Black's QB heads back to assist his KB in coping with the KRP.

61 K–Q3 B–R4   62 K–B2 B–K1!   63 N–Q8 B–R1

Black's defensive plan is to leave his King and QB where they are and tempo back and forth with his KB. He doesn't have to worry about the opposite–color Bishop endgame after 64 N–B7 BxN   65 BxB, as Black's King will always be able to get back to the Kingside to prevent penetration by White's King. Black can also hold the type of opposite–color Bishop endgames which result after a N–KN6 by White, as after the exchange . . . BxN, PxB, Black's King and remaining Bishop are able to blockade White's KNP and KRP.

64 B–B7 B–N4   65 N–K6?!

Tired out after the long non-stop effort (there was no adjournment at Move 40) White "blunders," allowing an immediate draw. Even so, there is no more win. Apart from entering one of the two opposite–color Bishop endgames discussed above, White's only other try is to queen his KRP starting with 65 B–N6. This allows Black to go after White's KP, however, and achieve the draw as follows: 65 . . . B–N2   66 N–B7 B–B3! 67 P–R8 = Q BxQ 68 NxB BxPch   69 K–N2 B–Q6!, and Black, with 70 . . . P–K5, P–K6, P–K7, will win back his piece and have complete equality.

65 . . . B–B3   66 K–Q3 Draw

After 66 . . . B–N4ch   67 K–B2 B–B3 neither side has anything better than to repeat the position with 68 K–Q3! B–N4ch! etc.

CHAPTER 26
King Activity for the Defense

Since the King is powerful and mobile in the endgame, sending it on a defensive assignment is a logical thing to do. Such use of the King in trying to hold an inferior position for a draw is, of course, routine and does not require any belaboring of the point. A typical example is the following, I. Csom–A. Groszpeter, Budapest 1978, after White's 34th move. White: K—f2 R—d1, d4 N—g2 P—a3, b4, c4, f4, g3, h2 Black: K—h8 R—b7, f7 N—g6 P—a7, b6, d7, e6, f5, h7. White does have the freer and more active position; the only potentially vulnerable point in Black's position, however, is the QP. Therefore Black rushes his King over to safeguard it:

34 . . . K–N2! 35 N–K1 K–B3! 36 N–B3 P–KR3! 37 K–K3 R–K2 38 R–Q6 R–QB2 39 R/1–Q4 K–B2! 40 K–Q3 K–K1! 41 K–B3 R–R2 Draw

The draw agreement is quite justified. With Black's QP safe, White has no meaningful attacking prospects.

Of greater teaching importance is the utilization of the active King for defensive purposes in order to help bring about an ultimate victory. For instance, consider the situation of Diagram 126, I. Csom–L. Barczay, Budapest 1978, after Black's 30th move. True, White is ahead a passed QRP. But how to do something with it? Black's Rooks have a total grip on the QR file and White's Rooks must remain on the second rank to guard the QRP. White comes up with an instructive winning maneuver: he sends his King to QN1; with the QRP sufficiently protected,

DIAGRAM 126

BLACK

WHITE

Csom–Barczay
Budapest 1978
after Black's 30th

White's pieces can then become coordinated for attacking purposes. The game continued:

31 K–B1! P–B3 32 P–R4 K–B2 33 K–K1! R–R1 34 K–Q1! R–KN1 35 N–Q2 P–N4 36 N–B3 B–R8 37 K–B1! P–N5 38 N–K1 B–K4 39 K–N1! R–QN1 40 R–B1

Black threatened 40 . . . R/1xNPch! (41 PxR?? R–R8mate). Black should now try to retain the status quo with 40 . . . R/1–QR1. The coming opening of the game works out in White's favor.

40 . . . P–K3?! 41 R–Q1! R–K1 42 PxPch RxP 43 R–Q5 R–R1 44 N–Q3 K–K2 45 P–R4 R–QB1 46 K–B2!

With its function on QN1 completed, the King selects a useful central location.

46 . . . K–Q2 47 K–Q1! R/K–K1 48 P–R5! K–B2 49 R–R2 R–QN1 50 R–R3 K–B3 51 K–B2 P–B4 52 P–R6

White's extra passed QRP is a power, and with all of White's pieces harmoniously placed, Black has no satisfactory defense. By trying for complications Black hastens the end; good advice is non-existent, however.

52 . . . P-B5 53 PxP B-Q5 54 P-N4! PxP 55 NxPch RxN
56 RxB R-QR1 57 R-R5 R-N3 58 RxQPch KxR 59 P-B5ch
K-B3 60 PxR KxP 61 R-R2 K-R2 62 K-Q3 Black resigns

Black had sealed 62 . . . R-K1 but resigned without resuming play. After 63 K-Q4, followed by P-B5 etc., White's win is elementary.

White has sacrificed a pawn to arrive at Diagram 127, V. Tukmakov–B. Gulko, 1977 USSR Championship, after White's 24th move. The immediate threat, of course, is 25 R-B8ch!, and after something like 24 . . . P-N3?!, White has excellent chances for getting both of his Rooks active on the 7th rank after 25 N-B4 BxN 26 R/1xB. However, Black extinguishes White's hopes by having the King participate in the defense of both the QP and the second rank:

24 . . . K-B1! 25 N-B4 BxN 26 R/7xB

DIAGRAM 127

BLACK

WHITE

Tukmakov–Gulko
1977 USSR
Championship
after White's 24th

After 26 R/1xB K-K1! Black threatens to trap the forward Rook with 27 . . . K-Q1 followed by 28 . . . N-B3.

26 . . . K-K1! 27 R/1-B2 K-Q1! 28 K-N2 P-QR4 29 R-B5 R-N1 30 P-Q5

White tries to bring about some complications. Otherwise Black exchanges a pair of Rooks with 30 . . . R–B1 and pushes the QRP to victory.

30 . . . PxP! 31 BxP NxB 32 RxN R–R1 33 R–B4 P–R5! 34 R–KR5 P–R3 35 R–KN4 R–R3! 36 RxNP R–N6 37 R–R7 P–R6 38 R/5xP R–R2!

With both Rooks on, the advance of the QRP is assured.

39 RxP R/N–N2!

The careless 39 . . . P–R7?? leads to a win for *White:* 40 R–R8ch K–B2 41 RxPch! KxR 42 R–R7ch, followed by 43 RxR.

40 R–R8ch K–B2 White resigns

White sealed 41 R–B3 but resigned without continuing, in view of the following variation: 41 . . . P–R7 42 R–B3ch K–Q3 43 R–R6ch K–K2 44 R–K3ch K–B2 45 R–B3ch K–N2 46 R/B–B6 P–Q3!.

Black had confidently aimed for the position below, A. Kotov–S. Reshevsky, Zurich Candidates Tournament 1953, after Black's 51st move, White: K—f3 N—e5 P—a3, b4, c4, f4, g3, h3 Black: K—d6 N—e4 P—a4, b6, e6, f5, g5, h5. in the expectation that his prospects for winning White's QRP gave him the superior chances. Yet a couple of deft moves by White's King show just the opposite to be true:

52 K–K3! P–N5

Best. Inferior are both (1) 52 . . . NxP? 53 N–B7ch K–K2 54 NxP, and the liberation of the Black Knight will require the sacrifice of the KRP, and (2) 52 . . . N–B6? 53 K–Q3! N–N8 54 K–B2 NxPch 55 K–N2 P–R5 56 KxN RPxP 57 N–B7ch! K–K2 58 NxP (Bronstein), and White wins.

53 PxP RPxP 54 NxP N–B6?

Again wrong, since White's King can trap the Knight. Required was 54 . . . NxP! 55 N–B2! N–B8ch! 56 K–Q3 P–K4 57 PxPch KxP 58 N–Q1 P–B5 59 N–B3 P–B6 60 NxP P–B7! 61 K–K2 N–Q7 62 KxP NxP (Stahlberg), with a draw.

55 N–K5 N–N8   56 K–Q3! NxP   57 P–N5!

It is important not to allow Black's Knight to free itself, as after 57 K–B3? P–N4!   58 P–B5ch K–Q4   59 P–B6 K–Q3   60 K–N2 N–B5ch   61 NxN PxN   62 P–N5 K–B2 the K and P endgame is drawn.

After the text move, 57 . . . K–B4 is met by 58 N–Q7ch K–N5 59 NxP K–N6   60 NxP!. Therefore, Reshevsky decides to sacrifice his Knight for two pawns, but White's active King easily carries the day.

57 . . . NxNP   58 PxN K–B4   59 N–B3 KxP   60 N–Q4ch K–N5 61 K–B2! P–K4   62 PxP K–B4   63 P–K6 K–Q3   64 K–B3 P–N4 65 K–N4 K–K2   66 K–B5! P–R6   67 K–Q5! Black resigns

CHAPTER 27
The King as a Generally Useful Piece

The single most important feeling that I want to impart to the reader is to have the desire, as if by second nature, to make some use of the King in the endgame. For instance, don't just think "what can I do with my Rook (or Bishop, or pawn[s] etc.)?" but equally "what can I do with my King to make it more useful in the play to come?"

Part of the time, general usefulness is what is involved. Diagram 128 shows M. Vukic–A. Karpov, Bugojno 1978, after White's 41st move. White has the more active position and Black's King on the second rank may turn out to be awkwardly placed. Yet note how easily Karpov achieves a perfectly sound position:

41 . . . P–N4!

The pawn march will gain some space for Black on the Kingside and the King will move up behind its pawns to a comfortable and useful location.

42 K–N2 P–R4! 43 P–R3 K–R3! 44 N–K3 P–B5! 45 Q–Q5

After 45 N–Q5 Black gains full equality with 45 . . . P–N5!.

45 . . . QxQ 46 NxQ PxP! 47 BxNP B–B1 48 K–B2 K–N3!

Black's King shifts over to the center, sends White's Knight away and gives Black total equality.

DIAGRAM 128

BLACK

WHITE

Vukic–Karpov
Bugojno 1978
after White's 41st

49 K–K2 K–B4 50 P–B3 PxP 51 PxP K–K3 52 N–K3 B–N2
53 B–K1 N–B1 54 B–Q2 N–N3 55 N–B1 N–B5ch 56 BxN
KPxB 57 N–Q2 Draw

If above the initial King activity was mostly general, in the
next example the need is more specific. The position below arose
after Black's 46th move in B. Spassky–A. Karpov, 1974 Candidates Match, Game 6. White: K—g3 R—d3 P—a4, b3, d6, g4
Black: K—e6 R—c8 P—a5, b6, e5, g5. Black is clearly better
because he is certain to win White's advanced QP. White's
drawing chances depend on getting counterplay and exchanging
pawns so that he can reach a theoretically drawn position,
though a pawn down. To achieve this, his King must do its part.
Correct therefore is:

47 K–B3!

Helping to hold back both Black's KP and King.

In the game White played 47 P–N4? and lost as follows: 47 . . .
P–K5! 48 R–Q4 (Or 48 R–N3 KxP 49 PxP PxP 50 K–B2 K–Q4 51
K–K3 R–B4 52 R–R3 K–K4 53 R–N3 R–Q4 54 R–B3 R–Q6ch,
with a won K and P endgame—Botvinnik) 48 . . . K–K4

49 R–Q1 PxP   50 R–QN1 R–B6ch   51 K–B2 R–Q6   52 P–Q7
RxP   53 RxP R–Q3   54 K–K3 R–Q6ch   55 K–K2 R–QR6 White
resigns. After 56 RxNP RxP White is defenseless against the coming
57 . . . K–B5.

47 . . . R–Q1   48 P–N4! RxP   49 R–N3 R–B3

After 49 . . . R–Q5 50 PxP R–B5ch White must play the active
51 K–K3! to draw. Losing is 51 K–N3? PxP 52 R–N6ch K–Q4 and
Black's active King will lead to a win.

50 PxP PxP   51 R–N5 R–B6ch   52 K–K2 R–B5   53 RxRP RxNP,
with a theoretical draw, as given by Botvinnik. Of course Black is
still better, but White can hold with correct play. Note the big
difference between this position and that in the game: here White
still has his QRP!

Some creative King prancing, though with a clear strategic
purpose, can be seen in the play arising from Diagram 129, H.
Wolf–A. Alekhine, Carlsbad 1923, after White's 31st move. White
is down a pawn and has a locked-in Bishop. Nevertheless he seems
to have set up an effective blockade, thus throwing into question
Black's potential win. As Alekhine demonstrates, the key to
winning is to break the blockade, and for this Black's King is to
play the major role:

31 . . . P–R4!   32 PxPch

After 32 P–N5 Alekhine gives the following win: 32 . . . BPxP 33
RPxP BxP 34 PxPch KxP 35 KxP P–KR5, with the passed KRP
decisive.

32 . . . KxP   33 PxPch K–B2!!

Aiming for the blockade–breaking K3 square. After 33 . . . KxP?
34 K–B5! the White King's active and blockading location may
well yield a draw.

34 P–R6

If 34 K–B5, the King will be chased back with 34 . . . R–KR1,
and then, after 35 K–N4, Black again plays 35 . . . K–K3.

34 . . . K–K3!   35 R–KN1 R–KR1   36 R–N6 B–B1 White resigns

DIAGRAM 129

BLACK

WHITE

Wolf–Alekhine
Carlsbad 1923
after White's 31st

The imminent 37 . . . RxP will chase away the Rook, whereupon 38 . . . P–B4ch will do the same to White's King, leaving Black with a decisive material and positional superiority.

And now for a lengthier example of making good use of the King throughout an endgame. Diagram 130 is V. Bagirov–Y. Razuvaev, Baku (USSR) 1977, after White's 24th move. Though much material still remains, the lack of direct danger to the respective Kings means that the position can be considered in endgame terms. Generally speaking, Black has a healthy advantage: he has the superior pawn formation, greater space and prospective attacking chances along the KB file. Still, without good King utilization not much can be achieved. Therefore:

24 . . . K–N2!

With the following strategic plan in mind: the King will go to KR3 from where it will protect both the Bishop and KRP. This will be followed by placing the KR on KB1 and maneuvering the Knight to K4. Black will then have an excellent attacking formation. In the coming play White defends as well as possible; for instance now inferior is 25 K–B1?! K–R3 26 K–K1 KR–B1, with a huge edge for Black.

DIAGRAM 130

BLACK

WHITE

Bagirov–Razuvaev
Baku 1977
after White's 24th

25 K–R3!? K–R3! 26 R–N2 R–K4!

Something of a change in plans. Black tries to chase the White King away from its KR3.

27 QR–KN1 B–K1 28 N–B1 B–Q2ch 29 K–R2 N–N5ch 30 BxN PxB 31 N–K3 K–N3!!

With this and the following King move Black neutralizes White's attack against the KNP.

32 K–N3 K–R4! 33 R–N1 P–N3 34 P–R4!? R–K2 35 P–R5 PxP 36 R–N7 R–B2 37 RxP

After 37 N–B5 Razuvaev demonstrates the following win: 37 . . . RxN 38 RxB R–B6ch 39 K–R2 R–R6ch 40 K–N1 R–QN1 41 R–N3 R–N8ch 42 K–N2 R/R–R8!.

37 . . . P–R5 38 K–R2 KR–KB1 39 K–N1 KxP 40 R–R6 R–B3?

An error just before time control which White could have exploited with the active 41 R–R2ch K–N4 42 R–R7! with good drawing chances. Correct was 40 . . . R–QN1!—as subsequently played in the game.

41 R–R7? R/3–B2   42 R–R6 R–QN1!   43 R–R2ch

Equally unsatisfactory is 43 RxQP R–N8ch   44 K–R2 (44 N–B1 P–K6!) 44 . . . K–N4!, with the threat 45 . . . R–R2ch.

43 . . . K–N4   44 RxP R–N8ch   45 K–N2

Or 45 N–B1 P–N6!   46 R–N2 RxNch!   47 KxR B–R6.

45 . . . R–N7   46 K–N1 P–R6   47 R–QR6 P–N6!   48 PxP RxR 49 KxR R–B7ch   50 K–N1 R–K7!   51 RxP

Hopeless too is 51 N–B1 P–R7 etc.

51 . . . RxN   52 R–R5 RxPch   53 K–B2 K–B5! White resigns

CHAPTER 28
Technical King Movements

SECTION 1. Opposition

The most important single concept of K and P endgames is that of "opposition." Take a look at the position below, noting that the Kings are opposite each other. White: K—e6 P—d6 Black: K—e8. For the technical meaning of "opposition" to apply, however, the Kings must be separated by an *odd* number of squares: 1, 3 or 5. A separation by 2, 4 or 6 squares has no particular meaning as far as "opposition" is concerned. Above we have an example of *vertical* opposition. This is the most common type. The other types are *horizontal* and the fairly rare *diagonal*. In chess terms, *that side is said to have "opposition" which is NOT on move*. In this position if it is White's move, *Black has the opposition*. Correspondingly, if it's Black's move, *White has the opposition*. In clear-board situations it is always favorable to have the opposition. Here, this factor is the decisive one in deciding the result of the game:

A) *Black is on move* (i.e. White has the opposition):

1 . . . K–Q1 2 P–Q7 K–B2 3 K–K7 White wins

B) *White is on move* (i.e. Black has the opposition):

1 P–Q7ch K–Q1 2 K–Q6 Stalemate

It is very important to know that K and P vs. K endgames *always* come down to the type of position shown above. The ultimate result then is dependent on who is on move.

The next two examples illustrate the basic methods of achieving the desired result when one has the opposition. The position below is a 1952 endgame study by J. Moravec: White to play and win: White: K—f1 P—g2 Black: K—c8 P—h5.

1 K–B2 P–R5!

The best try. After 1 . . . K–Q2?! 2 K–N3 K–K3 3 K–R4 K–B4 4 KxP K–B3 5 P–N4 K–N2 6 K–N5! White has the opposition and is sure to achieve our basic position with *Black on move.*

2 K–N1!!

Unfortunately the routine 2 K–B3? is met by 2 . . . P–R6!! with a draw: a) 3 PxP K–Q2 and the Black King gets to his KB1 with a book draw, b) 3 P–N4 K–Q2 4 K–N3 K–K3 5 KxP K–B3 6 K–R4 K–N3 7 P–N5 K–N2 8 K–R5 K–R2 9 P–N6ch K–N2 10 K–N5 K–N1! (The only correct retreat) 11 K–B6 K–B1, and Black has the opposition and the draw: 12 P–N7ch K–N1 13 K–N6stalemate. This last variation clearly shows that to hope to win K and P vs. K endgames, the stronger side's King must lead (i.e. be in front of) its pawn.

2 . . . P–R6!

Again, 2 . . . K–Q2 3 K–R2 followed by 4 K–R3 and 5 KxP gives a winning position similar to that of the note after Black's first move.

3 P–N3!

Instead 3 P–N4? allows the same draw demonstrated after 2 K–B3? P–R6!! 3 P–N4.

3 . . . K–Q2 4 K–R2 K–K3 5 KxP K–B3!? 6 K–R4!

Not 6 K–N4? K–N3! and Black, having the opposition, draws.

6 . . . K–N3 7 K–N4!

White has the opposition and wins:

7 . . . K–R3 8 K–B5 K–N2 9 K–N5! K–R2 10 K–B6 K–R3 11 P–N4 K–R2 12 P–N5 K–N1 13 K–N6! K–R1 14 K–B7 K–R2 15 P–N6ch White wins

Keeping in mind the concept of opposition allows White to draw from this position: White: K—b1 P—e4 Black: K—c5 P—d6.

1 P–K5!!

Routine play is hopeless: 1 K–B2? K–Q5 2 K–Q2 (2 P–K5!? KxP! 3 K–Q3 K–Q4!) 2 . . . KxP 3 K–B3 P–Q4! 4 K–Q2 K–Q5! and Black, having the opposition, wins.

1 . . . PxP 2 K–B1!!

Establishing *distant* vertical opposition is the only way to draw. Losing is 2 K–B2? K–B5! 3 K–Q2 K–Q5! 4 K–K2 K–K5! etc.

2 . . . K–Q4!?

Routine is 2 . . . P–K5?! 3 K–Q2 with a draw. After 2 . . . K–B5 3 K–B2! it is White who has the opposition and can draw: 3 . . . K–Q5 4 K–Q2 K–K5 5 K–K2.

3 K–Q1!!

Retaining distant vertical opposition holds the draw. All other King moves lose.

3 . . . K–Q5 4 K–Q2! K–K5 5 K–K2 Draw

The best that Black can get is the type of position shown in our first example, where White will have the opposition and therefore draw.

The concept of opposition is of recurring importance in practical play. A relatively simple illustration is from Diagram 131, L. Espig–Inkiov, Varna 1976, after Black's 53rd move. Though White is up a passed KBP, it is not possible to exploit this factor directly, e.g. 54 K–N6 K–N1 55 P–B7ch K–B1 56 K–B6??stalemate. To win, the pawn must be used solely for purposes of achieving the opposition:

54 P–B7!! KxP

The "fancy" 54 . . . K–N2 is parried by the "extra fancy" 55 P–B8 = Qch! KxQ 56 K–B6 etc.

DIAGRAM 131

BLACK

WHITE

Espig–Inkiov
Varna 1976
after Black's 53rd

55 K–B5!

White has the opposition and therefore wins, since Black can't prevent penetration by the White King.

55 . . . K–K2 56 K–N6 K–K1 57 K–B6 Black resigns

After 57 . . . K–Q2 58 K–B7 etc. White wins the QP and the game.

A whole series of "opposition opportunities" occur in the play arising from the position below, La Rouche–S. Weil, New York 1977, after Black's 55th move. White: K—c2 N—h5 P—b4, c3, d4 Black: K—e3 P—b5, c6, d5, g4. Black had sacrificed a piece to get this position, in the correct expectation that, after winning it back, he will have the better K and P endgame because his King has penetrated into White's position. Note that the Queenside pawns are essentially fixed; thus the question of opposition will determine whether Black will be able to win or whether White can hold. Play went:

56 K–B1

O.K., but perhaps simpler is the line discovered by Fred Sorensen: 56 N–N3! K–B7 (Equivalent is 56 . . . K–B6   57 N–B5! P–N6   58 K–Q2! P–N7   59 N–R4ch K–B7   60 NxP KxN   61 K–K2. White has the horizontal opposition for the draw.) 57 N–R5! P–N6 58 K–Q2!! P–N7   59 N–B4 P–N8 = Q   60 N–R3ch K–N7   61 NxQ KxN   62 K–K1, with White again having the horizontal opposition and the draw. White's 58th and 59th moves gained the tempo required to achieve the opposition.

56 . . . K–Q6   57 K–N2 K–Q7   58 N–N3

Still keeping the draw in hand, yet making the job more difficult. More accurate was 58 K–N3!, and only after 58 . . . K–B8, 59 N–N3. Then Black's King is one square further from the Kingside and this gives White sufficient time to achieve normal opposition thus: 59 . . . K–Q7   60 N–R5 K–K7   61 K–B2 K–B7   62 K–Q2 P–N6   62 NxP KxN   64 K–K3!. If now 64 . . . K–N7,   65 K–K2 etc., and after 64 . . . K–N5   65 K–K2! White has diagonal opposition and can transform this into horizontal or vertical opposition, e.g. 65 . . . K–B5   66 K–B2! K–K5   67 K–K2.

58 . . . K–K8   59 K–B2

An interesting alternative draw is to set up the distant horizontal opposition from the QR file: 59 K–N3 (59 K–R2 also works) 59 . . . K–B7   60 N–B5 P–N6   61 NxP KxN   62 K–R3!! (Sorensen). Two possibilities arise:

  (1.) 62 . . . K–B7   63 K–N2 K–K8   64 K–R1! (White must
       stay off the QB file where he doesn't have enough
       maneuvering room) 64 . . . K–Q8   65 K–N1! K–Q7   66
       K–N2 K–Q6   67 K–N3 etc.
  (2.) 62 . . . K–B6   63 K–N3! (Not 63 K–N2? because of 63
       . . . K–B7! and not 63 K–R2? because of 63 . . . K–K7!)
       63 . . . K–B7   64 K–N2 etc.

59 . . . K–B7   60 N–B5?

Finally, *the* losing move. Correct was the method given in the note to White's 56th move: 60 N–R5! P–N6   61 K–Q2!!.

60 . . . P–N6   61 NxP KxN   62 K–B1

White is lost, as he will not be able to prevent Black from gaining the opposition, e.g. 62 K–Q3 K–B6 63 K–Q2 K–B7! (64 K–Q1 K–K6; 64 K–Q3 K–K8). No better is 62 K–N3 K–B6 63 K–N2 K–B7! and Black wins, thanks to having the distant opposition. However, faulty would be 63 . . . K–K6? because of 64 K–R3! and 63 . . . K–K7? because of 64 K–R2!—in both cases White draws. White also has no time for 63 K–R3 because 63 . . . K–K6! (distant opposition!) wins: 64 K–N2 K–Q7; 64 K–N3 K–Q6; 64 K–R2 K–K7!.

62 . . . K–B6 63 K–N1 K–K6 64 K–R2 K–K7!

Gaining the distant horizontal opposition is the *only* way to win. After the inconsistent 64 . . . K–Q7? White draws with 65 K–N2, e.g. 65 . . . K–K6 66 K–R3!, and it is now White who has the opposition.

65 K–R3 K–Q8! 66 K–N3

Or 66 K–N2 K–Q7, and Black wins.

66 . . . K–B8 White resigns

If Black so chooses he can win all three of White's pawns—an excellent example of the power of the active King when it obtains the opposition!

Section 2. Triangulation

The term "King triangulation" refers to the King making a "triangular" run around its location in order to arrive again at its starting point, but in a position a move behind its opponent. The purpose of triangulation is to give the move to the opponent and is of significance only in *zugzwang* positions. Triangulation is only meaningful when the "triangulating" King has more maneuvering room than its counterpart.

The following examples will clarify this abstract sounding definition. The greatest effect of successful triangulation occurs in K and P endgames. An instructive case is shown in the following composition (Fine 1941): White: K—c3 P—b4, g3, h2 Black: K—h3 P—b5, c4. Though White is a pawn up, Black's protected passed QBP appears to ensure the draw, as it seems to prevent activity by White's King. Nevertheless, by some accurate King maneuvers, including two triangulations, White can get his pawns to the sixth rank. Then White's King will join its pawns for a mating attack. White plays and wins as follows:

1 K–Q4 K–N5   2 P–R4 K–R4   3 K–K3 K–N5   4 K–K4 K–R4 5 K–B4!

The immediate further advance of White's pawns is now assured. Note that from here White's King can still catch the QBP.

5 . . . K–N3   6 P–N4 K–N2   7 P–R5! K–R3

White's pawns now appear stymied. If Black, however, had to move again in this position, White's pawns could advance. Therefore White's King triangulates to achieve this position with Black to move.

8 K–K4! K–N4   9 K–B3! K–R3   10 K–B4 K–N2   11 P–N5 K–B2   12 P–N6ch K–B3!

Again Black seems to have stopped the pawns. But once more triangulation forces Black to give up control of his key KB3 square.

13 K–K3! K–N2   14 K–K4! K–B3   15 K–B4! K–N2

After 15 . . . K–K3 White wins as follows: 16 P–R6 K–B3   17 P–R7 K–N2   18 K–B5! P–B6   19 K–K6! P–B7   20 P–R8 = Qch! KxQ   21 K–B7, followed by 22 P–N7ch etc.

16 K–N5! P–B6   17 P–R6ch K–N1   18 K–B6 P–B7   19 P–R7ch K–R1   20 K–B7 P–B8 = Q   21 P–N7ch KxP   22 P–N8 = Qch K–R3 23 Q–N6 Mate

The active King won!

The usefulness of King triangulation may not appear as obvious for other endgames, but often is equally applicable. Consider first the position below, Sozin–M. Botvinnik, USSR 1929, Black on move. White: K—g3 B—g1 Black: K—e2 P—f5, g4, h3. White's position is most precarious, yet at the moment he is hanging on by a thread. If White was on move here, however, Black could make decisive progress. Therefore Botvinnik starts to triangulate:

1 . . . K–Q7! 2 B–R2

Allowing the main line. The alternative was 2 K–B2 K–Q6! 3 B–R2 K–K5!. Now 4 K–N3 K–K6 5 B–N1ch K–K7 leads to the game continuation, whereas 4 B–N3 leads to a routine loss after 4 . . . P–B5 5 B–R2 K–B4! 6 B–N1 P–N6 ch 7 K–B3 P–R7.

2 . . . K–K8! 3 B–N1 K–K7!

The triangulation is successfully completed, and White on move must give ground. If now 4 K–B4, Black's King penetrates the Kingside: 4 . . . K–B8 5 B–R2 K–N7.

4 B–Q4 P–B5ch!

And now the KBP can advance, since White's Bishop is no longer guarding his KR2 square.

5 K–R2 P–B6 6 K–N1 P–B7ch

Even simpler is 6 . . . P–N6.

7 BxP P–R7ch White resigns

After 8 KxP KxB 9 K–R1 Black wins with 9 . . . K–N6!.

Meaningful opportunities for triangulation often exist at higher material levels also. Diagram 132, W. Henneberger–A. Nimzowitsch, Winterthur 1931, after White's 48th move, shows a classic case of the "good Knight" vs. the "bad Bishop". Nevertheless, the position is so blockaded that it is difficult to see where Black can penetrate. To make progress, Black will have to resort to two triangulations. The first item on Black's agenda is to achieve the diagram position with White to move. Note that Black has two access squares from which his King can get to Q4; White has only one square from which to reach K3. Therefore Black has an easy case of triangulation:

48 . . . K–Q3! 49 K–K2 K–B3! 50 K–K3 K–Q4 51 K–K2 N–Q3 52 K–K3 N–N4 53 B–Q2 N–R6 54 B–B1

Forced, as 54 B–K1? allows a hopeless K and P endgame after 54 . . . N–B7ch 55 K–K2 NxB 56 KxN K–K5 57 K–K2 P–R6. After the text, however, White's Bishop will soon be stalemated.

DIAGRAM 132

BLACK

WHITE

Henneberger–Nimzowitsch
Winterthur 1931
after White's 48th

54 . . . N–N8!! 55 B–N2 P–R6 56 B–R1 K–Q3! 57 K–K2 K–B3! 58 K–Q1

After 58 K–K3 K–Q4 Black's King gets to K5 and then still farther in. If White tries to triangulate himself with 58 K–B2, Black's Knight is freed and he wins with 58 . . . N–Q7 (59 K–K2 N–K5; 59 K–N1 N–N6!). Winning the Knight is the best try.

58 . . . K–Q4 59 K–B2 K–K5 60 KxN K–B6 61 B–N2

As White is playing without the Bishop, Black would win easily on the Kingside. Therefore the text is the only chance, but Black still wins by a tempo:

61 . . . PxB 62 P–R4 KxP 63 P–R5 K–R7! 64 P–R6 P–N6 65 P–R7 P–N7 66 P–R8 = Q P–N8 = Qch 67 KxP Q–N7ch! 68 QxQch KxQ 69 K–R3 K–B6 70 K–N4 KxP 71 KxP K–K6 72 P–Q5 PxPch 73 KxP P–B5 74 P–B4 P–B6 75 P–B5 P–B7 76 P–B6 P–B8 = Q White resigns

In the R and P endgame below, I. Ivanov–V. Chehov, Vladivostok (USSR) 1978, after Black's 40th move, White: K—e2 R—c6 P—b2, c3, f2, g3, h4 Black: K—f5 R—d5 P—b5, c4, e5, g6, h5. White has two advantages: the active Rook and the superior pawn formation. Yet Black is just able to prevent any immediate damage. Seeing that Black presently has the optimum piece configuration, White forms the following plan: to give Black the move! Triangulation will do the job:

41 R–N6! R–B4   42 K–B3!

Premature is the immediate 42 P–B3?!, as Black gets good counterplay after 42 . . . R–Q4   43 R–QB6 R–Q6   44 R–B5 K–K3! 45 RxNP P–K5!   46 PxP RxNP.

42 . . . R–Q4   43 K–K3! R–Q6ch   44 K–K2 R–Q4   45 R–QB6!

Mission accomplished—Black is now forced to deactivate his Rook.

45 . . . R–Q2   46 R–B5 R–QN2   47 K–K3 R–N3   48 P–B3! P–N5

Passive defense is also hopeless: 48 . . . R–N1   49 P–B4! K–N5 50 RxKP KxP   51 R–N5ch KxP   52 RxKNP, and the passed KBP will win easily, since Black's King remains cut off on the KR file.

49 P–N4ch! PxP   50 PxP ch K–B3   51 K–K4!

Keeping the King active!

51 . . . PxP   52 PxP R–N8   53 R–B6ch K–B2   54 KxP R–KR8 55 R–B7ch K–K1   56 K–B6! RxP   57 RxP Black resigns

CHAPTER 29

Various Important Activities

Section 1. Preventing Threats

There are all kinds of potential threats and there are a large number of King movements possible to deal with them.

Perhaps the simplest one is the direct defensive move to parry an overt threat. An instructive example is offered by the play arising from Diagram 133, Gottschall–S. Tarrasch, Nuremberg 1888, after White's 79th move. Even though Black has only two pawns for the piece, he has a significant advantage because White's Knight is nothing but a defensive piece and Black can create connected passed pawns on the Queenside with . . . P–R4 and . . . P–N5. Black's actively placed Queen is another advantage, and to keep winning prospects he doesn't want to allow an exchange. At the moment, therefore, White has a definite threat: 80 Q–R3!, and if 80 . . . QxN, 81 Q–B8ch, with a perpetual check draw. Therefore the immediate 79 . . . P–R4? is faulty because the endgame after 80 Q–R3! QxQ? 81 NxQ P–N5 82 N–B2! is *at best* only drawn for Black. Tarrasch parries White's threat with the defensive:

79 . . . K–N2! 80 Q–R3

Not wanting to be smothered to death after 80 . . . P–R4 etc., White tries his luck with Queen activity. It will turn out that Black's King can evade the checks; White's approach however, is no worse than anything else.

80 . . . QxN 81 Q–K7 Q–B8ch! 82 K–K3 Q–K8ch 83 K–B3 QxBPch 84 K–N2 Q–Q7ch 85 K–R3 Q–R4! 86 Q–B6ch K–B1

DIAGRAM 133

BLACK

WHITE

Gottschall–Tarrasch
Nuremburg 1888
after White's 79th

87 Q–R8ch K–K2   88 Q–B6ch K–K1!   89 Q–R8ch K–Q2   90 Q–KB8 Q–Q1!   91 Q–B5

Nothing satisfies. The Black King escapes to safety after 91 Q–Q6ch K–K1   92 Q–B6ch Q–Q2   93 Q–R8ch K–K2   94 Q–R8 Q–K1!   95 Q–B6ch K–Q2; after 91 QxPch Q–K2   92 QxRP P–N5 the three connected passed pawns will triumph.

91 . . . Q–QN1   92 Q–N4 K–K1!   93 Q–B5 Q–N2   94 Q–R3 P–N5   95 Q–KB3 P–N6   96 QxRP P–N7   97 Q–R8ch K–Q2   98 Q–KB8 P–N8 = Q   99 QxPch K–B3!   100 QxPch K–N4 White resigns

Prevention of threat(s) by King aggressiveness is demonstrated in the play arising from Diagram 134, A. Alekhine–R. Fine, Kemeri 1937, after Black's 31st move. Black had hoped to get out of an unpleasant bind by the use of tactics directed against White's King, and he now threatens both 32 . . . N–N6ch and 32 . . . RxPch. Alekhine however, turns the hunted into the hunter with

32 K–B3!

Now 32 . . . RxP? loses a piece after 33 K–B4!. The Knight retreat 32 . . . N–Q2 loses material to 33 B–K7. Therefore Black's

DIAGRAM 134

BLACK

WHITE

Alekhine–Fine
Kemeri 1937
after Black's 31st

response is forced, and Alekhine quickly turns his overwhelming space advantage into a win.

32 . . . P–QN3   33 PxP PxP   34 BxN! PxB   35 P–N6! N–Q3 36 B–Q7!

With the plan of 37 B–B6,   38 P–N7 and 39 R–R8. Not wanting to witness this, Black commits suicide.

36 . . . RxB?!   37 R–R8ch Black resigns

Then there is the indirect—often "sneaky"—way of preventing a threat, as shown in the play arising from Diagram 135, M. Botvinnik–D. Bronstein, 1951 World Championship Match, Game 5, after White's 30th move. At first glance it may seem that White has little to worry about, since Black's forward doubled QP seems destined to be lost. Moreover, Black's attempt to retain a pawn advantage by 30 . . . NxP allows White approximate equality after 31 NxQP NxN   32 BxNch BxB   33 N–K7ch! K–B2   34 NxB, because White threatens 35 R–R1,   35 N–N6,   35 N–B7,   35 R–B1ch—and therefore wins back the pawn effortlessly. However, Bronstein has a devilishly sneaky way of preventing the threat to his QP:

30 . . . K–R1!!   31 R–K1?

DIAGRAM 135

BLACK

WHITE

Botvinnik–Bronstein
1951 World Championship
Match, Game 5
after White's 30th

Without the helpful *zwischen*-check on K7, it turns out that Black's QP is inviolate: 31 NxQP? NxN 32 BxN BxB 33 RxB P–N3! 34 N–K7 N–K6!, and White must choose between losing his Rook or his King.

Even so, the text also is unsatisfactory. White should save his QRP with 31 P–QR4!, retaining fair prospects for an eventual draw.

31 . . . NxP 32 N–Q6 B–B3 33 R–R1 N–B7 34 RxP P–Q5!

The ugly doubled pawn has developed into a power. If now 35 BxB, Black wins with 35 . . . NxP! 36 R–R8 RxR 37 BxR PxN.

35 N/3xP BxB! 36 KxB N–N5! 37 N–B5

There is no defense. Black also has a winning attack after 37 N–K4 N/B–K6ch 38 K–R3 P–N4! 39 NxNP (39 NxQP R–B7!! 40 NxR NxNmate!) 39 . . . R–B7 40 K–R4 RxPch 41 N–R3 N–B7.

37 . . . P–Q6 38 R–Q6

Hopeless too is 38 N–B3 P–N3 39 N–Q6 N/B–K6ch 40 K–R3 R–B7.

38 . . . RxN   39 RxP/7 N/B–K6ch White resigns

In the previous examples the threats were of the immediate tactical type. Equally important is to prevent the longer range strategic ones. An instructive case arises in the following position, E. Gufeld–Gavashelishvili, USSR 1977, after Black's 40th move. White: K—h2 Q—c5 P—b4, f2, g2, h3 Black: K—g8 Q—b2 P—e4, f5, g6, h5. Though material is even, White has a winning advantage because he is going to push his passed QNP to victory. Black's only chance is to loosen up White's King position by throwing his Kingside pawn forward and then hope that he can achieve perpetual check. White can win if he sees through and prevents Black's plan. However:

41 P–N5?

Both overeager and careless. Winning was 41 K–N3!!, with the King stopping the pawns long enough to allow the decisive march of the QNP.

41 . . . P–B5!   42 P–N6 P–K6!   43 PxP P–B6!   44 Q–Q5ch

The resulting Q and P endgame is unwinnable. More chances were offered by 44 Q–KN5! QxQNP   45 PxP, with the lack of symmetry in the interest of the stronger side.

44 . . . K–R2!   45 QxBP QxQNP   46 Q–B4 Q–N8   47 P–K4 Q–K8   48 P–R4 K–N2   49 P–K5 Q–B6   50 Q–B6ch K–R2   51 Q–K7ch K–N1   52 P–K6 Q–K4ch Draw

Black has a relatively easy perpetual check.

Section 2. Marking Time

Just as it was true in the middlegame, so also in the endgame the King is useful as a time–killing mechanism. Usually the prospects for formulating a concrete plan are better in the endgame than in the middlegame, and thus the opportunities for marking time are correspondingly fewer. Nevertheless they do occur, and even world champions do not hesitate to mark time when it suits their purposes. Enlightening in this respect is the course of play from the following position, A. Alekhine–J. R. Capablanca, 1927 World

Championship Match, Game 34, after Black's 51st move. White: K—g2 R—d4 P—a5, f2, g3, h4 Black: K—g7 R—a6 P—f7, g6, h6. At this point in the match Alekhine needed one more win to become world champion. Clearly his position, a pawn up, is significantly favorable. Yet the practical question always is: how to *ensure* the win? Alekhine now played

52 R–Q5!?

Alekhine characterizes his approach to the play over the next ten moves as follows: "White makes use of every opportunity, by repetition of moves, to gain time with the clock, so as to avoid a slip just before the capture of the title." Note that at moves 52–53 he uses the Rook for this; at moves 60–61 the King performs this function.

52 . . . R–KB3   53 R–Q4 R–R3   54 R–R4 K–B3   55 K–B3! K–K4 56 K–K3 P–R4   57 K–Q3 K–Q4   58 K–B3 K–B4   59 R–R2! K–N4 60 K–N3!? K–B4   61 K–B3 K–N4   62 K–Q4!

The definitive winning plan: the King heads for the Kingside to menace the Black pawns. In the ensuing play Alekhine does not find the absolutely fastest wins, but keeps the game in hand, anyway. If now 62 . . . K–N5, White plays 63 R–R1!, as 63 K–N6? allows White's King to get to the Queenside with 64 K–B5.

62 . . . R–Q3ch   63 K–K5 R–K3ch   64 K–B4 K–R3   65 K–N5! R–K4ch   66 K–R6 R–KB4   67 P–B4

White could have put Black into *zugzwang* by triangulating with his King as follows: 67 K–N7! R–B6   68 K–N8! R–B3   69 K–B8! R–B6   70 K–N7! R–B4   71 P–B4.

67 . . . R–B4   68 R–R3 R–B2   69 K–N7 R–Q2   70 P–B5 PxP 71 K–R6 P–B5   72 PxP R–Q4   73 K–N7 R–KB4   74 R–R4 K–N4 75 R–K4! K–R3   76 K–R6! RxRP   77 R–K5! R–R8   78 KxP R–KN8 79 R–KN5 R–KR8   80 R–KB5 K–N3   81 RxP K–B3   82 R–K7! Black resigns

Using the King for marking time so that the opponent is put into *zugzwang* is quite an important endgame strategy. The sophisticated movement called "triangulation" was examined in detail in Chapter 28. Periodically, "simple" King moves serve equally well. For instance, let's look at Diagram 136, S. Tatai–

DIAGRAM 136

BLACK

WHITE

Tatai–Keene
Skopje (Ol) 1972
after White's 42nd

R. Keene, Skopje Olympiad 1972, after White's 42nd move. Though Black is a pawn up, it is difficult to see how he can make progress, since his Bishop has little scope, and 42 . . . R–KB2 is parried by 43 N–Q2!. Yet note that White is actually in *zugzwang*: the only King move allows . . . P–B5ch; a Knight move allows . . . R–Q7; any Rook move allows . . . R–KB2. Therefore Black simply plays:

42 . . . K–N2!   43 R–B1 R–KB2!   44 R–B4 K–N3!!

Zugzwang once more! If now 45 K–K3 R–QR2   46 R–B2 P–B5ch or 45 R–B1 P–B5!   46 RxP R–B5ch   47 K–Q3 RxNch. Therefore White must allow Black's Rook to penetrate to the 7th rank.

45 N–K1 R–B7   46 N–Q3 RxP   47 R–B1

Allows a tactical end. Equally hopeless is 47 NxBP BxN   48 RxB R–KN7   49 K–B3 R–N7.

47 . . . P–B5!   48 NxP R–K7ch   49 K–B3 R–K6ch   50 K–N2 PxP White resigns

Another instructive *zugzwang* position is set up from Diagram 137, E. Bogolyubov–A. Alekhine, Hastings 1922, after White's

DIAGRAM 137

BLACK

WHITE

Bogolyubov–Alekhine
Hastings 1922
after White's 40th

40th move. Black has a slight material advantage, but to win he must loosen up the White pawn formation. He does this by putting the White pieces in *zugzwang* by:

40 . . . Q–K7! 41 P–Q5

The pieces can't move: 41 R–R3 (or 41 R–R1) N–N5!; 41 N–N4 NxN!; 41 N–R3 N–N5!.

41 . . . K–N1! 42 P–R5 K–R2! 43 P–K4

Forced, but now the White pawn structure disintegrates.

43 . . . NxKP 44 NxN QxN/5 45 P–Q6 PxP 46 P–B6 PxP 47 R–Q2 Q–K7!

Forcing an easily won K and P endgame.

48 RxQ PxR 49 K–B2 PxN = Qch 50 KxQ K–N2 51 K–B2 K–B2 52 K–K3 K–K3 53 K–K4 P–Q4ch White resigns

Section 3. Gaining Time

Capablanca has said that for success in endgame play, the need is for accuracy and time saving; thus major attention must be given to moves that gain or save time. In other words, gaining time (or tempos, as it is often expressed) is a major objective of endgame play. This makes sense in those positions where the strategic goal is clear and simple, e.g. queening a passed pawn or obtaining control of a key square.

It is therefore logical to expect that the king has a vital role to play in the fight for time (tempos). Many such instances are so clear as to be self-evident. What I shall discuss, therefore, are the more sophisticated methods of using king activity to gain time.

Both interesting and important is the type of maneuver employed in the play arising from this position, a 1952 endgame study by J. Moravec. White: K—a4 P—c5 Black: K—d8 P—h7. White seems to be in dire straits indeed, since his King can't catch Black's KRP, while White's QBP looks easy to stop. Nevertheless, White's King can gain a tempo and the draw as follows:

1 K–N5! P–R4

After 1 . . . K–B2   2 K–B4! White's King is close enough to the KRP.

2 K–B6!! K–B1

Otherwise White's King gets to QN7 and assists in queening the QBP: 2 . . . P–R5   3 K–N7 P–R6   4 P–B6 P–R7   4 P–B7ch etc.

3 K–Q5!! Draw

In effect White's King has gotten to Q5 in net two moves and therefore is again close enough to the RP: 3 . . . P–R5   4 K–K4 P–R6   5 K–B3 P–R7   6 K–N2.

The successful execution of a similar maneuver in a practical game occurs in the play arising from the position below, A. Bisguier–J. Tarjan, 1975 U.S. Championship, after White's 47th move. White: K—f2 P—a4, b2, c4, g3, h2 Black: K—g7 B—h1 P—e4, g4, h7. A simple count shows that Black's King can't get to the Queenside in time to stop the QRP. Sacrificing the KP with an early . . . P–K6ch also offers no prospects. Yet there is *a* way for Black's King to accomplish its objective:

47 . . . K–B3!   48 P–R5 K–K4!!

If now 49 P–R6? K–Q5!   50 P–R7 P–K6ch. Therefore White's

reply is forced, and this loss of time is just enough for Black's King to complete his journey successfully.

49 K–K3 K–Q3! 50 P–N4 K–B3 51 P–N5ch K–B4 52 P–R6 K–N3

An interesting, dynamically stable position has resulted. White's three passed pawns offer no winning chances because his King can't participate, as it must stay back to prevent the KP's advance. On the other hand, Black also can't win because his Bishop has insufficient offensive punch. In the play to come, Black tries various approaches, but White parries them all.

53 K–B2 B–B6 54 K–K3 B–N7 55 K–B2 B–R6! 56 K–K2! K–R2 57 K–B2 K–N3 58 K–K2 B–N7 59 K–B2 B–B6 60 K–K3 K–R2 61 P–B5 P–R3 62 K–Q4 P–R4 63 K–K3 B–Q8 64 KxP B–R5 65 P–N6ch! KxP 66 K–B4 K–N2 67 K–N5 B–K1 68 K–R4 K–B3 69 K–N5 K–N2 70 K–R4 K–N1!? 71 K–N5! B–B2 72 K–R4 K–B1 73 K–N5 K–Q2 74 K–R4 K–B3 75 K–N5 Draw

A somewhat similar concept, but with a different execution, occurs in the play arising from this position, V. Smyslov–V. Korchnoi, 1952 USSR Championship, after White's 48th move. White: K—g4 R—h8 P—a5, h3 Black: K—f6 R—f2 P—e3, f4, g6. Black's advanced, connected passed pawns, well supported by the Rook, appear invincible. A closer look, however, shows that Black's Rook can't help its pawns advance and stop White's QRP. For example, 48 . . . P–K7 49 R–K8 P–B6 50 P–R6 R–B8 51 P–R7 R–QR8 52 KxP, and White draws. What Black would like to do, therefore, is to keep his Rook where it is and stop the QRP with the King. Yet quite obviously the King is too far away for this. Black however, does have a tempo–gaining King route:

48 . . . K–K2!!

By taking away the K8 square from White's Rook, Black threatens the immediately–winning 49 . . . P–K7. To reestablish access to K8, White is forced to send Black's King exactly where it wants to go.

49 R–R7ch K–Q3! 50 R–R8 P–K7! 51 R–K8 K–B3! White resigns

Black's King stops the QRP while Black's Rook ensures the promotion of his passed pawn(s): 52 R–K6ch K–N2   53 P–R6ch K–R2   54 P–R4 P–B6   55 K–N3 R–B8 etc.

A different kind of sophisticated King movement occurs in the play arising from Diagram 138, J. Tarjan–L. Christiansen, 1978 U.S. Championship, after Black's 27th move. White has a significant advantage based on having the more active pieces, the passed QRP and Black's weak QP. At the moment Black threatens 28 . . . N–Q6ch. A King move is White's best remedy, but which King move?

28 K–B3!

DIAGRAM 138

BLACK

WHITE

Tarjan–Christiansen
US Championship 1978
after Black's 27th

This is more accurate than 28 K–B2, as it prevents Black's Rook from getting to K7 with check in variations such as 28 K–B2 N–B6 29 RxRch RxR   30 B–B4 R–K7ch.

28 . . . P–B4?!

Fundamentally weakening the Knight's status on K4. Also useless is 28 . . . B–B2?! because White plays 29 K–B2! and has, in effect, gained a move, since the line given above would now be fruitless for Black because the Bishop is *en prise*. Black's best defensive set-up was 28 . . . K–N2 followed by 29 . . . P–B3.

29 B–B4 K–B2   30 P–QR4! B–B2   31 K–B2! K–B3   32 P–R4 K–B2   33 P–QR5! R/K–Q1   34 P–R6 N–B6   35 R–K6 R–Q2   36 K–N2!

One more sophisticated King maneuver: White makes sure that Black never gets in . . . N–Q5 *with check*.

36 . . . R–QR1   37 NxB RxN   38 BxP R/2–B1   39 R–K7ch K–B3 40 R–K6ch K–B2   41 R–K7ch K–B3   42 P–R7 N–Q5   43 R–QN7 Black resigns

Section 4. Preparing Action

You want to do something, but the King is either in the way or of no help? Move it, so that you can then be ready for action!

First I'll consider the case where the King position makes a desirable plan impossible. Diagram 139 is K. Regan–P. Benko, 1978 U.S. Championship, after White's 25th move. A cursory look may lead to the conclusion that White has some advantage, due to the strong pressure against the KP and the passive placement of Black's KR. Yet note how quickly Black demonstrates the complete soundness of his position:

25 . . . PxP!   26 RxRP K–B1!

Black would like to activate his KR via KB4, but that move is not feasible because the KP is pinned. But after the text it will be both feasible and good.

27 K–B1 R–KB4!   28 RxRch?!

Why straighten out Black's pawn formation? Correct is 28 R–QR3, with equality.

28 . . . PxR   29 K–K2 P–B5   30 R–K4 P–N4   31 K–Q2 R–Q2ch 32 K–B2 B–N2   33 R–K5 P–KR3   34 P–N3 K–K2!   35 RxR KxR

Black has a slight advantage because of his outside passed pawn. Accurate defense by White, however, achieved a draw on Move 61.

The Endgame

DIAGRAM 139

BLACK

WHITE

Regan–Benko
1978 US Championship
After White's 25th

Moving the King so that it is placed at maximum advantage for the execution of a concrete plan is shown in the play arising from the position below, J. Mieses–A. Alekhine, Mannheim 1914, after White's 35th move. White: K—e2 R—g5 N—e5 P—e4, f3, g2, h3 Black: K—g8 R—c5 N—g7 P—b6, c7, f4, h4. Though material is even, Black's connected passed pawns offer great promise of success. But how to make progress? A . . . P–N4 (e.g. 35 . . . P–N4) leaves Black's Rook unprotected, and White can untangle himself with 36 N–B7! A surprising King move, however, puts an end to all of White's hopes:

35 . . . K–R2!! White resigns!

Black simply threatens to push the QNP to victory. With Black's King on KR2 the tactical N–B7 (either next move or subsequently) is parried by (after e.g. 36 N–B7) 36 . . . RxR! 37 NxRch K–N3!, with White's Knight trapped and lost.

A sophisticated example of a King move to prepare action is illustrated in the play arising from this position, V. Ceshkovsky–V. Savon, Baku (USSR) 1977, after Black's 41st move. White: K—g1 Q—d6 B—e3 N—f1 P—d5, e4, f2, g2 Black: K—h6 Q—c3 N—f4, h7 P—c5, e5, f6, g4. Black's position is just plain horrible. His King is in some danger, the KR2 Knight a strictly defense piece, QBP weak—and White's QP an obvious queening threat. In the game White played the immediate 42 N–N3?!, and after 42 . . . N–K7ch! 43 NxN Q–K8ch 44 K–R2 QxN Black had considerably lightened his defensive load, and after some further inaccuracies by White managed to squeeze out a 60 move draw. The following sophisticated King move would have left Black in a completely helpless situation:

42 K–R2!! with a won position for White.

White removes his King from the first rank, thus obviating any checks and pins. White now is ready to proceed with 43 N–N3 and the Knight stands very well here for both offensive and defense purposes. Black's best try is 42 . . . N–K7!?, anyway, after which White activates his Queen with 43 Q–K6!, leaving Black defenseless. For instance, 43 . . . Q–K8 44 N–N3 Q–N8ch 45 K–R3 N–B5ch 46 BxN NPxB 47 N–B5ch, and White mates first. After the game Savon ventured the opinion that since after 42 K–R2!! his prospects would have been so bleak, he might well have resigned immediately!

Section 5. Weaving Mating Nets

As I have said many times previously, one of the characteristic features of endgames is that the Kings can feel rather safe. Paradoxically, this means that one King can participate most effectively in trying to help bring down its unlucky counterpart.

Sometimes the King needs just a bit of effort to accomplish its objective. A good example of this occurs in the play arising from Diagram 140, E. M. Jackson–F. J. Marshall, London 1899, after White's 28th move. In previous play Black had sacrificed two pawns to chase White's King to the edge of the board. To complete the job he still needs additional help, and this is where his own King comes in:

28 . . . K–N2! 29 B–B4?

DIAGRAM 140

BLACK

WHITE

E.M. Jackson–F.J. Marshall
London 1899
after White's 28th

Meets a striking refutation. A better try was 29 K–R5, though Black should still win after 29 . . . P–B5ch   30 K–N4 PxP   31 KxP R–K3!   32 P–KR4 RxPch   33 B–N5 RxP (Marshall).

29 . . . KxP!!   30 B–N5

The frightful threats of 30 . . . B–K2ch and 30 . . . RxBch! need parrying, but now comes a real Marshall bombshell:

30 . . . R–B5ch!!   White resigns

His choice is between 31 PxR B–B7mate and 31 BxR B–K2ch   32 B–N5 BxBmate.

More work by a King succeeds in turning the tables in the play arising from the position below, I. Bondarevsky–A. Ufimtsev, Leningrad 1936, Black on move. White: K—f4 R–h1 B—b5 N—g6 P—d5, e4 Black: K—g8 R—c2 B—h3 N—f6 P—a7, b6, d6, g7. Black is two pawns up and in no apparent danger. Yet note how quickly everything changes:

1 . . . B–N7??

After this obvious response White has a forced win. Correct is 1 . . . R–B6!.

2 R–R8ch K–B2   3 B–K8ch!! NxB   4 K–N5!! Black resigns

Next comes 5 R–B8mate.

A considerably longer successful King trek ending in mate results from the following position, L. Schneider–J. Nogueiras, Júrmala (Riga) 1978, after White's 35th move. White: K—g1 R—c6 B—d6 P—e5, f2, g3, h2 Black: K—g8 R—f7 N—d5 P—b6, e6, g7, h7. Despite material equality, Black has a significant advantage due to the passed QNP and the superiority of his Knight over White's Bishop. Yet the decisive factor will turn out to be Black's super-active King:

35 . . . R–N2!   36 P–B4 K–B2   37 R–B8?!

It was better to centralize the King with 37 K–B2!. The Rook just wastes time.

37 . . . K–N3!   38 R–K8 P–N4!   39 B–B5 R–QB2!   40 B–N6 R–B3!   41 B–R5 R–R3   42 B–K1 K–B4!

The start of the decisive march.

43 R–KN8 K–N5!   44 P–B5!? PxP   45 RxPch K–B6 46 R–N5 N–K6 White resigns

He is defenseless against the coming 47 . . . R–R8, e.g. 47 P–R4 R–R8   48 K–R2 RxB   49 P–K6 N–N5ch   50 K–R3 R–R8mate.

The direct attempt at mate does not always lead to that conclusion. Such a threat, however, is very often successful in achieving a specific objective some place else. In the following two examples, the ability to see mating opportunities is of decisive influence in the game's result. In the first example Black spies such an opportunity and this allows him to consolidate his material advantage successfully; in the second case White's inability to notice a similar opportunity allows his opponent to escape with a draw.

Diagram 141 is J. Timman–L. Ljubojevic, Amsterdam (IBM) 1978, after White's 40th move. Though a pawn down, White had counted on the imminent capture of Black's QP to give him sufficient counterchances for a draw. Yet Black has foreseen that he can stop all of White's hopes with the surprising:

DIAGRAM 141

BLACK

WHITE

Timman–Ljubojevic
Amsterdam (IBM) 1978
after White's 40th

40 . . . K–K2!!

The obvious 41 RxPch leaves White's King helpless after 41 . . .
K–K3!. The threat is 42 . . . B–B8ch and e.g. 42 R–Q1 leads to 42
. . . BxP 43 B–B4ch K–B3 and there is nothing to be done about the
threat of 44 . . . P–N4mate. Therefore White's King must now go
through some contortions to save itself.

41 K–K5 R–K6ch   42 K–B4 R–K5ch   43 K–B3 P–Q3!

Black has consolidated his position and, after winning the QNP,
will be up two sound pawns. The further play is routine.

**44 B–B6 RxP   45 R–Q3 B–N7   46 P–R5 R–QB5   47 R–K3ch
B–K4   48 B–N7 R–QR5   49 P–R6 P–N4!   50 P–R3 P–R4   51 R–K2
P–N5ch   52 K–N2 P–B5   53 R–Q2 R–R6 White resigns**

An unusual deployment of forces is depicted in this position, G.
Sosonko–A. Miles, Bad Lauterberg 1977, after Black's 33rd move.
White: K—h1 R—b3, c6 P—b2, b6, f2, f4, h2 Black: K—f5 R—
b7, h8 P—f7, g7, h7. Though White is up two pawns, both of these
are isolated and doubled, thereby significantly decreasing their
value. White, however, also has several strategic pluses: a very
strong advanced passed QNP, active Rooks, and Black King's

uncomfortable situation in the middle of the board. The way to win is to take advantage of the last factor:

34 K–N2!

With the devastating threat 35 K–B3! and 36 R–N5mate.

Instead, in the game, White rushed things with 34 R–B7?, and Black managed to draw after 34 . . . KR–QN1 35 RxR RxR 36 R–N4 K–K3 37 K–N2 K–Q4 38 P–B5?! (The non-weakening 38 K–B3! still retained winning chances) 38 . . . K–B4 39 R–N3 P–B3! 40 P–R4 P–R4 41 K–N3 K–B5 42 R–B3ch K–Q4 43 R–Q3ch K–B4 44 R–R3 RxP 45 R–R7 K–Q4! 46 RxP K–K4 47 R–K7ch KxP 48 R–K2 R–N6ch 49 P–B3 R–N5 Draw. Black's King turned out to be *safe and active!*

34 . . . KxP

Everything else is worse. For instance, 34 . . . R–K1 loses to 35 R–N5ch! KxP 36 R–B4ch R–K5 37 R–B7! RxR 38 PxR R–B5 39 R–N4!.

35 R–N5! P–B4! 36 R–B4ch K–N4 37 P–R4ch K–R3 38 R–B6ch P–N3 39 RxBP, with a won position for White

White has succeeded in exchanging one of his weak doubled KBPs for Black's healthy KBP, and, by retaining his material advantage and positional bind, can look forward to a fairly easy win.

CHAPTER 30
Correct/Incorrect King Moves

You're in check or, for other reasons, must make a King move. But where to move? Of course, the best way to proceed is to examine all the alternatives carefully and then choose the correct one. Yet if time is short or the position is too complicated for a definitive analysis—what to do then? The best approach is to rely on some valid general principles, i.e. if in doubt, play according to them and, most of the time, things will turn out fine. Five particularly important ones will be illustrated below.

1. *Don't be greedy—especially when in time pressure!*

Diagram 142, N. Gaprindashvili–U. Andersson, Dortmund 1978, after Black's 33rd move, shows a position in material and dynamic balance. White has an extra pawn on the Queenside; Black on the Kingside. The normal way to mobilize White's Queenside is 34 N–B3, forcing 34 . . . PxPch. Noting that Black is in serious time trouble, White tries a trickier approach:

34 PxPch!? KxN??

Usually the Swedish GM is among the most conservative of players. But here, caught by complete surprise, he loses his cool. Did he really think that White had left the Knight hanging? The only correct recapture—strategically and otherwise—was 34 . . . KxP!. Then, after 35 N–B3ch K–B3 36 K–B4 N–K3! 37 P–N3 N–B2, the position remains equal.

35 PxP N–K3

Or 35 . . . K–B3 36 P–N5ch K–B2 37 P–N6ch K–B3 38 P–R7 K–N2 39 P–R6ch. Should it really be a surprise that three well mobilized passed pawns quickly bring down a lone King?

DIAGRAM 142

BLACK

WHITE

Gaprindashvili–Andersson
Dortmund 1978
after Black's 33rd

36 P–R7 N–B2   37 P–N5 Black resigns

The likely end would have been: 37 . . . N–R1   38 P–N6
K–B3   39 P–R6, followed by 40 P–N7.

2. *Prevent all unnecessary counterplay.*

In Diagram 143, A. Mihaljchishin–V. Jansa, Vrnjacka Banja
1978, after Black's 27th move, White has a nice material advantage, as well as the positional pluses of a passed QP and well
coordinated pieces. The only potential danger is to White's
King, particularly as a result of the far advanced KBP. Correct
therefore is:

28 K–R1!

But not 28 K–B1? R–N7!, followed by doubling Rooks on the
KN file with excellent counterchances for Black. After the text
move White's Rook can participate in defending White's KN1
and the win becomes fairly routine. Note that in this case the
general principle of centralizing the King is replaced by the need
to prevent counterplay.

28 . . . R–N5   29 R–Q1 P–N4   30 P–Q6 R–Q1   31 B–N6 R–Q2
32 B–B7 P–N5   33 N–Q5 P–B6   34 PxP PxP   35 NxQBP R–QB5   36

DIAGRAM 143

BLACK

WHITE

Mihaljchishin–Jansa
Vrnjacka Banja 1978
after Black's 27th

**R–Q3! R–B5   37 N–Q5 R–B5   38 RxP K–K3   39 N–N6 R–B8ch   40
K–N2 R–N2ch   41 R–N3 Black resigns**

*3. Whatever the choice, avoid positions which must be
mathematically lost.*

One of the requirements for success in practical play is to hold
inferior positions for a draw. Inferior positions always require
choosing between a number of evils. It is imperative to be able
continually to select the minor ones. Part of the time this can be
done by a process of elimination. Avoid those moves which *must*
turn out badly; of the other(s), whatever will be, will be—and
there is no use in worrying about it!

Let's see how this type of thinking can be applied to the position
below, E. Mednis–J. Begovac, Sombor 1974, after White's 34th
move: White: K—g1 B—d5 N—d4 P—b4, f2, g3 Black: K—g8 B—
d3, d8 P—g7, h7. White is up a passed QNP, yet the win is in no
way assured because there are few pawns left and Black's Bishop
pair is well placed to cope with the QNP. But first things first:
Black's King is in check and must go to one of two possible squares.
Where?

34 . . . K–B1?

Not here! Though superficially logical ("heading towards the center"; "to be closer to the QNP" etc.), it is bound to be wrong since it allows by force a same–color Bishop endgame which must be certain death for Black. For better or worse, 34 . . . K–R1! had to be played. As a follow-up Black puts the KB on QN3 and then tries to free his King with . . . P–N3 and . . . K–N2. As discussed earlier Black's drawing chances remain considerable.

35 N–K6ch K–K2   36 NxB!

Clear and consistent: White aims for that endgame where he is sure of the win. Inferior is 36 NxP?!, since Black's Bishops and King may well capture the QNP. If so, White's Kingside pawn advantage would be insufficient for the win.

36 . . . KxN   37 P–B4 K–B2   38 K–B2 P–R3   39 K–K3 B–B7   40 B–K4 B–N6   41 K–Q4 K–N3   42 B–Q3 Black resigns

The game was adjourned here, and Black resigned without continuing it. The QNP binds down Black's King to the Queenside and White's King gets to the Kingside via K5 to win the pawns there.

4. *Keep out the enemy King.*

Since the King is an endgame power, it is logical enough to prevent the enemy King from penetrating into one's own territory. This fairly obvious point should give us sufficient guidance in selecting Black's correct move in this position, A. Nimzowitsch–M. Tchigorin, Carlsbad 1907, after White's 53rd move. White: K—d4 P—f4, g4, h2 Black: K—d6 P—d5, f6, h6. White is for choice because he has the more active King and is able to put pressure on Black's isolated QP. Black now must choose between 53 . . . K–B3 and 53 . . . K–K3:

A) 53 . . . K–K3? = Wrong!

This is the game continuation and must be patently wrong since White's King penetrates on the next move. Black's QP becomes immediately indefensible.

54 K–B5 P–B4   55 P–R3! PxP   56 PxP P–Q5   57 KxP K–Q3   58 P–B5 Black resigns

B) 53 . . . K–B3! = Right!

Black can now hold the game. At the moment this is not obvious, but is the only viable *practical* approach since 53 . . . K–K3? must be hopeless.

54 P–R3!

Black has fewer problems after 54 P–R4 K–Q3 55 P–R5 K–K3! 56 K–B5 P–B4 57 P–N5 PxP 58 P–R6 K–B2! 59 PxP P–B5 60 K–Q4 K–N3, with a draw.

54 . . . K–Q3 55 P–R4 K–B3! 56 P–R5

The break 56 P–N5 is insufficient: 56 . . . BPxP 57 BPxP PxP 58 P–R5 P–N5 59 K–K3 (Or 59 P–R6 P–N6 60 K–K3 P–Q5ch 61 K–B3 P–Q6 etc.) 59 . . . K–B4! 60 P–R6 P–Q5ch 61 K–B2 P–Q6 62 P–R7 P–N6ch, and both sides will queen.

56 . . . K–Q3 57 P–N5 BPxP 58 PxP K–K3!!

It is possible Tchigorin didn't notice that Black has this surprising defense. Even so, what he played was demonstrably worse, not only from a theoretical standpoint, but also from a practical one.

59 P–N6 K–B3 60 KxP K–N2 61 K–K6 K–N1

Keeping the opposition makes good general sense but Black could also draw here with 61 . . . K–B1. In all possible cases, White has many ways to stalemate Black's King—but that's all he can achieve!

62 K–B6 K–B1 Drawn

5. *When in doubt, be active!*

Often enough the choice between having an active or passive King comes down to psychological factors. Even though there seems to be nothing wrong with an active King move, "wouldn't it be better to play it safe?." As a general principle, the answer is "No!"—the King can be very powerful in the endgame, therefore, activate and use it! An excellent illustration occurs in the play arising from Diagram 144, A. Alekhine–E. Cohn, Stockholm 1912, after White's 47th move. Black has a slight material advantage, a

DIAGRAM 144

BLACK

WHITE

Alekhine–Cohn
Stockholm 1912
after White's 47th

passed KP and a very active Rook. White's only hope for salvation are his connected passed pawns. How should Black react to them?

47 . . . K–B3?

The "safe," passive way is the losing way, because now White's King can be activated and the team of King, Knight, QNP and QBP will be too much for Black to handle. As Alekhine pointed out, Black could have won with the active 47 . . . K–B5!, e.g. 48 P–B6 R–R6! 49 N–K4 R–R2!, and White's pawn(s) have been stopped.

48 K–Q3 R–KB8 49 P–N3!!

White does know the value of the active King. By preventing the check on Black's KB5, White has ensured QB4 for his King.

49 . . . P–R4 50 K–B4 P–R5 51 P–N5ch K–Q2 52 PxP R–B5ch 53 K–Q5 RxP 54 P–B6ch K–B2 55 K–B5! RxP 56 P–N6ch K–N1 57 N–N5 Black resigns

Note how the change in the role of the Kings totally changed the result of the game.